# CONCISE ENCYCLOPEDIA OF THE
# AMERICAN INDIAN

# CONCISE ENCYCLOPEDIA OF THE
# AMERICAN INDIAN

**Revised Edition**

## BRUCE GRANT

**Illustrated by Lorence F. Bjorklund**

**WINGS BOOKS**
New York/Avenel, New Jersey

Originally published as *American Indians Yesterday and Today*.

Copyright © 1958, 1960 by E.P. Dutton & Co., Inc.
All rights reserved.

This 1994 edition is published by Wings Books,
distributed by Random House Value Publishing, Inc.,
40 Engelhard Avenue, Avenel, New Jersey 07001,
by arrangement with E.P. Dutton, a division of NAL.

Random House
New York · Toronto · London · Sydney · Auckland

Printed and bound in the United States of America

**Library of Congress Cataloging-in-Publication Data**

Grant, Bruce, 1893-
    [American Indians, yesterday and today]
    Concise encyclopedia of the American Indian/by Bruce Grant;
illustrated by Lorence F. Bjorklund.
        p.    cm.
    Reprint. Originally published: American Indians, yesterday and
today. New York: Dutton, 1958.
    Includes bibliographical references.
    Summary: Presents descriptive alphabetical entries on Indian
tribes, territories, customs, tools, activities, and famous leaders.
    ISBN 0-517-69310-0
    1. Indians of North America—Dictionaries and encyclopedias—
Juvenile literature.  [1. Indians of North America—Dictionaries
and encyclopedias.]  I. Bjorklund, Lorence F., ill.  II. Title.
E76.2.G73   1989
973′.0497—dc20                                              89-17936
                                                              CIP
                                                               AC

15  14  13  12  11  10  9

# CONTENTS

For my nephew Bruce Grant II

# CONCISE ENCYCLOPEDIA OF THE
# AMERICAN INDIAN

A

**ABNAKI** (ab-nah'-kee) (Sometimes spelled Abenaki). A group of Indians who lived in what is now the states of Maine and New Hampshire. These Indians were among the first to come in contact with the white man and early gave the New Englanders the word "wigwam," which the white man thereafter applied to all Indian dome-shaped dwellings.

The Abnaki are famous in history as having been the Indians who gave the Massachusetts colonists much trouble in the early eighteenth century. They were believed to have been incited by a French Jesuit missionary, Father Rale or Rasles, who ran a mission at Norridgewock, on the upper Kennebec River. The English sent an expedition against Norridgewock in 1722, and after much fighting the Indians were defeated and Norridgewock destroyed. Father Rale was killed and among his papers was found an Abnaki dictionary he had prepared.

The Abnaki confederacy consisted of the Penobscot, Passamaquoddy, and Malecite tribes, and descendants of these still live in Maine. At the time the colonists met them they lived in villages, enclosed by palisades, and hunted and fished and also raised maize, or corn. They used fish to fertilize the soil, placing one or two dead fish at the roots of each stalk of maize. Their wigwams—"houses," in their language—were dome-shaped and covered with birch bark or woven mats. Each tribe had a war chief and also a chief to keep order in the village.

The Abnaki believed their good god, *Kechi Niwaskw,* created the first man and woman out of stone and, not being satisfied with them, destroyed them and made another pair out of wood.

The Abnaki claimed to be descended from these original wooden Indians. See MICMAC, PASSAMAQUODDY, PENNACOOK, PENOBSCOT, WIGWAM, WOODEN INDIAN.

**ACOMA** (ak′-o-ma). A pueblo, or village, inhabited by the Acoma Indians. Located on a rock mesa about sixty miles west of the Rio Grande in Valencia County, New Mexico, Acoma is recognized as the oldest inhabited settlement in the United States. The pueblo is difficult to reach, being 375 feet high on a sheer, bare rock and approached by a dangerous and dizzy trail. The village has three rows of tiered houses and narrow streets, as well as an old church.

The Acoma Indians live much like other Pueblo Indians. They have never vacated their pueblo, and after many centuries still live there today. Acoma was mentioned as early as 1539 by the Spanish and was visited the following year by Coronado's army. These Indians fought many bloody battles with the Spaniards. They are a farming people, cultivating and irrigating their fields of corn, wheat, melons, and gourds today much as they did in ancient times. They also raise sheep, goats, horses, and donkeys. Their farm lands are around Acomita and Pueblito, about fifteen miles from Acoma. See KERESAN PUEBLO, PUEBLO INDIANS.

14

**ACORN.** The fruit of the oak tree. The acorn was highly prized as a food by the California Indians. Whole villages would turn out to gather the crop. The acorns would be hulled and mashed in a mortar. The acorn nut is bitter and contains much tannic acid, which had to be eliminated before the nut could be eaten. A shallow hole was dug in clean sand and lined with dough made from acorn meal. Hot water was poured in, and as it seeped through the dough and sand it carried away most of the tannic acid. Indians made bread by baking the dough, or soup by mixing the meal with hot water. Some Indians flavored their acorn soup with mint leaves. See FOOD, METATE.

**ADIRONDACK** (ad-i-ron'-dak). An Algonquian tribe of Indians who formerly lived north of the St. Lawrence River. The Mohawk gave them the name *Adirondack*, which meant "They Eat Trees," as these Indians were in the habit of eating the bark of certain trees in times when food was scarce. The Adirondack sided with the French in the latter's war with the Iroquois. Their most famous chief was Pieskaret. The Adirondack Mountains in New York are named after these Indians. The name also was applied by some historians to the Chippewa. See PIESKARET.

**ADOBE** (a-doh'-bee). Large sun-dried bricks much used by the Pueblo Indians in building houses and garden walls. Not until the sixteenth century when the Spaniards visited the Indians did they learn to mold these bricks in wooden frames. Until that time their method was to set fire to a pile of sagebrush twigs and sedge grass, let it burn down to half coals and ashes, then throw in a quantity of dirt and water and mix it together. This mixture was formed into balls, which hardened when dry. These "stones" were set together with a mortar of the same mixture, unhardened. After the Spanish taught the Pueblo Indians to grow wheat, they added the straw to strengthen their bricks.

Because much water is needed in brickmaking, the Indian pueblos usually are located near streams. Both the bricks and the houses from which they are made are called "adobes." Generally the bricks are eighteen inches long, ten inches wide and six inches thick. When molded, they are set on edge with a slight slant to shed the rain. Adobe colors vary from gray to a rich reddish brown. Indian women use their hands to plaster the walls. The interior and borders of the windows are sometimes whitewashed. Adobe, or 'dobe houses are ideal for the hot dry climate in which they are used, being cool in summer and warm in winter.

In the Southwest, where the average rainfall was not great, structures built of adobe lasted a long time, with little need of repair. When there was rain, the greatest damage was done to the base of the walls. See PISÉ, PUEBLO INDIANS.

**ADOBE WALLS.** A trading post on the Canadian River in the Texas Panhandle where the famous battle between Indians and buffalo hunters was fought in June, 1874. There were twenty-eight white men and one white woman at Adobe Walls when some seven hundred Comanche, Cheyenne, and Kiowa-Apache Indians attacked under Chief Quanah Parker. The Indians wanted to destroy the whites because

they were killing off the buffalo. The small band of white men, with their powerful buffalo guns, drove back the Indians. More than one hundred Indians and only three white men were killed. Three days after the battle one of the most remarkable shots in the history of the West was made by Billy Dixon, a buffalo hunter. At a distance of 1,538 yards—only 185 yards less than a mile—he shot and killed an Indian horseman on a bluff. Among the defenders of Adobe Walls was Bat Masterson, later marshal of Dodge City, Kansas. See PARKER (QUANAH).

**ADZE.** A cutting, scraping, and gouging tool used by Indians. Early adzes had blades of stone, shell, bone, and sometimes copper. Later the Indians learned from the white man to use iron. The adze was most frequently employed in hollowing out or shaping wood after it had been charred by fire. See DUGOUT.

**ALEUT** (al'-eh-oot). A branch of the Esquimauan family living in the Aleutian Islands and on the north side of the Alaska Peninsula west of the Ugashik River. While they differ in appearance and language from the Eskimo, authorities have determined that they are a part of the Eskimo family. They furnished the name for the Aleutian Islands, and from their language is derived the word Alaska. In the early days before the Russians took possession of the islands, they were densely populated. Fish and sea mammals abounded off their coasts and furnished one of the best food supplies of that region. See ESKIMO.

**ALGONKIN** (al-gong'-kin). A small tribe which formerly lived where the present city of Ottawa, Ontario, Canada, now stands. They early attached themselves to the French but during the troubles with the Iroquois many were driven out of their country. Some fled to Mackinac and into Michigan where they consolidated and became known as the Ottawa. Their chief importance is that they gave their name to the great Algonquian family. See OTTAWA.

**ALGONQUIAN FAMILY.** One of the eight chief language groups of Indians in the United States, which formerly occupied a greater area than any other in North America. Their territory reached from the eastern shore of Newfoundland to the Rocky Mountains and from the Churchill River in Canada to Pamlico Sound in North Carolina.

**ALIBAMU** (ah-li-bah'-moo). Indians of the Creek Confederacy who formerly lived in southern Alabama. The state received its name from these Indians. The Alibamu fought against early white aggression. While relations became more friendly later, nevertheless they threw away everything left at a meal at which a white man had eaten, and washed everything he had used. They had a strange custom of flogging all their boys and girls during their festival season after which they were lectured by one or more of the older men. A few Alibamu still live in Oklahoma, and there is a small settlement of them in Polk County, Texas. See CREEK.

**ALLOTMENT ACT.** An act passed in 1887 which gave the President of the United States power to divide any Indian Reservation into individual allotments, on which a twenty-five-year trust period was to be imposed, and surplus lands not allotted were authorized to be sold. The act has been considered unjust to the Indian, because his lands of 155,000,000 acres have shrunk to about 47,000,000 acres since its adoption; the Indians themselves sell their allotments and "surplus lands" can legally be sold by the Government. See BUREAU OF INDIAN AFFAIRS, INDIAN REORGANIZATION ACT.


**ALTAR.** A term meaning in its broadest sense a place where sacrifices were made or offerings laid, or around which some other act of worship was performed. Some Indian altars were of the simplest nature, being an excavation in the earth, a pile of rocks, a fire, or perhaps merely a buffalo skull. Others were more like the altars of civilized people. Some tribes had altar-shrines near springs, rivers, caves, rocks, or certain trees. The term altar was also applied to the pipe bowl of the calumet. See CALUMET.


**AMERICAN.** A name the early colonists gave to the Indians from that of the country in which they lived. The English used this term to mean the original inhabitants of America and called the white men "colonists." Some time ago the Indian was referred to as the "vanishing American," a term which is not fitting today because Indians are increasing in numbers. Indians had no general name for themselves. See AMERIND, INDIAN.


**AMERICAN HORSE.** A chief of the Oglala Sioux. As spokesman for his tribe he signed the treaty in 1887 by which the Sioux reservation in Dakota Territory was reduced by half. Almost half of his tribe objected, and excited by the news of the killing of Sitting Bull, supposed

19

leader of the Ghost Dance uprising, they withdrew from the council and prepared to fight the Government. American Horse finally persuaded them to submit to the terms of the treaty. In 1891 he headed a delegation from the Pine Ridge Reservation to Washington and succeeded in obtaining living rations and better treatment for his people. See DAKOTA, GHOST DANCE, SITTING BULL.

**AMERIND.** A word made up of the first syllables of the words "American" and "Indian" suggested in 1899 by Major J. W. Powell as a substitute for the word "Indian." Sometimes used in scientific and popular literature. See AMERICAN, INDIAN.

**ANTELOPE.** A prong-horned, deerlike animal native to the western Plains. The antelope was an important animal to the Indian both for food and for clothing. The buckskin was used for moccasin tops and vests, the hair for stuffing pillows and mattresses, and the shinbones were fashioned into pipes. The horns were made into various tools and implements. The meat was highly prized at certain seasons. Indians especially liked the raw liver, which they ate with a little of the animal's gall sprinkled over it. The brains were cooked by roasting the entire head, after the horns had been broken off. See BUCKSKIN.

**APACHE** (a-pach'-ee). A fierce and warlike tribe of Indians of the Southwest. The Apache were among the first Indians to ride horses. They were living in New Mexico when the early Spaniards arrived, and already had gained a reputation as raiders and killers, swooping down on the Pueblo villages and settlements of agricultural tribes in Arizona. The Zuñi gave them the name *Apachu,* or "Enemy." After the Apache obtained horses and firearms, they were more dangerous than ever, and were the white man's greatest enemies in the desert country. New Mexico and Arizona were known as the dreaded "Apache Country" or "Apache Territory."

The Apache were assigned to a reservation in 1870 but a band under Cochise refused to live there and gave much trouble. Three years later the United States troops had rounded up some 3,000 of these Indians and placed them on reservations. But bands broke out and continued their old life of killing and plundering. Victorio led one troublesome band until he was killed in 1880. Geronimo became the new leader of the hostile bands. After three years of warfare Geronimo was defeated, and the Indians returned to the reservation. But they left again and continued their warfare until Geronimo surrendered in 1886.

There were eight or more tribes under the general name of Apache, chief among them the Kiowa Apache, Mescalero, Jicarilla, and Chiricahua. Several tribes, including the Chiricahua, were grouped under the name of the White Mountain Apache. One troublesome tribe in Texas was called the Lipan Apache. The Apache gained such a bad reputation that the French gave the name to their Parisian gangsters.

Except for some Apache in Mexico and a few Lipan with the Tonkawa and Kiowa in Oklahoma, most of them are now concentrated on reservations in Arizona and New Mexico. The name Apache has been given to villages in Arizona and Oklahoma and to a place, Apache Creek, in New Mexico, as well as to the Apache Mountains in Texas and Apache Peak in Arizona. See COCHISE, COYOTE, DOG, GE-RONIMO, JICARILLA, MESCAL, PIMA, PRAYER STICKS.


**APACHE MOON.** A western term for a full moon. Plains Indians, and especially the Apache, attacked at night only by the light of the moon. They had a superstition that when a warrior went to the next world he found there the same conditions that existed on earth when he was killed or died. The Indian believed that if he were killed in darkness his spirit would wander in continual darkness in the hereafter. See HAPPY HUNTING GROUNDS.


**APALACHEE** (a-pa-lach′-ee). One of the early native tribes of Florida, formerly living in the region north of what is now Apalachee Bay. These Indians were visited by De Soto in 1539 and found to be a farming people, industrious and wealthy, with a reputation for their fighting qualities. Later, upon siding with the Spanish, they began to suffer from raids by the wild Creek tribes, who were sent against them by the English government of Carolina.

In 1703 white colonists and their Indian allies raided the Apalachee country, destroying towns and missions, killing more than two hundred Apalachee warriors and carrying 1,400 of the tribe into slavery. Another expedition a year later completed the destruction. The remnants of the tribe became fugitives among friendly tribes and some fled for protection to the French at Mobile, Alabama.

In 1804 a few were reported living as a group in Louisiana, but today the tribe is extinct. Their name, however, has been preserved in Apalachee Bay, Florida, and in rivers in Florida, Georgia, and Alabama, but most prominently in the Appalachian Mountains. Tallahassee, capital of Florida, is from the Apalachee word meaning "Old Town." There is a post village, Apalachee, in Georgia.

**APPALOOSA** (ap-a-loo'-sa). The white man's name for the war pony of the Nez Percé Indians. The name came from the Palouse Valley of the Palouse River in Washington and Oregon, which was formerly inhabited by a portion of the Nez Percé. The Appaloosa is a fine sturdy horse and beautifully marked with spots. When the Nez Percé Indians were rounded up by Government troops in 1877 and placed on reservations, some of the horses were killed and others taken from the tribe. However, today stock breeders have succeeded in continuing the line. See JOSEPH, NEZ PERCE.

**ARAPAHO** (a-rap'-a-ho). A famous raiding tribe of Plains Indians who have been associated with the Cheyenne for more than a century. They were horse Indians and buffalo hunters when the white man first came across them. They observed the Sun Dance like the Cheyenne and Sioux and had similar military societies. The Arapaho are noted for their beadwork. Each design is supposed to tell a story, unlike most other Indian designs which are merely for decoration.

A brave and warlike people, the Arapaho are believed to have lived originally in what is now northern Minnesota, moving out toward the Plains about the same time or shortly before the Cheyenne did. Although they lived with the Cheyenne, and members of the two tribes intermarried, they never learned the Cheyenne language, and they kept their own tribal customs. For example, they buried their dead in the ground, while the Cheyenne placed theirs on rafters. With the Cheyenne, the Arapaho ranged eastern Wyoming and eastern Colorado. At one time they split into three groups—the Northern Arapaho, the Southern Arapaho, and the Gros Ventre of the Prairies, or Atsina.

The name Arapaho has been given to a county and a mountain in Colorado; to localities in Nebraska, North Carolina, Colorado, and Wyoming; and to the county seat of Custer County, Oklahoma. See CHEYENNE, GROS VENTRE, OTTER, SIGN LANGUAGE, SUN DANCE.

**ARIKARA** (a-ree'-ka-ra). These Indians, related to the Pawnee, were known to the white man also as the Arickaree and Ree. The name *Arikara* means "Horns" or "Elk," and refers to the ancient manner in which these Indians wore their hair with two pieces of bone standing up, one on each side of the crest.

The Arikara originally came from the Platte Valley in Nebraska. In early days they were considered hostile to the white man. For a long time they were allied with the Mandan and Hidatsa after smallpox and wars with the Dakota had reduced their number. Later they were grouped with these tribes under the general name of "Fort Berthold Indians."

They were accomplished farmers, and long preserved the seed of a peculiar type of small-eared corn. They respected corn and called it "Mother," as the giver of life. They were expert swimmers and sometimes captured buffalo disabled in a river while a herd was crossing. They lived in earth lodges. In 1900 the Arikara became citizens of the United States. Arickaree in Washington County, Colorado, carries on the name. See MANDAN, PAWNEE, REE.

**ARIZONA.** Name of a state derived from "Arizonac," a former Papago *rancheria* or small village in Sonora, Mexico, just below the boundary line at the present city of Nogales. Arizonac meant "Small Springs" in Papago. In 1836-1841 there was a rush of treasure-seekers to the Southwest when balls of silver of enormous size were found. The territory was called Arizona and when New Mexico was divided from it, the name was retained for the remaining portion.

**ARKANSAS.** A state and river named for the Quapaw Indians, who were known as the Arkansas by the Illinois Indians. Some say the French first termed them *Arkansa,* having placed the word *arc* meaning "bow," before the name Kansa. See QUAPAW.

**ARROW.** A long slender shaft, pointed on one end and feathered on the other, to be shot from a bow. Arrows of various types were common to practically all American Indians, who used the bow and arrow in hunting and in war.

The main part of the arrow is the shaft which is made of some pithy reed or cane, or stem of wood. Indians selected these shafts with great care. They tied them tightly in bundles and hung them in their wigwams or tepees high above the fire to straighten and season them. When ready for use, they were straightened further and smoothed with stone implements.

Most Plains Indians cut shallow grooves along the length of the shaft. These were known as "lightning marks" or "blood grooves," since they allowed the blood to flow from the wound of an animal. This would not only weaken the animal but would also leave a trail of blood the Indian hunter could follow. These grooves also kept the arrow shaft from warping, and Indians believed they helped to keep the arrow straight in flight.

Feathers for arrows came from the wings of various birds, chiefly from the eagle and the wild turkey. Feathers from the same wing were used on one arrow. When split and fastened to the arrow these feathers gave it a twisting or spiral motion like that of a bullet fired from a rifle. Tail feathers were not good for arrows. Some arrows had no feathers and others had two, but the majority were fletched with three, set at equal distances around the circumference of the shaft. The Eskimo used the entire feather, but most Indians split the feathers before placing them on the shafts. Feathers were fastened with glue and lashed with sinew. In many cases the middle part of the feather was free, only the ends being tied down.

There were many types of arrowheads. The early Indians used flint or other hard rocks, flaked and shaped; also bone, antler tips, and

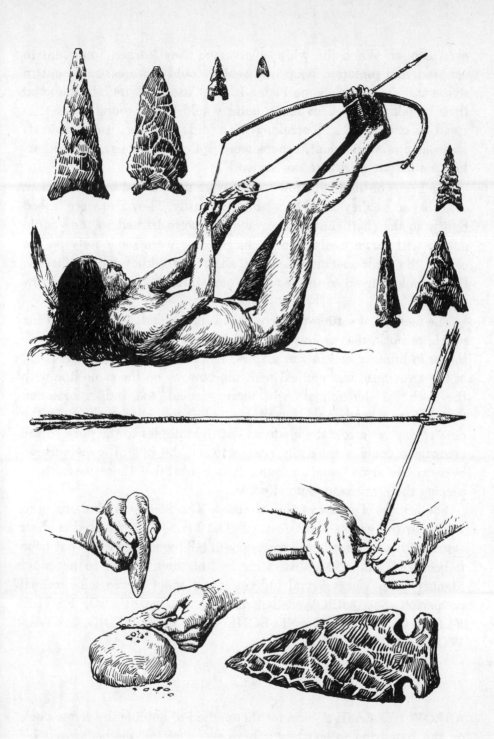

even copper. When the white man came they learned from him to use iron, and preferred hoop iron which could more easily be cut to shape and sharpened. Some Plains Indians used stiff buffalo sinew on their buffalo arrows. This sinew point would bend around a bone instead of striking it and breaking. For birds and very small animals some arrows were blunt, others were split into prongs, and others had a stick set crosswise on the end.

The heads of hunting arrows often were not barbed but were more oval-shaped, so they could be withdrawn easily. They also were lashed tightly to the shaft. But war arrowheads were barbed so they could not be withdrawn easily, and in many cases were set loosely on the end of the shaft so that when the shaft was withdrawn the arrowhead would remain in the wound. Some Indians poisoned the arrow tips.

The method of setting the arrowhead in the shaft in relation to the notch, or nock, that groove into which the string fitted, was also different in hunting and in war arrows. In the hunting arrow the blade of the arrowhead was vertical with the bow, or on the same line with the nock. As the animal's ribs were vertical, the Indian reasoned that the arrowhead could thus more easily pass between them. In the case of the war arrow the blade was at right angles to the nock so the arrowhead could more easily pass between the ribs of a man. However, as the arrow spun in flight, it is doubtful if these methods of placing the arrowhead were effective.

The arrows of various tribes differed. The Southwest Indians used a long arrow with a short feather. The Plains Indians used a short arrow with a long feather. Experts could tell by an arrow to what tribe it belonged. An Indian always marked his own arrows so he could identify them, since several Indians might shoot at the same animal or person. See ARROW RELEASE, BOW, BUFFALO, EAGLE, FLINT, GLUE, HORN AND BONE CRAFT, HUNTING, METALWORK, QUIVER, SINEW.


ARROW RELEASE. A term for the method of holding the arrow nock on the bowstring in shooting. There were several methods used by

Indians. The simplest form was one that still is used by small white boys when they first shoot bows and arrows. The nock-end of the arrow is pinched between the thumb and first joint of the forefinger. This is known by students of archery as the "primary release," preferred by the Navajo, Chippewa, Micmac, and Penobscot Indian tribes.

The second method is called the "secondary release." Here the arrow is pinched as before, but the middle and third fingers are laid along the string. This was the method used by the Ottawa, Zuñi, and some of the Chippewa.

The third, or "tertiary release," consisted in holding the nock-end by pinching it between thumb and forefinger, with the forefinger and second finger hooked over the string. The Omaha, Arapaho, Cheyenne, Assiniboin, Comanche, Crow, Siksika, and some Navajo tribes used this method.

A fourth method, and one used by the white man in archery, is known as the "Mediterranean release." In this the string is drawn with the tips of the first, second, and third fingers, with the nock-end resting between the first and second fingers. The Eskimo generally used this type of release. See ARROW, BOW, BOWSTRING.

**ASSINIBOIN** (a-sin'-i-boin). A tribe of Indians sometimes known as the Rocky Mountain Sioux. While their language is almost identical with that of the Dakota Sioux and they belong to the same family, the two tribes were bitter enemies from early history. The Jesuits in 1640 found the Assiniboin a distinct tribe from the Dakota. Although they originally roamed Canada, they later came down into North Dakota and Montana. The Assiniboin at one time joined the Chippewa (who gave them their name signifying "one who cooks by the use of

hot stones") and Cree in fighting the Dakota for control of the buffalo country. In dress and custom the Assiniboin resembled the Cree, despite their Sioux background. They suffered a sad fate in 1840 when smallpox killed off many of them, reducing 1,200 lodges to only 400. See CHIPPEWA, CREE, DAKOTA. See also illustration, page 12.

**ASSOCIATION ON AMERICAN INDIAN AFFAIRS.** An organization with a national membership and with both Indian and non-Indian directors, which was active in obtaining passage of the Indian Reorganization Act and in various court cases which established that Indians were not wards of the Government. The Association also won the right to vote for Indians in Arizona and New Mexico. See INDIAN REORGANIZATION ACT.

**ATAKAPA** (ah-tah'-kah-pa). An extinct tribe of Indians, belonging to the Siouan language family. They occupied the region near Middle or Prien Lake in Louisiana. Their name in Choctaw meant "Man-Eaters," and they were said to have been cannibals, because they and some of the tribes to the west of them ate the flesh of their enemies.

**ATHAPASCAN** (ath-a-pas'-kan) **FAMILY.** One of the eight chief language groups of Indians in the United States and the most widely distributed of all the language families of North America. This group of fifty-three tribes formerly lived in parts of the continent from the Arctic Coast down into northern Mexico and from the Pacific to Hudson's Bay at the North.

**ATLANTIS** (at-lan'-tis). A mythical continent or island believed to have existed in ancient times, stretching from Central America and

Mexico far into the Atlantic Ocean. Before recorded history this island is supposed to have sunk into the ocean; the Canaries, Madeiras, and Azores being the only parts which did not disappear. Those who hold to the theory of Atlantis claim the American Indians were among those who survived when Atlantis sank. The Atlantic Ocean was not named for the lost continent of Atlantis, but for the Atlas Mountains in North Africa.

**ATSINA.** See ARAPAHO, BLACKFOOT, GROS VENTRE.

**ATTACAPAN** (ah-tah'-ka-pan) **FAMILY.** A small language family group composed of two tribes in southern Louisiana and northeast Texas.

**AWL.** A pointed instrument for making holes. The awl was the Indian's "needle." Awls were fashioned from hard wood, thorns, bone, and metal. In using an awl, holes were punched at regular intervals in skins to be sewed together and then the sinew was passed through these holes. When not in use, awls were kept in sheaths of hollow wood, bone, or metal.

**AX.** A sharp-edged tool for chopping, usually made from a hard tough stone. Indian axes averaged from 1 to 6 pounds in weight, but some were as heavy as 30 pounds. Often made from a wedge-shaped rock, sometimes grooved for attaching the handle, the Indian's ax was most effectively used for chopping wood that had first been charred. When Europeans introduced the iron ax, the Indian quickly adopted it in preference to the stone one. See CELT, TOMAHAWK.

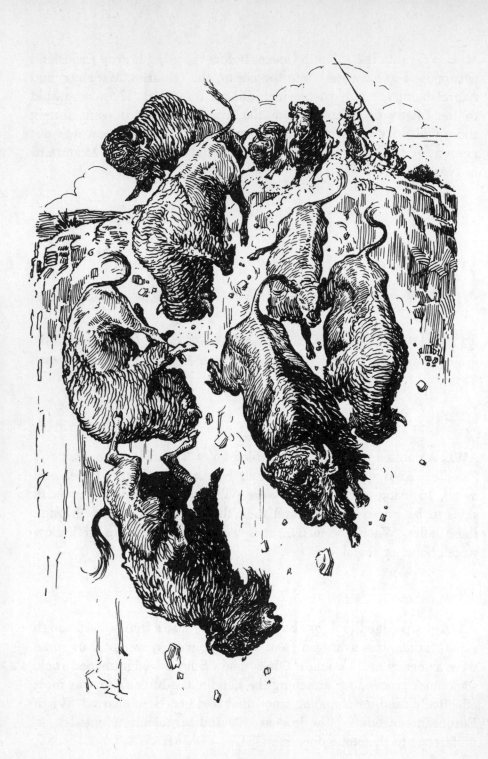

**BABICHE** (ba-beesh'). A thong or string cut from eelskin, deerskin, or caribou hide. After being softened it was used as string or lacing, or woven into nets and bags. Babiche was made into skeins and carried by Indians and northern trappers to be used for many purposes where string or cord was necessary. The word is believed to have come from the Micmac Indian word *ababich,* meaning cord or thread. Some tribes of the Athapascan family were known as "Babiche People." See CARIBOU, FISHING, RABBITSKIN WEAVING, RAWHIDE.

**BAGS AND POUCHES.** Having no pockets in his clothes, the Indian carried his toilet articles, paint, medicine, tobacco, pipes, trinkets, sewing tools, and other prized possessions in small bags or pouches. These were made from rawhide, bird skins, buckskins, babiche, hair, bark, grass, and other materials. Larger bags, joined together like the cowboy's saddlebags, were used on horses for transporting heavy articles and supplies. Most bags were highly decorated with beadwork, quillwork, or painted designs. See BARK CRAFT, BASKETS, BEADS, PARFLECHE, QUILLWORK.

**BAKING STONES.** Slabs of stone used by the ancient Indian tribes of Southern California. They were usually of soapstone, hollowed out on one side and rounded on the other. A fire was built under the rounded portion. Many such stones have been dug up and today are in museums. They are similar to the flat baking stones which the Hopi and other Pueblo Indians use in making their paper or wafer bread. See HOPI, PAPER BREAD.

**BALSA.** A form of boat or raft made by tying bundles of rushes together in a cigar shape. Balsas were used by Indians of California, as on Cedar Lake among the Pomo and Tulare Lake among the Yokut. Sometimes balsas were made of tule grass, like those used on Pyramid Lake in Nevada. The name is from the Spanish *balsa,* which means a raft or float for conveying people or goods across a river.

**BAND.** Usually a term to denote a group of Indians smaller than a tribe. Many so-called tribes were divided into clans, or groups of people descended from the same ancestors. Tribes often split into smaller groups, some of them composed of clans, while other groups from the same tribe would break off and follow a leader of their own choice. These were usually called bands. See CLAN, TRIBE.

**BANNER STONES.** Polished and often decorative stones lashed on throwing sticks used in hurling spears. These stones gave the sticks, or *atlatls*, the proper balance. Throwing sticks with their stone weights went out of use in North America around 500 A.D. when the bow and arrow came into use. Banner stones, sometimes termed butterfly stones, were about five inches in length and weighed from one-half to three-quarters of a pound. See THROWING STICK.

**BANNOCK.** A Shoshonean tribe, related to the Northern Paiutes, who once ranged southeast Idaho and western Wyoming. They had little trouble with the white man during their early history, and in 1869 the Fort Hall Reservation in Idaho was set aside for them and for a large number of Shoshoni. Nine years later, the loss of hunting grounds and the decrease in buffalo herds led to a Bannock uprising which was known as the Bannock War. A vigorous campaign under General O. O. Howard ended in the defeat and capture of the Bannock in the fall of 1878 and, since then, they have lived peacefully on their reservation. The Bannock gave their name to a river, a range of mountains, and a county in Idaho. See SHOSHONI, UTE.

**BAREFOOT INDIANS.** Term applied to tribes of southeast Texas, where Indians went without moccasins, occasionally wearing sandals. See MOCCASIN.

**BARK CRAFT.** Indians used the bark of trees for many purposes and were expert in making it into useful articles. The inner bark of cedar, elm, and other trees was shredded, twisted, and spun or woven. Certain tribes ate bark in the spring, the time of the greatest food scarcity. Willow bark was smoked in ceremonial pipes. A mixture of bark and tobacco was known as *kinnikinnick*. Red cedar bark was used in secret-society rites by the North Pacific Coast Indians.

The most valuable bark for the Indian was that of the white birch tree, which is found in the north woods of the United States. From this he made his canoe, buckets, coverings for his wigwam, mats, pots and kettles for cooking with hot stones, and many other articles. Juices of some barks were utilized as medicine.

The birch bark was removed from the tree only in the spring and early summer. The Indian felled his tree, cut a straight gash lengthwise the full length of the trunk, and peeled the bark off in sheets. He then rolled it inside out, and weighted the bundle with stones. Indians used the inside or the brown side of the bark outward, as this is more durable and firm and does not peel.

Indians also used—and still use—the bark of the elm, basswood, poplar, cottonwood, and the root of the wild cherry tree. Basswood bark is especially valuable. It is taken from the trunk of the standing tree, usually in strips about four inches wide. The bark is first loosened by pounding on it, then a cut is made and it is pulled upward and outward, separating high in the tree. The bark is soaked for about five days, after which time the inner bark can be peeled from the rough outer bark. This inner bark is next separated into lacings by running the fingernail along the edge. It must be wet when worked and in this state can be twisted into rope or twine, or used as a flat thong. Good bark lacings also are made from slippery elm, hickory, white oak, red cedar, osage orange, and buckeye.

Some strong barks are used for bowstrings. The bark house was common to the Chippewa. When they moved camp, the bark roof was rolled up and carried along. They chopped down poles and made another house frame when they camped. The Iroquois constructed their famous long house from bark. Bark also was used for floors, beds, and partitions in houses. See BAGS AND POUCHES, BASKETS, CANOE, COSTUME, DISHES, FISHING, GLUE, IROQUOIS, KINNIKINNICK, STONE BOILING, TOBACCO, WIGWAM.

**BASKETS.** Basketmaking in some fashion was practiced by almost every Indian tribe in the United States. The early Mound Dwellers were basketmakers, as is shown from impressions found in mound excavations.

Indians were familiar with all the materials suitable for making baskets such as roots, grasses, barks, and other fibers. They knew when to gather the materials, preserve them, and prepare them for making their baskets.

There were two general types of baskets—woven and coiled. In the woven types there was a frame, or warp, consisting of a coarser material onto which was woven the weft, or woof, of finer fibers which went crosswise. In the coiled type baskets, coils of the material were built up in spiral fashion.

Strange as it may seem, baskets were much used for cooking in olden times. When lined with pitch they became watertight, and some believed the art of pottery grew out of baskets lined with clay. When the clay hardened from the heat, the Indian found this clay vessel could be used alone. From California to Alaska Indian women wove baskets which were watertight. Cooking in such baskets was done by the stone-boiling method, or by dropping hot stones into the liquid contained by the basket.

The Indians of the Great Lakes region used birch-bark containers in place of baskets. Willow and cane were utilized in the South, while farther north splint wood, or flat pieces of wood, were woven into baskets. The Nez Percé made soft bags which were woven after the fashion of baskets. The Tlingit Indians made baskets of spruce roots. Apache baskets are among the finest.

37

Indians became expert in decorating their baskets. They took their designs from nature. Basketwork also was employed in making fences, fish weirs, houses, trays, mats, shields, and cradles, as well as many other things. See BAGS AND POUCHES, BARK CRAFT, BIGIU, DISHES, FISHING, MOUND BUILDERS, POTTERY, ROOTS AND ROOTCRAFT, STONE BOILING.

**BAT HOUSE.** An ancient pueblo of the Hopi, situated on the northwest side of the Jeditoh Valley in northeast Arizona. It is called the Bat House because it was built, and formerly occupied, by the Bat Clan of the tribe. See HOPI.

**BATON.** A ceremonial wand used by a chief, song leader, or other high-ranking person. Most Indian batons were highly carved and decorated and made of wood, ivory, or even flint.

**BAYETA** (bah-yeh'-tah). A dull red blanket made by the Navajo Indians by using wool from a Spanish trade cloth. The word means "baize" in Spanish and is applied to the cloth itself, which was introduced in the nineteenth century as a trade item. The Navajo unraveled the cloth and used the wool to make their blankets, which were the most highly prized of all Navajo blankets. See BLANKET, NAVAJO.

**BAYOU.** A sluggish stream forming the inlet or outlet of a lake or bay, or connecting two bodies of water or a branch of a river flowing through a delta. The word is from the Choctaw *báyuk*, meaning "small river" or "a river forming a delta."

**BEADS.** Small spheres or cylinders with a hole, which were strung on threads or attached to fabrics. Before the colonists brought over glass and porcelain beads, almost every tribe of Indians used some form of this decoration. Beads were made from many kinds of mineral substances, including quartz, turquoise, soapstone, and copper; from the stems and roots of plants; from nuts and berries; shell, bone, horn, teeth, and claws of animals; and even the beaks of some birds, and claws of eagles and hawks. The Eskimo used walrus ivory and teeth of various animals. In Virginia a cheap kind of bead, called *roanoke,* was made from the clamshell. The claws of the bear and teeth of the elk were highly prized.

Beads were worn in the hair as a decoration or hung in strings from the ears, on the neck, arms, wrists, waist, and lower limbs. They were attached to bark, wood, or buckskin; were woven into belts; and were used to cover leggings, headdresses, moccasins, and other articles of dress. As ceremonial pledges, or wampum, they were used in councils of war and peace, also as money. In many instances vast quantities were buried with the dead.

39

In the early part of the last century a large china bead called the "pony bead" was popular among the Plains Indians. It was made in Venice, Italy, and was known as the pony bead because it was brought overland by pony pack trains. This bead was about twice the size of the "seed bead" which was introduced later, in 1840. The pony beads were first used on bands to decorate skin robes, shirts, pipe bags, cradles, saddlebags, moccasins, and the headbands on war bonnets. The seed bead was used for finer work and soon the pony bead disappeared from use. About 1870 the translucent beads became popular with the Indians, and fifteen years later they worked with glass beads, which were colored silver or gilt and cut with facets.

The great period of Indian beadwork flourished between 1860 and 1900. Experts on beadwork can tell the date when an article was made by the type of beads used as well as by the coloring of some of the beads. Many Plains Indians made a long tubular bone bead which was used on breastplates, and which traders duplicated and termed "hair pipes." See BAGS AND POUCHES, BREASTPLATE, COSTUME, KNIFE SHEATH, MOCCASIN, PAPOOSE, PORCUPINE, QUILLWORK, QUIVER, ROANOKE, SINEW, WAMPUM, WOMEN.

**BEAR.** A large meat- and fruit-eating animal inhabiting the forest and mountain areas of the United States. The grizzly bear was the largest and fiercest of these animals. Some weighed as much as 1,000 pounds. The black bear was the most common and was smaller than the grizzly

bear. Black bears weighed from 200 to 300 pounds. The cinnamon bear was a color phase of the black bear. All bears except the grizzly could climb trees. They lived on fruits, roots, insects, honey, and meat. During the cold winter months they slept in caves or hollow trees.

The bear was one of the most useful animals to the Indian. It was hunted for its flesh, and especially for its fat or grease, which the Indian preserved in skins. Heavy winter robes were made from the pelts, and moccasins cut from the skins. Thongs of twisted bears' guts were used for bowstrings, and the bows were rubbed with bears' oil. The oil was used freely on the hair and sometimes on the entire body. Paints were mixed with bears' grease. Bear claws were prized as ornaments.

The bear was held in great reverence and admired for its strength and courage. Some Indians were superstitious about the animal and would not kill it, and a few writers have said that this was because these Indians feared the bear. Another reason given was that Indian women did not care to work over bearskins as this gave them sore throats. The bear was used as a totem for many clans, and therefore could not be killed.

A wounded bear was one of the most ferocious animals, and the Indian could not always kill him outright with his simple weapons. See BOW, FOOD, HAIR, MOCCASIN, PAINT, TOTEM.

BEAVER. A member of the rodent family, related to squirrels and marmots, but which lives in and near the water. This small, industrious animal was a great favorite with the Indian and was praised by him in song and story.

Indians believed that beavers could think like men—that they lived in colonies ruled over by a chief and had their own laws and language. Some Indian tribes ate the beaver, and its skin was used for making clothing and, especially, pouches. Beaver teeth, with which the animal could cut down large trees, were prized by the Indian, who would set them at the end of a stick and use this as a weapon or tool. Beaver skins, with their glossy fur, were favored articles of trade.

The beaver is found west of the Mississippi River—less frequently to the east of the river—and to the south of the Great Lakes. The lodge of the beaver is round or oval, and built so that it is about two-thirds out of the water. It is plastered with clay so that it is almost airtight. The entrance is below the surface of the water and deep enough so that when ice forms on the water in winter, the beaver can come and go at will.

Indians often caught the beaver by cutting a hole in the ice. When the animal came up for air, the hunter grabbed it by the paws and pulled it out on the ice and killed it. Indians also trapped the beaver or caught it in nets. See FUR TRADE.

**BELL.** A hollow instrument of metal or other material which gives forth a pleasing sound when struck. Indians, especially the Pueblos, were familiar with bells before the time of Columbus. The Indian metallic bell is believed to have evolved from the rattle made of shells or molded clay. Copper bells with stone tinklers have been dug up in Arizona and New Mexico. English colonists used copper and bronze bells in trading with the Indians. Bells were especially popular in dance ceremonies, and Indians wore rows of them strapped around their legs. See DANCE, METALWORK, MOTHER-IN-LAW TABOO, MUSICAL INSTRUMENTS.

**BIG HEART.** Indian term for "brave." Indians spoke of "keeping their hearts big" and having no fear. See BRAVE, INDIAN LANGUAGE.

**BIGIU.** The Chippewa Indian term for "pitch" or "gum," obtained from evergreen trees such as the fir and the cedar. It is used for waterproofing baskets, repairing canoes, and making torches for night hunting. See BASKETS, CANOE.

**BIG MOUTH.** A chief of the Brûlé Sioux. His tribe regarded him highly for his manly and warlike qualities. He was a bitter enemy of the white man. When Spotted Tail, a Brûlé Teton chief, after being entertained in Washington and other eastern cities, returned with friendly feelings toward the white man, Big Mouth ridiculed him. Spotted Tail killed him in 1874. See SPOTTED TAIL.

**BILOXI.** A small tribe of the Siouan language family, formerly living in what is now the lower part of Mississippi. They spoke an entirely different language from any of their neighbors. They are noted as the tribe that met the expedition to Louisiana to establish the first French colony. They furnished the names for the first two capitals of Louisiana, Old and New Biloxi; that of the present Biloxi, Mississippi; and Biloxi Bay. A few still live in Rapides Parish, Louisiana, and there are said to be some with the Choctaw Nation in Oklahoma, but the tribe is practically extinct.

**BIRCH BARK.** See BARK CRAFT, CANOE.

**BLACK DRINK.** See YOPON.

**BLACKFEET SIOUX.** A name applied to a band of Indians who lived near the Standing Rock Agency and Reservation on the Missouri River. They are not to be confused with the Siksika, or Blackfoot. Captain W. P. Clark, author of *The Indian Sign Language*, said there were two stories of how they obtained their name. One was that a chief, jealous of his wife, had the soles of her moccasins blackened so he could trail her wherever she went. The other was that some of the band, after an unsuccessful chase of a band of Crow Indians, lost everything, including their ponies, and had to return home over country that had been burned, and arrived with blackened moccasins and feet. See DAKOTA.

**BLACKFOOT.** A confederacy of Indians of the northern Plains, belonging to Algonquian stock. They were known as one of the largest and most warlike groups of that region, and were next to the Dakota in prominence. Their name is from the native word, *siksika*, meaning "black foot," which formerly was thought to have been given them because of the discoloration of their moccasins by ashes of prairie fires. However, it is now believed that they originally dyed their moccasins black.

The Blackfoot consisted of the Siksika, or Blackfoot, the Blood, and the Piegan. Under their protection were two smaller tribes—the Atsina (Gros Ventre) and the Sarsi. When the white man first knew them, they were distinguished by the beadwork on their moccasins—a design ending in three prongs, which designated the three tribes.

At one time the Blackfoot held most of the territory from the North Saskatchewan River in Canada to the southern headstreams of the Missouri River in Montana, and from longitude 105° to the base of the Rocky Mountains. They were roving buffalo hunters, living in tepees. They early acquired the horse and the gun. While warlike and aggressive and continually fighting with their neighbors, the Cree,

Assiniboin, Sioux, Crow, and Flatheads, they were never regularly at war with the United States. Nevertheless they were always hostile to the white man.

The Blackfoot observed the Sun Dance, as well as a spectacular ceremony known as the Horse Dance. In this latter dance they appeared mounted in full war gear—bonnets, shields, guns, lances, with faces and bodies painted and ponies decorated—and circled, charged, yelled, and fired their rifles. They had secret societies and many sacred bundles of tribal "medicine," while every warrior had his own personal "medicine." They also had military societies like other Plains Indians.

While most writers term them Blackfoot, their agency in Montana is called the Blackfeet Agency. The Blackfoot have given their name to a town, creek, and mountains in Idaho, and to a river and village in Montana. See GROS VENTRE.

**BLACK HAWK.** A famous chief of the Sauk and Fox Indians and leader in the Black Hawk War of 1832. He was known to his tribesmen as "Black-Big-Chest." Black Hawk was one of several Indian medicine men who rose to be great chiefs.

Black Hawk was born in 1767 in the Sauk village at the mouth of the Rock River in Illinois. At the age of fifteen he was a warrior and took his first scalp before he was seventeen. In an early raid on the Cherokee his father, keeper of the tribal medicine, was killed and Black Hawk did not go to war for five years, spending his time fitting himself to become a medicine man.

In the War of 1812 the Sauk and Fox split, Black Hawk and his Sauk followers joining the English, while Keokuk and his tribe went with the Americans. Despite a treaty made in 1802 providing that the Indians would remove to the west side of the Mississippi, Black Hawk would not go, claiming that his people had been deceived.

This led to trouble, which reached a climax in the Black Hawk War. Abraham Lincoln was a captain in this war. The Indians were defeated in the summer of 1832 and Black Hawk fled to the north, but was later captured and confined for a time in a Virginia prison. After his release he lived in an Indian village on the Des Moines River, where he died October 3, 1838. His body was buried Indian-fashion on the surface of the ground. He was dressed in a uniform given him by General Jackson. Later the body was stolen and carried to St. Louis, but subsequently was sent to Quincy, Illinois, where the bones were made into a skeleton. Black Hawk's son protested, and the bones were sent to Iowa where they remained in the Burlington Geographical and Historical Society Museum until they were destroyed in 1855 when the building burned down.

A noble statue of Black Hawk, made by Loredo Taft, stands today on the east bank of the Rock River at Oregon, Illinois. With folded arms, the great chief majestically and eternally surveys part of the domain over which he once ruled. See BURIAL, KEOKUK, KICKAPOO, KING PHILIP, MEDICINE MAN, SAUK AND FOX, SHABONEE, WINNEBAGO.

**BLACK HOOF.** A principal chief of the Shawnee, born about 1740. His Indian name was *Catahecessa*. He was one of the greatest chiefs of the ferocious Shawnee throughout the period when they were the most dreaded enemies of the colonists. He was at General Braddock's defeat in 1755 and took a prominent part in the desperate battle with the Virginia militia at Point Pleasant in 1774. When Mad Anthony Wayne broke the power of the Indian Confederation and peace was signed in 1795, Black Hoof's fighting days came to an end. From that time on he was a friend of the Americans and as head chief of the Shawnee kept the majority of his tribe from joining Tecumseh and the British in the War of 1812. He died at Wapakoneta, Ohio, in 1831. See SHAWNEE.

**BLANKET.** A heavy covering made by Indians from wool, hair, fur, down, bark, cotton, and other materials. They were worn as articles of clothing, served as bed and covering at night, and for hangings, partitions, doors, and sunshades. Indian women used them as spreads on which to dry fruit, as cradles for their babies, and as containers.

Most Indians manufactured blankets of some sort. Robes were made from bearskins and buffalo hides. The Nez Percé made a decorated blanket by weaving goats' hair with a warp of vegetable fiber, as well as by weaving rabbitskins. Others used soft barks, wild hemp, down, and plumes or feathers of birds.

The most famous blankets were made by the Navajo Indians. The finest of these was made from yarn unraveled from the Spanish *bayeta*. Later, when they owned sheep, they sheared them, colored the wool with native dyes, and spun it. No two designs of the Navajo blanket were ever the same. The chief's pattern consisted of wide bars of black and white—black being the "male color," while blue was the "female color." Navajo women purposely made a "mistake" in the design somewhere in the blanket, as they did not want to compete with the gods in making something perfect.

When the white man came, he quickly saw the possibilities of the manufactured blanket for Indians. He traded blankets to Indians who formerly had used robes, and as furs became scarcer, blankets were in greater demand and like furs were used as money. In 1831 a plant was established in Buffalo, New York, for the manufacture of the heavy Mackinaw blanket. Indian delegations visiting Washington during the last century wore this blanket and it attracted much attention. See BAYETA, BLANKET INDIAN, CARIBOU, COSTUME, MACKINAW FORT, NAVAJO, PAINT, RABBITSKIN WEAVING, WOMEN.

**BLANKET INDIAN.** A term applied to an Indian who was unwilling to adopt the white man's dress or accept his customs. This term came into use during the last century when members of Indian delegations visiting Washington and eastern cities insisted on wearing their blankets at all times. See BLANKET.

**BLANKET SIGNAL.** See SIGNALS.

**BLOOD.** See BLACKFOOT.

**BLOWGUN.** A hollow cane or wooden shaft through which was blown a dart, sharp on one end and with thistledown on the other. The blowgun was used by the Cherokee, Iroquois, and Muskhogean tribes for killing birds and small game.

**BONE CRAFT.** See HORN AND BONE CRAFT.

**BOONE, DANIEL.** American pioneer, trapper, and Indian fighter. Boone was born November 2, 1734, near the present city of Reading, Pennsylvania. When he was seventeen, he moved with his father to Davie County, North Carolina, and here he spent much of his time hunting and trapping. He was a wagoner with the English general, Braddock, when the latter was defeated by the Indians in 1755.

Twelve years later Boone first roamed Kentucky with several companions, collecting bear, beaver, and deerskins. In 1775 he led a party of settlers to Kentucky where he founded Boonesborough. A few years later he and several companions were captured by the Shawnee, taken to Detroit, and adopted into the tribe. Boone escaped and returned to Boonesborough in time to notify the settlers of a planned Indian attack. As a result the Indians were repulsed.

When Kentucky was admitted to the Union, Boone lost title to his land. He moved to a place in what is now Missouri, about forty-five miles west of St. Louis. He died September 22, 1820, at Charette, Missouri. Later his remains were taken to Frankfort, Kentucky, where a monument was erected to him. See DARK AND BLOODY GROUND, TRAILS.

**BOSTON.** Chinook name for "America." The prominence of Boston in the early history of the United States led to its name being used for "America" or "American" on both the Atlantic and Pacific coasts. The Micmac Indians still call the United States *Bostoon,* and an American is a *Bostoonkawaach.* Many western Indians picked up the Chinook term. See CHINOOK JARGON.

**BOW.** The chief weapon of the early American Indian. Bows were made from many types of springy woods, as well as from bone and horn, and were of different lengths and shapes. The Indian prized his bow and took good care of it, keeping it unstrung and in a bow case when not in use. Even after he had acquired firearms, he usually carried his bow whether in war or on the hunt.

There were four general types of bows in use by the Indians. One was the self-bow, made of one long length of wood, popular with the eastern Indians. Then there was the compound bow, made of several layers of wood, bone, or horn, glued and lashed together, used by some Plains tribes. The third was the sinew-wrapped bow, made of a brittle wood which was wrapped from wing to wing with sinew. This bow was used among the Alaskan tribes. The last type was the sinew-backed self-bow strengthened by a strip of sinew or rawhide, glued and lashed to the back of the bow, much used by the California tribes.

The Eskimo made a bow out of whales' ribs, set on a wooden grip. The North Pacific tribes used a short bow with flat wide wings and a round grip. The Florida Indians' bow was as long as the height of the man who used it. Bows of the Plains Indians were shorter than most, as they usually were shot from horseback. Some Plains tribes, as well as the Apache, bent back the tips of the wings in the shape of a cupid's bow. Pueblo Indians made small painted bows to be used in religious ceremonies and to be buried with the dead.

Bows were made of the wood of the Osage orange (*bois d'arc*), found west of the Mississippi, ironwood, second growth hickory, cedar, dogwood, white ash, and mulberry.

Indians learned the use of the bow from childhood. Many stories have been told of how Indians could shoot four or five arrows, one after the other, before a man could reload his gun. When the Spanish *conquistadores* found that an arrow would go through a coat of mail they adopted as armor the quilted cloth of the Mexican Indians.

50

The University of California tested the distances arrows could be shot. These tests showed: Osage bow, 92 yards; Apache bow, 120 yards; Blackfoot bow, 145 yards; Cheyenne bow, 165 yards; Yaqui Indian bow (from Mexico), 210 yards; English long bow, 250 yards. See ARROW, ARROW RELEASE, BEAR, BOWSTRING, BUFFALO, ELK, HORN AND BONE CRAFT, HUNTING, QUIVER, SINEW.

**BOWSTRING.** The string on a bow which springs the bow and sends forth the arrow. Indians made their bowstrings from sinew, rawhide, and twisted vegetable fiber. Bears' guts, too, made strong bowstrings, and southern Indians preferred squirrel hide. One end of the bowstring was tied fast to the end of one wing of the bow and the other end of the string was made into a loop which could be slipped up to engage the nock on the other wing when the bow was to be sprung. See ARROW RELEASE, BOW.

**BRANT, JOSEPH.** A famous Mohawk chief, who sided with the English in their fight against the American colonists. Joseph Brant, whose Indian name was *Thayendanegea*, was born on the Ohio River in 1742 when his parents were on a hunting expedition. His father was a full-blood Mohawk chief and his mother was believed to have been half white. His father died when he was young and his mother married an Indian known to the white man as Brant. Joseph Brant's sister, Molly, became the Indian wife of Sir William Johnson, and the small boy went to live in the household of the Englishman.

At the age of thirteen Brant joined the Indians under Sir William at the Battle of Lake George in 1755. Sir William took an interest in the boy and sent him to school at Lebanon, Connecticut, where he learned to speak and write English. Brant later married the daughter of an Oneida chief and in 1765 settled at the old family home at Canajoharie Castle, New York. When his wife died, he married her half-sister. He was with Sir William in the Niagara Expedition of 1763 and took part in the Pontiac War in 1763. In 1775 he visited England where he was entertained royally and made a colonel in the British army.

During the Revolutionary War he fought with the English and took part in several battles, notably the massacre of the whites at Cherry Valley, New York. Following the war he retained his English commission, drawing half pay, and was granted a tract of land six miles wide on each side of the Grand River in Ontario.

Brant was an intelligent man and during his old age translated the New Testament into the Mohawk language. He died November 24, 1807, and was buried near the little church he built on the Grand River, three miles from Brantford, Ontario. There is a monument over his grave, said to have cost $30,000, with the inscription:

"This tomb is erected to the memory of Thayendanegea, or Capt. Joseph Brant, principal chief and warrior of the Six Nations Indians, by his fellow-subjects, admirers of his fidelity and attachment to the British Crown." See HALF-BREED, MOHAWK, PONTIAC, RED JACKET.

**BRAVE.** A term applied to an Indian warrior, undoubtedly first used by the early Spanish. *Bravo* means savage, wild, fierce, and in the strict sense is applied only to animals, but the term *Indios bravos* is found in early Spanish writings. An Indian spoke of having a "brave time" when he overcame great dangers and hardships. Thus Dull Knife, the great Cheyenne chief, journeying with his people eighteen days in a subzero climate and eating nothing but a few dried rosebuds and snow, spoke of having a "brave time." See BIG HEART, DULL KNIFE.

**BREASTPLATE.** An ornament or protective covering worn by Plains Indians. It was made of long bone beads, known to traders as "hair pipes." See BEADS, COSTUME.

**BREECHCLOTH.** Also called breechclout. A strip of material a foot wide and about six feet long, passed between the legs and under the front and rear part of a belt. Some were made of buckskin; others of woven fabrics; and, in the extreme South, of Spanish moss. Women also wore them to form a sort of apron in front and behind. The breechcloth sometimes was decorated with beadwork and had fringed ends. See COSTUME.

**BRIGHT EYES.** An Indian woman, Susette La Flesche, daughter of a former chief of the Omaha, who did much to better the condition of Indians on reservations. After the Government had forcibly removed the Ponca Indians from the Omaha Reservation to Indian Territory in 1877-1878, Bright Eyes and her father went there to help care for sick and dying relatives. This case attracted nationwide interest and it was in connection with this removal that Judge Dundy rendered his famous decision that "an Indian is a person."

Bright Eyes toured the country appealing for humanity toward her race. The Government was requested, as a result, to permit no more forcible removal of Indians to reservations, and this policy was more or less observed from that time. Bright Eyes later married Thomas Henry Tribbles, a white man who had become interested in her work. She died at Lincoln, Nebraska, in 1902. Tribbles later wrote a book, *Buckskin and Blanket Days*. The manuscript was left to a daughter, but it was not until 1957 that Tribbles' grandson finally interested a publisher in it. See INDIAN, STANDING BEAR, WOMEN.

**BRÛLÉ SIOUX.** See DAKOTA.

**BUCKSKIN.** A softened and smoke-treated raw-hide, sometimes known as smoked leather. Buckskin was one of the most valuable materials of the Indian and combined the good qualities of both cloth and leather for making articles of clothing, bags and pouches, and many other useful things.

Buckskin is usually thought of as softened deer-skin, or the skin of the buck, or male, deer. Deer-skin makes a superior quality of buckskin, but the Indian also made buckskin from many other hides and skins—from that of the buffalo, the moose, the elk, and even smaller animals. Sometimes the hair was left on and the softened skin or hide used as a robe.

Buckskin is not a tanned leather—although the white man's modern "buckskin" is usually tanned sheepskin, and he even tans a deerskin with chemicals and terms it buckskin. But not the Indian. His buckskin is made directly from rawhide, without tanning agents.

While there were some slight differences in the procedure among various tribes, in general the method of making buckskin was about the same. Taking his dehaired rawhide, the Indian softened it by working into it the brains of the animal, adding perhaps a little of the liver. This had been made into a suds by boiling it in water. Southern and southwestern Indians found that green young maize, mashed up, served the same purpose, and others used cornmeal and eggs. The hide or skin was then pounded in a mortar or kneaded and stretched and pulled. After this treatment it was soft and white and some Indians used it in this fashion, especially for women's clothes.

Since this type of skin became hard after being wet, the Indian treated his hide or skin with smoke. A pit was dug in the ground and a fire made from white cedar, corncobs, buffalo chips, or rotted wood. The skin was sewed into a cone shape and suspended over the fire, or laid over it on a bower of bent poles. Care was taken that the fire did not blaze, and the skin was smoked for an hour or so. With old white cedar the Indian got a dark tan skin; with young white cedar he obtained a light yellow or buff color. Corncobs and buffalo chips also produced a yellow.

Sometimes the Indian dyed the skin by steeping it a day in a solution in which red oak bark had been boiled. This gave a yellow-reddish color. A bright red was obtained by soaking the skin in a solution of red wild-peach bark. Finished, or smoked, buckskin is soft and pliable, can be easily cut and sewed, washes like cloth and never becomes hard. It is windproof and a protection against thorns and brush. See ANTELOPE, COSTUME, DEER, FIRE MAKING, MOCCASIN, RAWHIDE.

**BUFFALO.** The American bison, misnamed "buffalo" by the early white man, was the most important animal to the Plains Indian. It provided him with everything he needed—food, clothing, weapons, shelter, and warmth.

Not so long ago there were millions of buffaloes ranging the Plains and prairies west of the Mississippi River from the Canadian border to the Gulf of Mexico. In earlier history they are said to have been found as far east as Ohio. All tribes within the range of the buffalo were in constant contact with the great herds during the summer and winter migrations. They regulated their habits, tribal customs, and even religious rites to conform with the ways of the buffalo.

Strict regulations were observed during the tribal or ceremonial hunts, which occurred in June, July, and August. The flesh of the buffalo was then the best for eating.

Such hunts were organized under leaders, and rules were made so that every member of the hunting party had an equal chance. Individual hunting, or what was known as "still hunting," was forbidden and sometimes punished by death. An individual might scatter an entire herd and thus cause suffering to the tribe.

The "buffalo surround" was one of the most common methods of hunting on the Plains. A large circle was formed around the herd and then the hunters rushed in and killed the animals with arrows and lances—later with firearms. Squaws followed and skinned and dressed the carcasses on the spot. Other times a hunter would disguise himself in a buffalo hide and act as a decoy for the herd, leading the buffalo to the edge of a precipice where they were driven over to their death. The place where this was done was known as a "buffalo fall."

In hunting, Indians marked their arrows so they could tell which animals they had killed. Sometimes when several arrows were found in a buffalo, the animal was divided accordingly. The hide and certain parts of the carcass went to the man whose arrow had apparently killed the buffalo, while the remainder was divided among the helpers, the poor, and the disabled of the tribe. In winter the buffalo was hunted mainly for his thick pelt, from which were made robes, bedding, and the thicker and heavier garments. The winter hunt was not a tribal or ceremonial hunt, but one of small, independent, but organized parties.

Every portion of the buffalo was used by the Indian. The hide was made into a covering for his lodge, or bed, or into a robe, as explained. Or the rawhide was thickened by heating it beneath a fire in the ground to make it arrowproof—and even bulletproof—for a shield. Or it was softened for use as horse gear, bags and pouches, and numerous other articles. Stretched on willow withes, the hide formed a bullboat with which to cross streams. Buffalo hair was woven into ropes and used for ornaments.

Every part of the flesh was eaten. The hump ribs were the finest meat the Plains offered. The Indian ate the inner parts right on the spot—the liver was consumed after being sprinkled with a little gall.

The stomach was cleaned and dried and used as a container for cooking by the stone-boiling process. The meat was jerked, or cut into narrow strips and dried. Dried meat was pounded into pemmican. Marrow bones, or the bones of the hind legs, were roasted. They were then cracked open and the marrow eaten. Bones of the forelegs were of no value as marrow bones, as they contained no marrow. The buffalo had two stomachs. The contents of the first were believed to be a remedy for skin diseases and especially frostbite. Sinew was used for thread and for backing bows, as well as for tipping buffalo arrows. Buffalo chips were used as fuel.

The buffalo was also a totem or clan-symbol animal. He was believed to be the instructor of the medicine man, teaching him where and how to find healing plants and herbs. Some Indians believed the buffalo had been created by a Supreme Being especially for them. The head and horns of the animal were used by some tribes in religious ceremonies.

The great Indian uprisings of the West came because of the wanton slaughter of the buffalo by the white man. Millions were killed, often merely for the tongues, which were considered great delicacies, or for the robes. The white man never fully understood what the buffalo meant to the Indian—to every aspect of his life, his culture, and even his religion. See ARROW, BOW, BULLBOAT, DISHES, FOOD, GLUE, HUNTING, JERKED MEAT, PAINT, PEMMICAN, RAWHIDE, STONE BOILING. See also illustration, p. 32.

**BUFFALO (WHITE).** The albino buffalo, held in great awe and reverence by the Plains Indians. It provided medicine men with material for many of their mythical stories. The white buffalo was supposed to be able to transform itself into a white hawk, a gray fox, or more commonly, a beautiful woman. Its hide was used in a sacrifice to the gods.

**BUFFALO ROBE.** See BLANKET, BUCKSKIN.

**BULLBOAT.** A circular, basketlike or tub-shaped boat made by Indians for crossing streams. Willow or other withes were woven into a frame and covered with rawhide, usually from the buffalo. The seams were closed with tallow and ashes. These boats were used by the Sioux, Mandan, and other tribes on the Missouri River. See BUFFALO, RAW-HIDE.

**BULL-ROARER.** An instrument for producing a whizzing or roaring sound. Some Indians thought it produced the sound of the Thunderbird, a mythical bird supposed to cause lightning and thunder. It was made from a narrow slat of wood, from six inches to two feet long, and from one-half to two inches wide. It was hung by a cord in one end, and the Indian produced the roaring sound by swinging it in circles above his head. Also called a whizzer, whizzing stick, or lightning stick, it was used as a rain-making instrument by some Indians. See MUSICAL INSTRUMENTS, THUNDERBIRD.

**BUREAU OF INDIAN AFFAIRS.** A Government bureau, also called the Office of Indian Affairs, which provides public services to the Indians. It combines the functions performed by all other federal agencies, by state governments, by counties, by municipalities, and even by private organizations.

The Federal Government first became interested in Indian welfare through the regulation of trade. Benjamin Franklin had reported to the Albany Congress in 1754 that "Many quarrels and wars have arisen between the Colonies and the Indian nations through the bad conduct of traders who cheat the Indians after making them drunk."

In 1775 the Continental Congress took over Indian affairs, and when the Federal Constitution was adopted, the states gave to the national government the duty of regulating commerce not only with foreign nations, and among the states, but with the Indian tribes. It said: "The utmost good faith shall always be observed toward the Indians; their land and property shall never be taken from them."

Upon the establishment of the War Department in 1879 all Indian affairs were placed under its jurisdiction. In 1824 the Bureau of Indian Affairs was created within the War Department, but in 1849, owing to much criticism in the West of the way the military branch administered Indian affairs, the Bureau was transferred to the newly created Department of the Interior, where it is today.

The Bureau's function was then one of guardianship, and in a sense the Indian was considered a ward—although the Indians themselves never liked this term. The original purpose of the Bureau was to civilize the Indian and prepare him for full citizenship, and to insure that the Government fulfilled its promises to the various Indian tribes in more than 400 treaties. With the years, the aim of the administration of Indian affairs has changed gradually.

In 1924 all Indians had become citizens and could vote. However, as the Bureau still has certain trustee obligations for Indian property, and because it will take time to adjust the many-sided relationship between Indians and the Federal Government, the Bureau continues to provide services to Indians.

The Commissioner of Indian Affairs is appointed by the President. The Bureau has an agency for one or more reservations. Agencies are supervised by area offices, which in turn are supervised by the Central Office. The Central Office acts as a go-between with Congress through the Secretary of the Interior and the President.

As many Indians are leaving reservations and going to cities to work, the Bureau operates relocation centers in Chicago, Denver, Los Angeles, and Oakland, California. It is planning many other such centers and already thousands of Indians have been placed in jobs. The Bureau also operates 365 Indian schools with an enrollment of 43,616 Indian children.

More than half the Bureau's 9,500 regular employees have Indian blood. To complete its services to the Indians, the Bureau has become a huge business enterprise. It handles large estates. It is in the oil industry. It is interested in bonuses and royalties, and the disposition of great timber areas. It conducts a large cattle business and is even in the fishing industry. It arranges leases of tribal lands and carries on a big banking business. See ALLOTMENT ACT, INDIAN REORGANIZATION ACT, INDIAN RESERVATION, INDIAN SCHOOLS.

**BURIAL.** Indians had many different ways of burying their dead. Sometimes each tribe had several forms of burial. The most common modes were the placing of the dead in pits, graves, or holes in the ground; in stone caskets; in mounds; and under or in cabins, wigwams, houses, lodges, and in caves.

Among the Chippewa, Sioux, Siksika, Mandan, Gros Ventre, Arapaho, and others the dead person was placed on a scaffold or in a tree. In the Northwest the deceased was put in a canoe and the canoe placed on posts or in the forks of trees.

Some tribes of the South wrapped the corpse in a cane matting and put it in a reed coffin and buried it in the ground. Others mummified or embalmed the corpse before burial. Cremation was observed by some Pacific Coast tribes. The Creek and Seminole buried their dead in a circular pit in a sitting position, and the Mohawk made a large round hole and placed the body in it in a squatting position.

Some tribes of the Great Lakes region dug up their dead at certain periods and placed all the bones in a common pit.

The totem-pole-makers of the Northwest were in the habit of cutting off the heads of their medicine men, placing them in boxes with their magical equipment, and storing the box in a dry cave.

Most tribes placed food and weapons near the burial place and a few even killed slaves and horses, believing the dead would need these things in the next world.

Mourning the dead was customary. Among a few tribes the name of a dead person was never mentioned. Others observed the mourning period by cutting off their hair, wailing loudly, throwing away all ornaments and neglecting their persons, or carrying around a bundle representing the deceased. Cheyenne widows slashed their arms and legs.

Some famous Indian chiefs have had a difficult time resting in their graves. The bodies of Sitting Bull and Quanah Parker have been dug up and reburied in other spots. Black Hawk's remains were disturbed several times, only to be destroyed at last by fire. Red Jacket's body was hidden by a relative for years before it was properly buried. Comcomly's skull was sent to England and exhibited there for more than a century, and only recently was returned to this country. See BLACK HAWK, COMCOMLY, PARKER (QUANAH), RED JACKET, SITTING BULL.

**BURY THE HATCHET.** An expression used to mean that peace has been made between tribes or between the white man and Indian. The expression is said to have come from the custom of inserting the blade of the pipe-tomahawk in the ground before lighting the pipe. These pipe-tomahawks were traded to Indians by the white man. See CALUMET, TOMAHAWK.

**BUSK.** The green-corn dance of the Creek—a kind of New Year ceremony. See CREEK, YOPON.

C

**CADDO** (kah'-do). An Indian tribe whose members were of dark complexion and medium height. They pierced their noses, wore rings in them, and practiced tattooing. Their grass lodges were conical-shaped.

Originally of the Red River section of Louisiana, the Caddo moved to the extreme Southern Plains area, where they became buffalo hunters. They were the leading tribe of what the white man termed the Caddo Confederacy, which included the Wichita, Kichai, Tawakoni, and Waco. They obtained horses early from the Spaniards and traded these animals as far north as Illinois.

At one time the Caddo were known to the Spaniards as the *Tejas* or Texas Indians, but this term was applied to many tribes in the Southwest as it meant simply "friends." The Caddo remained loyal to the Federal Government during the Civil War and sought refuge in Kansas. In 1902 each man, woman, and child was given an allotment of land and was also made a citizen of the United States.

The name has been given to a parish in Louisiana; a county in Oklahoma; to Caddo Gap in Arkansas; villages in Oklahoma and Texas; and to Caddo Mills, in Texas. See CONFEDERATION, TEXAS, WICHITA.

**CADDOAN** (kad'-o-an) **FAMILY.** A language family group of nine tribes, scattered over the states of Texas, North Dakota, and Nebraska.

**CALENDAR.** Indians had no calendar as the white man knows it, but some tribes did keep a time record by the use of notched sticks or knots tied in a string, while others kept a record by pictures painted on skins. Among the latter were the so-called calendars of the Dakota and Kiowa. The Dakota calendar, known as the "Lone-Dog Winter Count," said to have originally been painted on a buffalo robe, covered the events from 1800 to 1871 by figures or pictures.

Indians divided their day into four periods—the rising of the sun, noon, the setting of the sun, and midnight. Full days were known as "sleeps," or nights. Months were calculated by moons, the month beginning on the new moon. An Indian thus spoke of so many moons.

The year was made up of moons, some tribes basing it on twelve moons and others on thirteen. The Creek counted twelve and one-half moons to the year, adding a moon at the end of every second year. But almost all Indians spoke of a year as a winter.

Indians usually recognized four seasons, which were either determined by the budding, blooming, leafing, and fruiting of vegetables and plants, or the actions of birds and animals. Indians of Virginia had five seasons: spring was when the buds appeared on the trees; the next season was that of the earing of corn or roasting-ear time; summer came when the sun was highest; fall was when the leaves fell off and corn was gathered; and winter began with the first snow or frost. Some tribes began their year with spring and others with fall.

Age was dated from some important event in the history of the tribe or in nature itself which was within the memory of the parents. Few Indians could calculate their age according to years, or winters. See COUNTING, PICTURE WRITING, POWHATAN.

**CALIFORNIA INDIANS.** See MISSION INDIANS.

**CALUMET** (kal'-yu-met). Usually termed the "peace pipe" by the white man, the calumet or Grand Pipe was one of the most profoundly sacred objects to the Indian from the East Coast to the Rockies. It was important in all religious, war, and peace ceremonies. It was a war pipe as well as a peace pipe.

The calumet was smoked by representatives of tribes to seal a peace pact and to assure a friendship which already existed. It was used to bring about good weather and ideal conditions for journeys and for the hunt. It also was smoked to bring rain. Its use banished evil and brought about good. It assured victory and the death of enemies who were named during a chant while it was smoked. A dance was sometimes held in honor of the calumet.

When the early French explorers came into the Mississippi Valley, they were received by the Indians with the "Dance of the Calumet." Those presented with a calumet were able to approach all other Indians as friends, simply by holding the pipe out in front of them. The flag which General John Charles Frémont, "The Pathfinder," used when he crossed the continent first showed a bundle of arrows. This meant war to the Indians, and he soon changed the symbol to that of a calumet crossed with arrows in the talons of an eagle, and was then received as a friend.

The calumet was at first simply a bunch of sacred reeds or a shaft. (The white man's word comes from the French term, which was derived from the Latin *calamus*, meaning tube or reed.) Later the Indians' bundle of reeds was combined with an altar, or pipe bowl, in burning tobacco to the gods. Thus when the calumet was smoked, friendship was sanctioned by the gods.

The calumet shaft usually was highly decorated with feathers, skins and heads of birds, hair, quillwork, or beadwork. When war was planned, feathers on the shaft were painted red. The pipe bowl was often highly carved.

Stone pipes were used by many Indians. They made journeys to the Pipestone Quarry in southwest Minnesota to obtain a red clay-stone. This was first noted by the American traveler, George Catlin, and after that the stone bore the name of "catlinite" in honor of him. The Comanche, Ute, Bannock, and Shoshoni used a rather soft stone of greenish color. The shinbones of the deer and antelope were also used, and some Plains tribes employed the thick neck muscles of the buffalo and bull elk, twisted into shape and dried.

The white man manufactured a pipe-tomahawk for trade with the Indians. It had a steel head and hollow handle. See ALTAR, BURY THE HATCHET, CATLIN, FEATHERWORK, HAIRWORK, MOUND BUILDERS, QUILLWORK, TOBACCO.


**CAMAS** (kam'-as). A root which was one of the chief foods of the Shoshoni, Bannock, and Flatheads. It was found in the high mesas of the Rockies. It was sometimes called wild hyacinth and *pomme des prairies* (apple of the prairies). The roots were placed in the ground and a fire built over them. It required about three days of cooking before they could be eaten. Also spelled *camass*. See ROOTS AND ROOTCRAFT.


**CAMP.** A temporary community or village usually located on or near the hunting grounds. To the unpracticed eye an Indian camp would look as if each family had pitched its lodge or erected its dwelling where it fancied, but in reality such camps were carefully laid out.

Plains tribes on an annual hunt camped in a circle which

was a quarter of a mile or so in diameter. Sometimes there were circles within circles. Each circle represented a family or political group. The Dakota, who called themselves the "Seven Council Fires," formed their camps in two groups, one composed of four circles and the other of three.

The Omaha camped in a wide circle, with each of the ten families in its accustomed place. In time of danger the ponies were driven within this circle. When the Kiowa, Cheyenne, and others held their annual sun dance or other ceremonies, they camped in a larger circle than usual, with each political division in a fixed and regular order.

No matter what position a lodge might have in a circle it always opened to the east. When on the warpath the Indian had no order about his camp. Then he sometimes erected a rude shelter known as a wickiup. See CHEYENNE, DAKOTA, KIOWA, LODGE, OMAHA, SUN DANCE, TEPEE, WIGWAM, WICKIUP.

CANOE. The canoe was one of the most important gifts from the Indian to the white man and to civilization. The birch-bark canoe was light and easily carried over portages, drew very little water, and so could be paddled in shallow streams. The method of paddling the canoe enabled the Indian to move quietly and stealthily.

The framework of the canoe was of sprucewood; the covering was of white birch-bark, sewed together and made watertight with pitch. The inside, or toughest part of the bark, was outside, instead of the "pretty side" being outside as usually is pictured. The canoe was pointed at both ends with the bow and stern greatly rounded up.

Canoes were used on rivers and streams east of the Rockies and especially in the Great Lakes region. They varied in size from small river canoes, which were handled by two men, to the Montreal, or voyageur's canoe, which was thirty-five to forty feet in length. This latter canoe was much used on the Great Lakes, and was handled by from eight to ten men. A smaller canoe than this, twenty-four feet long, was used on inland lakes and rivers, and was usually handled by four or five men. See BARK CRAFT, BIGIU, DUGOUT, GLUE.

**CANOE BURIAL.** See BURIAL.

**CANONICUS** (ka-non'-i-kus). A sachem of the Narragansett, who treated the Pilgrims at first with great arrogance. He is remembered as the haughty chief who sent Governor Bradford a bundle of arrows tied in a snake's skin, which was a challenge of war. Governor Bradford sent the skin back filled with gunpowder and bullets. The superstitious Indians took this for some fatal charm and passed it from village to village until finally they sent it back to Plymouth as a token of peace. After that Canonicus was a friend to the whites. The chief, who lived on Canonicus Island, opposite the site of Newport, Rhode Island, died in 1647 at the age of eighty-two. See NARRAGANSET, PILGRIMS.

**CAPTAIN JACK.** Chief of the Modoc Indians. See MODOC, RIDDLE.

**CAPTIVES.** Persons captured in an Indian raid usually were considered the property of the man or men who had actually captured them. If several claimed a prisoner, he might be owned by them all, or if there was much argument about ownership the prisoner was tortured to death.

White women captives were well treated by tribes east of the Mississippi River, but the opposite often was true when they were taken by tribes west of the river, on the Plains, and in the Southwest. Children commonly were treated tenderly and often adopted into the tribe. Indians, as a rule, loved children.

When some tribes were at war and warriors of the enemy side were captured, they were usually made to run the gantlet, or they were tortured to death, and sometimes even eaten. Often the captive's fate was decided by the warrior who had made the capture. He might want to adopt the prisoner or make a slave of him. As most tribes disowned a man who had been taken prisoner, a captive would gladly become a member of the tribe of his captor. If a prisoner was adopted it was usual to give him the name and allow him to fill the place of some kinsman who had died. He brought this person "back to life" in the eyes of the relatives. See INDIAN NAMES, PAPOOSE, SLAVES, TORTURE.

CARIBOU (kar'-eh-boo). A large animal of the reindeer family, of a dull dun color in summer and a smoky-white in winter. It had large antlers and was found from Maine to Lake Superior. The caribou was an important food animal for the northern Indians. The hide was used for clothing and robes, and was also made into rawhide and, particularly, babiche. This type was known as the woodlands caribou. A Barren Ground species was found farther north in the Arctic regions. See BABICHE, BLANKET, RAWHIDE.

**CARLISLE INDIAN SCHOOL.** The first school for Indians established by the Government off a reservation. It was located at Carlisle, Pennsylvania, and was founded by General R. H. Pratt, United States Army, while a lieutenant in charge of Indian prisoners of war at St. Augustine, Florida, in 1875-1878. When the release of these prisoners was ordered, twenty-two of the Indians requested further education. They were placed in schools at Hampton, Virginia, and several other localities.

Finally an order was issued transferring the Carlisle Barracks near Harrisburg, Pennsylvania, from the War Department to the Department of the Interior for Indian school purposes.

A law to establish such an institution was passed in 1882. General Pratt, who was in charge of the school, became known as the "Father of the Indian School System." His idea was "to get the Indian away from the reservation into civilization, and when you get him there, keep him there." The school was continued until World War I, when it was closed and the buildings returned to the War Department as a hospital for convalescents. Many prominent Indian athletes were graduated from there, including the famous football star, Jim Thorpe. See INDIAN SCHOOLS, THORPE.

**CARSON, CHRISTOPHER (KIT).** A great American frontiersman, scout, and Indian fighter. He was born in Madison County, Kentucky, on December 24, 1809. When he was a year old, his parents moved to Missouri. Orphaned at an early age, young Kit served as a saddler's apprentice at Old Franklin, an outfitting post on the Santa Fé Trail. At the age of seventeen he ran away, joining a caravan on its way to Santa Fé, but upon reaching there he went on to Taos, New Mexico.

For the next fourteen years Kit made his living as a professional guide and hunter for exploring parties and for a time shot game for the garrison at Bent's Fort in the Territory of Colorado.

At St. Louis in 1842 Kit Carson joined General John C. Frémont on his exploring expedition, and three years later was employed by Frémont on his expedition to California. He fought in the War with Mexico, and after the Gold Rush of '49 hired out to guide immigrants and drovers across the Plains and mountains.

Tiring of this life, Kit Carson decided to settle down and raise sheep at Taos. But because of trouble with the Navajo he was forced to give this up and continue his life as an Indian fighter. In 1853 he was appointed Indian Agent at Taos and had much influence in controlling the warlike Navajo. Ten years later he rounded up some 8,000 of the Indians and held them prisoners on a reservation.

During the Civil War he fought on the Federal side and was chief scout in charge of various groups of irregulars and rangers engaged in the constant border warfare. In the Texas Panhandle he repulsed an attack by Comanche and Kiowa warriors who greatly outnumbered his troops. This battle at Adobe Walls was a half-mile from the Adobe Walls attacked some years later by Quanah Parker and his Indians.

Carson rose to the rank of brigadier general and was cited for gallantry and distinguished services. After the war he again took up his duties as Indian agent. He died at Fort Lyon, Colorado, on May 23, 1868. His old home at Taos has been preserved as a museum. See FUR TRADE, INDIAN SCOUTS, LONG WALK (THE), NAVAJO, TANOAN PUEBLOS.

CATAWBA (kah-taw'-ba). One of the important eastern Siouan tribes. At one time they were considered the most powerful tribe in the Carolinas. While they were an agricultural people and friendly to the whites, in their early days they were constantly at war with the Iroquois, Shawnee, Delaware, and other tribes of the Ohio Valley.

Two hundred years ago the Catawba numbered as many as 5,000 in North and South Carolina, but war and smallpox in time reduced their population to a few hundred. Although they had assisted the Americans in the defense of South Carolina against the British in the Revolutionary War, years later they found themselves without a home in that state. Their reservation there was almost wholly leased to whites in 1826 and in 1840 they sold the remainder of it. When North Carolina refused to set apart any land for them, they returned to South Carolina where finally 800 acres were given them. The few remaining live there today.

The Catawba gave their name to a variety of northern fox grape they utilized. The name also has been preserved in a county and town in North Carolina, and places in West Virginia, Kentucky, Ohio, Missouri, New York, Oklahoma, South Carolina, and Wisconsin, as well as by an island in the Ohio River, and the Catawba River of the Carolinas. See TRAILS.

**CATLIN, GEORGE.** Famous authority on the life and customs of the American Indian. Catlin was the first great painter of the Indian, and he not only made the Red Man renowned on canvas but in literature.

Catlin was born in Wilkes-Barre, Pennsylvania, in 1796, and was educated as a lawyer. He practiced two years in Philadelphia, but preferring art he gave up practice and set up a portrait studio in New York. Believing like many that the American Indian was disappearing, he decided to spend his life painting them and writing about them.

He lived among Indians, learning their languages, habits, and customs and making many notes and studies for paintings.- In 1841 he published the *Manners, Customs and Conditions of the North American Indians* in two volumes, illustrated with 300 engravings. Three years later he brought out *The North American Portfolio* with 25 plates of Indian hunting scenes and amusements in the Rockies and on the Plains.

His great collection of paintings is now in the Catlin Gallery of the National Museum in Washington, D.C.

Catlin first brought to attention the quarry in southwest Minnesota where the Indians obtained the red pipestone used in making their sacred calumets. Indians believed this stone represented living flesh and blood. It now bears the name of catlinite in honor of Catlin.

Catlin died in Jersey City, New Jersey, December 22, 1872. See CALUMET, MANDAN.

**CATLINITE.** See CALUMET, CATLIN.

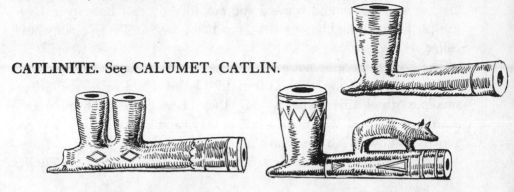

**CAT'S CRADLE.** A game played with string, especially popular with the Zuñi and Navajo. See GAMES.

**CATTLE.** The Indian thought of cattle in much the same way he did of any other animal whose flesh could be used as food, and hide made into clothing and robes. In fact the Algonquin, who called the buffalo *beezhike,* applied the same name to cattle when they first saw them.

Indians did not raise cattle as the white man did. The Plains Indians preferred buffalo meat to cow meat, and it was not until the white man had killed off the buffalo that Indians began to raid the white man's herds of cattle.

During the great cattle drives from Texas to the railheads in Kansas, the Indians living on reservations in Oklahoma demanded a certain share of the cattle as payment for the driving of the herds across their territory. They called the cow *wohaw,* from the terms "whoa" and "haw," which they had heard used by bull-whackers in driving their teams of oxen. See COWBOY.

**CAYUGA** (kah-yoo'-ga). See IROQUOIS.

**CAYUSE** (ky-oos'). A western tribe associated with the Nez Percé and Wallawalla Indians, formerly ranging the territory at the heads of the Wallawalla, Umatilla, and Grande Ronde rivers from the Blue Mountains to the Deschutes River in Washington and Oregon. The Cayuse were brave and warlike and considered great horsemen. Cayuse ponies were highly prized by cowboys, and in Texas a pony was called a "cayuse."

The Cayuse became notorious during the early days of the settlers in Washington. They were unfriendly to the white man, and when smallpox struck their tribe in 1847, they blamed the white man and murdered Marcus Whitman, a missionary, and several other settlers at what is now Whitman, Washington.

A town in Oregon is named Cayuse. See JOSEPH, NEZ PERCÉ.

**CELT.** Stone, metal, or other hard material shaped in the form of an ax or hatchet, but without the handle grooves. Celts have been found weighing from half an ounce to twenty pounds. Most were made from serpentine and other hard stones. They were shaped by grinding. They were used as axes, scrapers, skinning knives, meat cutters, and in some instances as weapons of war. See AX, FLINT.

**CHAPARRAL COCK.** The road runner, a cuckoo-like bird of the Southwest, which was called the "Medicine Bird" by some Indians. This small bird with short wings was considered "good medicine" by the Plains Indians. The skin, or even some of the feathers, hung in an Indian lodge was believed to bring good luck to the occupants. Indians also used the feathers of this bird on their whistles in the Medicine Dance.

The road runner, also known as *paisano*, or "fellow countryman" along the Border, is the deadly enemy of the rattlesnake. There are tall stories that when it darts toward the snake it catches up a mouthful of chaparral thorns, and weaving in and out as the snake strikes, stuffs the thorns into the reptile's mouth. It then pecks out the snake's eyes.

The chaparral cock is the state bird of New Mexico. See DANCE, FEATHERWORK.

**CHARBONNEAU, JEAN BAPTISTE.** Son of Sacajawea, the Bird Woman. See SACAJAWEA.

**CHATTANOOGA.** A Cherokee word meaning "crow's nest," which has given its name to a city in Tennessee, a creek in Georgia, as well as towns in Ohio and Oklahoma.

**CHEMEHUEVI** (chem-a-wa'-ve). A small desert tribe believed to have been at one time a part of the Paiute. They once roamed the eastern half of the Mojave Desert and later the Chemehuevi Valley along the Colorado River in California. Today a few remain, living among the Paiute in California. See PAIUTE.

**CHEROKEE.** One of the most powerful tribes of the Iroquoian stock, and one of the most famous in all North America because of its size and strength and the prominent part it played in the history of the United States.

Separated from the other Iroquois in the early days, the Cherokee roamed the mountain region of the South Alleghenies in southwest Virginia, west North Carolina, South Carolina, northern Georgia, and northeast Alabama, claiming territory to the Ohio River. They were first encountered by De Soto in 1540. During the Revolutionary War they sided with the English, but they did not wage actual war against the colonists. In 1820 they had adopted a regular form of government modeled after that of the United States. They were then known as the Cherokee Nation.

The Cherokee were respected by the white man. They were people of high character, and were the first to own farms and accept the white man's schools. In 1825 it was recorded that forty-seven white men and seventy-three white women had married into the tribe. It was the gifted Sequoya, son of a white man and a Cherokee woman, who painstakingly created the first written Indian alphabet—an alphabet of the Cherokee language—so that his people could learn better the ways of the white man. It was the only case of the creation of a system of writing without the aid or prompting of the white man in the history of the Indian.

When gold was discovered in Georgia, the white man sought the removal of the Cherokee from this part of the country. The state of Georgia began to claim their lands, and some of the whites destroyed their farms and took their horses and cattle. In 1838-1839 the United States Army rounded up most of the Cherokee population and marched them west. One-fourth of the unhappy Indians died on the way.

The survivors were established in the Indian Territory. They reorganized their government and joined with the Chickasaw, Choctaw, Creek, and Seminole to form the Five Civilized Tribes. As many were slaveholders and had thousands of Negro slaves, they joined with the Confederate States during the Civil War.

One small group of Cherokee had refused to be moved west and fled into the mountains of North Carolina and Tennessee. After many difficulties they finally were able to obtain sufficient land upon which to live, and today their homes are on the Qualla Reservation in the Smoky Mountains of North Carolina.

The name Cherokee is widespread throughout the United States. There is a Cherokee county in Alabama, Georgia, Iowa, Kansas, Oklahoma, North and South Carolina, and Texas. There are also place names in some of these states, as well as in California, Kentucky, and Arkansas. There is a Cherokee City in Arkansas, a Cherokee Dam in Tennessee, and a Cherokee Falls in South Carolina. Several prominent Americans have descended from the Cherokee, notably Senator Robert Owen and Will Rogers, the actor. See FIVE CIVILIZED TRIBES, MOUND BUILDERS, SEQUOYA, TATTOOING, WAMPUM, WARD.

**CHEROKEE ALPHABET.** See SEQUOYA.

**CHESAPEAKE** (chess'-a-peek). An Algonquin word meaning "place where there is a great body of water spread out." It is the name of a bay off the coast of Maryland, and a town in Ohio.

**CHEYENNE** (shy-en'). One of the most famous tribes of the Plains. The Cheyenne formerly lived in what is now Minnesota and later moved to the present state of North Dakota. From here they were driven west by the powerful Chippewa, who destroyed their settlement. It was after this that they are believed to have joined with the Arapaho, with whom they were ever after allied.

The Cheyenne, divided into what are called the Northern and the Southern Cheyenne, were a powerful, athletic race, and of a superior mentality. The men were noted for their bravery and the women for their virtue. They were horse Indians and buffalo hunters and lived in tepees.

The Cheyenne were continually at war with both their red and white neighbors. In 1876 they joined the Dakota under Sitting Bull and were present at the famous battle fought with General Custer. Two years later they were defeated by Government troops and placed on a reservation in Oklahoma. The climate did not agree with them and many died, until finally in September, 1878, they made an epic break for freedom under the leadership of Chief Dull Knife. They were pursued, but outfought and outmaneuvered the best of the United States troops, only to be overcome at the Dakota border.

Dull Knife once more led his people in an attempt to escape from Fort Robinson, Nebraska, only to be recaptured.

The efforts of this proud and freedom-loving people to regain their hunting grounds and live their roving, carefree existence make one of the saddest annals in Indian history. They were eventually confined to reservations in Oklahoma and Montana and gave little trouble until the Ghost Dance religion swept over the Indian country.

The great tribal ceremony of the Cheyenne was the Sun Dance. They also observed a Buffalo Head ceremony. They had a bunch of four sacred arrows, each of a different color, which they claimed they had possessed since the beginning of the world. No woman, white man, or half-breed was allowed to come near this bundle. It is still preserved by the Southern Cheyenne.

The Cheyenne had several war societies, the most noted of which was the "Dog Soldiers." As the white man sometimes referred to the entire tribe as Dog Soldiers, some thought the name Cheyenne came from the French *chien*, meaning "dog." However, it is from the Teton Sioux *Shahiyena*, meaning "People of Alien Speech."

Today the Northern Cheyenne live at the Tongue River Agency in Montana; the Southern Cheyenne and the Arapaho in Oklahoma.

The name is preserved by the state capital of Wyoming and by a river in South Dakota; counties in Colorado, Nebraska, and Kansas; the Cheyenne Mountains and Cañons in Colorado; by a river and a town in North Dakota, both spelled Sheyenne; by Cheyenne Wells in Colorado, and towns in Oklahoma and Texas. See ARAPAHO, CAMP, CUSTER'S LAST STAND, DOG SOLDIER, DULL KNIFE, GHOST DANCE, HORSE, HORSE INDIANS, KIOWA, MILITARY SOCIETIES, ROMAN NOSE, SACRED BUNDLES, SAND PAINTING, SIGN LANGUAGE, SUN DANCE.

**CHICKAHOMINY** (chick'-a-hom'-i-ni). A band of the Powhatan, of whom a few survive today in Virginia. They gave their name to the Chickahominy River in Virginia. The name means "turkey lick," or "place where turkeys are plentiful." See POWHATAN.

**CHICKASAW** (chik'-a-sah). A tribe of the Muskhogean family closely related to the Creek and Choctaw in the early days. They are noted as one of the warlike tribes of the Gulf area, and the one tribe encountered by the Spaniards who came nearest to destroying De Soto's army in 1451.

The Chickasaw formerly ranged a section which is now in northern Mississippi and portions of Tennessee. They were a slaveholding people, but when the Civil War ended they freed their slaves and adopted them into the tribe. They became members of the Five Civilized Tribes after they were moved to Oklahoma by the Government.

The Chickasaw language, similar to that of the Mobile Indians, served as a means of commercial and tribal intercourse for all tribes along the Mississippi River. Their chiefs were called "mingos." Today they are in Oklahoma. There are towns of the name in Alabama and Ohio and a Chickasha in Oklahoma. See FIVE CIVILIZED TRIBES, MINGO, MOBILE.

**CHIEF.** In many tribes the title of chief was inherited. In others it could be won only by brave acts or by wealth and influence. The Iroquois had chiefs who were given office as a reward for some great deed. These were known as "the solitary pine trees," and when they died the office was not filled. A chief had no legal status and obedience to him was voluntary.

There were several grades of chiefs, who were organized into a tribal council. Many tribes had peacetime, or civil chiefs, who had to resign their offices if they wished to follow the war chief into battle. Each clan had a chief, and this office remained in the clan or family, the descent usually traced through the mother. Each wandering band also had its own chief. In some tribes, mainly those of the Plains, a courageous and wealthy warrior might proclaim himself chief.

In confederations the head man usually was known as "head chief," but where the confederation was powerful the man might be known as "king" or "emperor." The English frequently gave these Indian chiefs such royal titles. It was only the Natchez who had a ruler, "The Great Sun," who actually was what might be termed a king. See NATCHEZ, POWWOW, SACHEM, TRIBE.

**CHILE** (chil'-ly). A hot red pepper used by Indians of the Southwest.

**CHINOOK** (sheh-nook'). A tribe, noted as traders and fishermen, living on the Columbia River on the West Coast. In their contact with other tribes and with the white man, especially with the fur traders at Astoria, Oregon, the Chinook Jargon was developed, as the Chinook language itself was difficult to learn and pronounce.

The Chinook used dugout canoes and lived in wood houses. They were taller than most other Pacific Coast Indians and had wider faces and high narrow noses. They deformed their skulls by pressure when young, and considered a naturally formed skull a disgrace, permitted only to slaves.

The name has been given to towns in Washington and Montana. See CHINOOK JARGON, CLATSOP, COMCOMLY, FLATHEADS, FUR TRADE.

**CHINOOK JARGON.** An Indian trade language of the Columbia River section, also known as the Oregon Trade Language, a combination of Indian, English, French, and a few Russian words. First noted by fur traders on the West Coast around 1810, it served the same purpose in the Northwest as the Mobile language did in the Gulf States and the Indian sign language on the Plains.

Examples of Chinook Jargon: American was *Boston Man;* Amusement was *He-He;* Broom was *Bloom;* Buffalo was *Moos-Moos;* Christmas Day was *Hy-as Sunday;* Clock, *Hy-as Watch;* Eat, *Muck-a-Muck.* See BOSTON, CHINOOK, INDIAN LANGUAGE, MOBILE, SIGN LANGUAGE, SIWASH, TRADING LANGUAGES.

81

**CHINOOK WIND.** A warm southwest wind which usually comes in winter and suddenly melts the snow. There are three types of chinook winds: a wet chinook, a dry chinook, and a chinook which is in between. The term is said to have first been given to a wind which blew over the Chinook Indian camp toward the trading post established by the Hudson's Bay Company at Astoria, Oregon.

**CHIPPEWA** (chip'-ee-wa). A Woodland tribe, one of the largest and most important of the Algonquian family, which formerly ranged both shores of Lakes Superior and Huron across Minnesota to North Dakota. They were also known as the Ojibwa.

The Chippewa were once a part of the Potawatomi and Ottawa, and with them were known as the "Three Fires." But they separated in the westward movement of the group. They early obtained guns from the white man and were able to stop the expansion of the warlike Dakota and the Fox, who sought to take from them their valuable wild rice fields. They beat the Fox so badly that the latter took refuge with the Sauk, with whom they were ever after allied.

They were first known only as the Ojibwa—and, in fact, most of the Indians themselves use this term today—but the name was twisted about in mispronunciation until it became Chippewa, which became the favorite of historians. Ojibwa, meaning "to roast until puckered up," had been given them by other tribes because the tops of their moccasins were puckered at the seam in sewing.

The Chippewa were not prominent in the early history of the United States. This was because they were remote from the frontiers during the colonial wars. They have been on friendly terms with the white man since their treaty of 1815.

The Chippewa, a handsome, intelligent tribe, in the old days lived in wigwams made of birch bark and grass mats. Expert in the use of the canoe, they were good fishermen. Their main food was wild rice.

Henry R. Schoolcraft, the great Indian authority, lived among them and married a Chippewa woman. He wrote much about them, and Longfellow further popularized them by using Schoolcraft's material in his poem *Hiawatha*. While the name Hiawatha was drawn from Iroquois sources, the stories are nearly all from the Chippewa.

The name is preserved by streams is Wisconsin, Ohio, and Michigan; by counties in Michigan, Wisconsin, and Minnesota; and by place names in Pennsylvania, New York, Wisconsin, Michigan, and Ohio. There is a Chippewa Bay in New York, a Chippewa Falls in Wisconsin, and a Chippewa Lake in Ohio. There is a town named Ojibwa in Wisconsin. See ASSINIBOIN, CONFEDERATION, HOLE-IN-THE-DAY, LONGFELLOW, MENOMINEE, OTTAWA, POTAWATOMI, SAUK AND FOX, SCHOOLCRAFT, TATTOOING.

CHOCTAW (chok'-taw). The largest tribe belonging to the southern branch of the Muskhogean family. They were farming Indians, formerly of the middle and southern sections of what is now Mississippi. Their name is said to have come from the Spanish word *chato*, which means "flat," because of their custom of flattening their heads.

The earliest historical record of these Indians is when they were found by De Soto in 1540. They were friendly to the French when the latter settled the Louisiana Territory, and were always at peace

with the United States Government. The Choctaw began to migrate to the Indian Territory in 1835 when they ceded most of their lands to the government.

They had a strange custom in burying their dead. They first cleaned the bones before putting them in boxes and baskets in their bone houses. This work was done by "old gentlemen with very long nails." They allowed their fingernails to grow long just for this purpose. Another unusual custom among the Choctaw was that of the men wearing their hair long, and for this reason some of their neighbors gave them the name of "Long Hairs."

A jargon of the Choctaw language was called the Mobile trade language, also known as the Chickasaw trade language. The Chickasaw and Choctaw languages were similar. There were reports that during World War I the Choctaw language was used as a code language by intelligence officers. A Choctaw would be placed at each end of a field telephone and would transmit messages in his own tongue. A similar report came out of World War II.

The Choctaw joined with the Cherokee and others as a member of the Five Civilized Tribes. The tribe has furnished the name for counties in Alabama, Mississippi, and Oklahoma, and settlements in the same states, as well as in Arkansas. See FIVE CIVILIZED TRIBES, MOBILE, MOUND BUILDERS, TRADING LANGUAGES.

**CHUCK.** An Algonquian word for food. It is still used in the West by the white man.

**CHUNKEY.** A game played by southeastern Indians. See GAMES.

**CLAN AND GENS.** The unit of a tribe. Members of a clan or gens were those descended from the same ancestor. In some cases this was through the father, a son or daughter belonging always to his or her father's gens. But in other cases it was through the mother, and a child belonged to its mother's clan. Marriages were not allowed within the clan or gens. Frequently each clan or gens had an animal "totem," or symbol, such as the Wolf, Deer, Turtle, or Snipe clans of the Iroquois. Each clan or gens also had its own chief. See BAND, POWWOW, TOTEM, TOTEM POLES, TRIBE, WOMEN.

**CLARK, CAPTAIN WILLIAM.** See LEWIS. See also illustration, page 180.

**CLATSOP.** An Oregon tribe, related to the Chinook, who lived along the Columbia River. Their name meant "dried salmon." A town and county in Oregon are named for them. See CHINOOK.

**CLIFF DWELLERS.** A term usually applied to the early Pueblo Indians of what is now New Mexico, Arizona, Utah, and Colorado. Long ago, before recorded history, they lived in houses that were cut out of rock on ledges, or in natural niches in the faces of cliffs, usually in the walls of canyons. Homes built in these places were difficult of access by marauding tribes. The most famous of the houses were at Mesa Verde in Colorado, where apartments were built in the crescent-shaped hollows of cliffs. See PUEBLO INDIANS.

85

**COCHISE** (koh-chees'). A famous Chiricahua Apache chief who led the revolt of his tribe against the whites in the 1870's. Cochise had resisted when efforts were made to place the Apaches on a new reservation in New Mexico. With fewer than 200 warriors he held off the United States Army for more than four years and forced the Government to make peace with an unconquered enemy. Then, after a reservation was established in Arizona, he brought in his warriors.

Cochise, although one of the fiercest Apaches of them all, proved in peace to be a very wise man. He did not want his people on a reservation, and had said: "Let my people mingle with the whites, in their farms and communities, and let us be one people." But the Government said no. It was many years before the white man realized the wisdom of Cochise's reasoning and decided that Indians and whites should be one people.

Cochise died peacefully on June 8, 1874. A county, town, and mountains in Arizona are named for him. See APACHE.


**COCKAROUSE** (kok'-a-rous). A word used by the old-time Virginia Indians to mean a person of importance. It has been adopted by the white man to designate a leader or big man.

**CODY, WILLIAM FREDERICK (BUFFALO BILL).** A famous scout, Indian fighter, and showman. See DAKOTA.

**COFITACHIQUI** (ko-fit'-a-chee-kee), **THE LADY OF.** A gracious and friendly Indian girl, niece of the chieftainess of Cofitachiqui, a town of the Muskogee Indians, on the Savannah River, in what is now Georgia. When De Soto visited this place in 1540, he was welcomed by the "Lady of Cofitachiqui" on behalf of her aunt, and she presented him with a valuable string of pearls. This friendship was ill returned by De Soto, who carried her away as a hostage to protect his party from attacks of Indians under her influence. After two weeks of captivity the "Lady" managed to escape in the mountainous region of northeast Georgia, and in leaving carried away a box of pearls De Soto had seized, much to the Spaniard's chagrin. See WOMEN.

**COLUMBUS, CHRISTOPHER** (1446-1506). Italian navigator and explorer who discovered America for Spain on October 12, 1492. Columbus was known as the "Admiral of the Ocean Sea," the Atlantic being known as the "Ocean Sea" at that time to distinguish it from the Mediterranean Sea.

It was Columbus who gave the natives of America the name "Indios," or "Indians," first mentioned in his journal of October 17, 1492, after landing at San Salvador or Cat Island in the Bahamas. After describing the natives he wrote: "All these Indians I am taking with me."

Columbus thought at the time that he was cruising among the islands of the eastern Indies off the Asiatic Coast, and that the people he saw were therefore Indians. See INDIAN.

**COLVILLE.** A division of Salish Indians on the Columbia River in Washington. They were named for Fort Colville, a post of the Hudson's Bay Company at Kettle Falls.

**COMANCHE** (ko-man'-che). One of the most famous tribes of the Plains. They were typical Plains Indians—expert horsemen, buffalo hunters, and warlike in character. When the Comanche came into history they had the horse and were considered the finest horsemen of the Plains, with dash and courage.

They were believed to have been an offshoot of the Shoshoni of Wyoming. When the Shoshoni were beaten back into the mountains by the powerful Dakota, the Comanche were driven south. In early times the Comanche, Kiowa, and Shoshoni were all termed Snakes, and sometimes Horse Indians. The three tribes formed a long line from Montana to Mexico—the Shoshoni in the north, the Kiowa between Denver and Amarillo, and the Comanche south and east of Amarillo. As Plains Indians, each tribe needed a ranging area of from 500 to 800 square miles.

The Comanche, bitter enemies of the Texans, carried on a war with them for almost forty years. In 1867 they agreed to go to a reservation between the Washita and Red rivers in southwest Oklahoma. But some, led by their chief, Quanah Parker, refused. Not until the last outbreak of the southern tribes in 1874-1875 did they and their allies, the Kiowa and Kiowa Apache, finally settle on the reservation.

The Comanche language was a trade language in the Southwest and understood by most neighboring tribes. It has a nice, flowing sound, with a rolling "r."

In 1901 the Comanche reservation was thrown open to settlement, and today they are attached to the Kiowa Agency in Oklahoma. Counties in Kansas and Texas are named for them, as is a mountain in Texas and a river in Colorado. There is a Comanche in Montana, Texas, and Oklahoma. See HORSE, HORSE INDIANS, INDIAN LANGUAGE, KIOWA, KIOWA APACHE, PARKER (QUANAH), SHOSHONI, TEXAS, TRADING LANGUAGES, TRAILS.

**COMANCHEROS** (ko-man'-cher-os). A rough class of frontiersmen who banded together several times a year and went into the Plains Indian country to trade for horses and mules. Usually the trinkets they carried for trade never exceeded twenty dollars in value, but they did an enormous business. Frequently the Indians stole back the animals they had traded the comancheros. As much of their trade was in Texas with the Comanche, they thus gained their name. See HORSE.

**COMCOMLY** (kom-kom'-ly). A famous chief of the Chinook Indians. He was a friend of the whites and welcomed the Lewis and Clark expedition when it reached the mouth of the Columbia River on the Pacific Coast in 1805. Later, when the Astor expedition arrived to take over the country for the United States, Comcomly gave his daughter as wife to Duncan M'Dougal, who was at the head of the expedition.

Although it was charged that Comcomly was connected with a plot to massacre the garrison and seize the stores, the chief redeemed himself by offering to fight on the side of the Americans in 1812 when the British arrived to capture the fort. A peaceful transfer of the fort was made, however.

Comcomly was a regal chief and always traveled in style. Usually 300 slaves or more went ahead of him and carpeted the ground with beaver and otter skins for him to walk upon. He died in 1830, and his flattened skull was sent to England as a medical curiosity. It was on exhibition at the Royal Naval Hospital from 1835 to 1952 when it was presented to the Clatsop County (Oregon) Historical Society. See BURIAL, CHINOOK.

**CONESTOGA** (kon-es-toh'-ga) **HORSE**. A heavy draft horse which was bred in Pennsylvania in the late 1700's. It was a cross of the Flemish carthorse and an English breed. The horse was named from Conestoga, a village in Lancaster County, Pennsylvania, which was called after one of the Iroquois tribes of that section. These horses were much used with the famous Conestoga wagon. See CONESTOGA WAGON, SUSQUEHANNA.

**CONESTOGA WAGON.** A large, heavy wagon which was covered with canvas. This wagon was favored by emigrants who went to settle in the Far West. It was usually drawn by oxen, but in the East it was drawn by six or more Conestoga horses. Called a *wagon-tipi* by the Indian, it was named for Conestoga, a village in Lancaster County, Pennsylvania, where it was first built. See CONESTOGA HORSE.

**CONFEDERATION.** A league of two or more Indian tribes, formed for mutual protection, especially in time of war. The most famous confederation was that of the Iroquois. Lesser confederations were headed by the Chippewa, the Powhatan, the Dakota, and the Caddo. See CADDO, CHIPPEWA, DAKOTA, IROQUOIS, POWHATAN, TRIBE.

**CONNECTICUT.** A state which gets its name from the Indian word meaning "Land of Long Tidal River," the Connecticut River. Indians called the country along the banks of this river, *Quinnehtugut,* and Roger Williams in 1643 called these Indians the Quintikoock. Quonoktacut Lake in Maine is a name from the same source.

**COOPER, JAMES FENIMORE** (1789-1851). American novelist, born in Burlington, New Jersey. His novels of the frontier were among the most popular of his writings. These included his *Leatherstocking Tales: The Deerslayer, The Last of the Mohicans, The Pathfinder, The Pioneers*, and *The Prairie*. See MAHICAN, MOHEGAN, UNCAS.

**CORN.** See MAIZE.

**CORNPLANTER.** A famous Seneca chief who was the son of an Indian woman and a white man. He was also known as John O'Bail and was born in the 1770's on the Genesee River in New York.

Cornplanter was brought up among the Seneca, believing himself a true Indian. But when his playmates spoke of the difference in color of his skin and theirs, his mother finally told him his father was a white man and lived in Albany, New York. He visited his father who was then married to a white woman. The elder O'Bail treated him kindly "But gave me nothing to carry back," Cornplanter later said.

While fighting on the side of the British in the Revolutionary War, Cornplanter captured his father and tried to persuade him to live with him. But his father refused and was taken back to his home.

Like the other Seneca Indian chief, Red Jacket, Cornplanter was forgiven his part in the Revolution when he sided with the United States in the War of 1812. He offered to lead his tribe against the British, but was not allowed to because he was thought too old to fight. His son, Henry O'Bail, served as a major with the United States Army.

Years later Cornplanter, who had been honored by the colonists for his friendship, said the Great Spirit had told him to have nothing more to do with the whites. He burned a belt and broke a beautiful sword which had been given him. He died at about the age of ninety, and years later, in 1866, a monument was erected to his memory on his reservation by the state of Pennsylvania. See HALF-BREED, IROQUOIS, ORATORS, RED JACKET.

**CORNSTALK.** A celebrated Shawnee chief who lived from 1720 to 1777. He first came into notice by his leadership of the Indians in the Battle of Point Pleasant, West Virginia, on October 10, 1774. He was defeated by the settlers, but his generalship won him their praise. Three years later he went with his two sons to Point Pleasant to inform the people that the Indians might rise against them and he might be drawn into the war. He and his sons were held as hostages and later were treacherously murdered. A monument was erected to his memory in the courthouse yard at Point Pleasant in 1896. See SHAW-NEE, TARHE.

**CORONADO, FRANCISCO VASQUEZ DE.** A Spaniard who first explored the southwestern part of the United States. He set out in 1540 to find the famed "Seven Cities of Cibola," which are believed now to have been the Zuñi pueblos in New Mexico. He expected to find much gold and wealth. With a part of his force he found and conquered the "Seven Cities," but did not find the supposed wealth.

In search of another wealthy Indian settlement, told of by an Indian guide, "The Turk," his army wandered as far north as Kansas. The route followed by Coronado and his men is thought to have been followed later by the famed Santa Fé Trail when it was established. Coronado was the first to meet and report on many of the Pueblo tribes. See HOPI, HORSE, TURK (THE), ZUÑI.

**COSTANOAN** (kos-tah-no'-an). A tribe of Pacific Coast Indians who at one time lived between San Francisco and Point Sur. Their name is from the Spanish *Costaños*, "Coast People." Today the tribe is believed to be extinct.

**COSTUME.** The clothing, or costume, of the Indian consisted mainly of skins, feathers, and woven materials. He procured everything he needed right from nature. Being a great hunter, he killed his game with the idea of supplying himself not only with food, but also with clothing, tools, and utensils, as well.

For clothing, the Indian used the skins and hides of the deer, buffalo, bear, caribou, and other animals. He made robes from the woven skins of smaller animals. He made decorations from the quills of the porcupine, and beads from shells, bone, claws, teeth, and even berries. He used the coarse hair of animals for braiding and decoration. Feathers of birds were made into robes, dresses, and headdresses.

The moccasin covered and protected the Indian's feet. The Timber or Woodland Indians had a soft-soled moccasin made entirely from one piece, sewed to a tongue or flap at the top. The Plains Indians had a moccasin made of two pieces, one of rawhide for the sole and the other of soft buckskin for the upper part. Indians decorated their moccasins with gayly colored beads and porcupine quills.

The Indian loved bright colors. In many cases the colors and designs on his clothes, or those he used on his face and body, had a meaning. He had colors for male and female, for the four points of the compass, and for war and peace.

Men were usually fully dressed when they wore moccasins, breechcloth, leggings, and robe. Women wrapped a wide piece of softened skin or woven material around their waists for a dress, and sometimes wore a jacket. The Algonquian women wore the slit skirt long before the white women. Women also wore moccasins and legging-moccasins.

Indians gave particular attention to their hair, greased it with bear oil, and decorated it with fur, feathers, beads, and other things. Some wore a band of some skin about the head with bangles or a row of feathers. Some wove this band from grass. Other Indians wore fur turbans. The Dakota and many western tribes wore drooping feather headdresses. Some wore only one or two feathers, for all such feathers had a meaning and usually had to be won by some brave act.

Because the Dakota Indian's dress is picturesque it has come to symbolize the dress of all Indians. Even paintings of Indians receiving the Pilgrim fathers show the red man dressed as the Dakota. A Seminole Indian marching in the Presidential Inaugural Parade at Washington might be dressed as a Dakota chief. One artist painted Pocahontas in the dress of a Sioux bride.

No Indian worried about clothes until he was ten or more years old. His own skin was satisfactory. Even when older he wore as little as possible. A blanket sometimes was his chief article of dress.

To get rid of lice in his clothes, the Indian might leave everything he was wearing on an anthill for a day or so. This was his cleaning establishment. Some Indians preserved their furs and pelts from moths by drying the body of a bird, either the martin or the "fisher," pounding it into a powder, and then sprinkling it over the fur. See BARK, BEADS, BLANKET, BREASTPLATE, BREECH-CLOTH, BUCKSKIN, DAKOTA, DEER, EARRING, HAIRWORK, HEADDRESS, HORN AND BONE CRAFT, HORSE, IROQUOIS, LEGGINGS, MOCCASIN, OTTER, PAINT, PORCUPINE, QUILLWORK, WAMPUM, WOMEN.

COUNCIL. See POWWOW.

**COUNTING.** The system of tens generally was used by Indians in counting. The white man calls this the decimal system. The Indians called it the finger and hand count.

In the Indian sign language, in counting from one to ten the usual way was to hold the closed right hand in front. For one the little finger was extended; two, the third finger; three, the second; four, the index; five, the thumb. To continue to ten the left hand was brought up. The thumb was extended for six; the index finger for seven, and so on. The little finger of the left hand indicated ten.

For twenty, both hands were brought up and the fingers and thumbs extended twice. For twenty-five the fingers of both hands were extended twice and those of one hand raised once, and so on. Among some tribes, such as the Eskimo and Tlingit, twenty was counted on the hands and feet—or on all fingers and toes—"the complete man," as they said. The Zuñi counted the second ten back on the knuckles.

Many Indians could count to one thousand, but few could imagine a greater number than this. Most of them could not imagine numbers greater than two or three hundred. The Cherokee called one thousand the "great one hundred." Among the Iroquois it was "ten hand clasps," that is ten hundreds. The Kiowa called it "the whole-hand hundred." See CALENDAR, POWHATAN, SIGN LANGUAGE.

**COUNTING COUP.** Taking credit for a victory over an enemy, or relating deeds of valor. The true coup was counted for being the first to strike or touch an enemy while alive. See COUP, COUP STICK.

**COUP** (koo). A term used by Plains Indians for a brave deed or victory over an enemy.

The bravest act was that of touching an enemy while he was alive. For this purpose the warrior might rush in and strike the enemy with his gun, quirt, bow, lance, or a long coup stick, or even with his bare hand. If he also killed his enemy, after touching him while alive, and finally scalped him, he could count three coups.

Stealing a horse from an enemy would entitle a warrior to count coup. He also could count coup by dashing into the enemy's village and striking or touching a tepee or lodge. He was said to have "captured" the tepee, and whatever design or symbol was painted on the enemy tepee the warrior could paint on his own.

Should a warrior count coup on an enemy tepee, enter and touch a live enemy, finally kill and scalp him, and on his way out of camp steal a horse he would have plenty to boast about.

In general, it was a higher honor to touch a live enemy than to kill him or even scalp him. The Assiniboin said: "Killing an enemy counts nothing unless his person is touched or struck." The Cheyenne permitted three men to count coup on an enemy—the first who touched him, of course, gaining the greatest honor. The Crow, Assiniboin, and Arapaho allowed four men to count coup. The Cree believed that killing a man while out in the open was more honorable than killing him from ambush. To kill him with a club rated higher than killing with a rifle or bow and arrow.

Various decorations were worn for each brave deed by a warrior. The Assiniboin who had killed enemies wore an eagle feather for each deed. The Dakota had exploit feathers, each indicating the feat the warrior had accomplished. The Blackfoot coup-striker wore white weasel skins. The Crow wore wolf tails at the heels of his moccasins. A gun-snatcher put ermine skins on his shirt. A subchief trimmed his shirt and moccasins with hair. See COUNTING COUP, COUP STICK, HEADDRESS, INDIAN NAMES, SCALPING, TEPEE. See also illustration, page 62.


**COUP STICK.** A long stick, bent on one end and decorated with otter fur, used by a warrior to count coup on a live enemy. The Cheyenne claimed that "an old woman in a cave" told them long ago how to make a medicine coup stick. When they carried it into war, the enemy could not hit them with bullets or arrows, but the man who carried the coup·stick could easily touch his enemy with it. This stick was handed down from father to son. See COUNTING COUP, COUP, OTTER, WAR DANCE.

**COWBOY.** The Indian and the cowboy had one thing in common—the horse. But while the Indian taught the cowboy many things, the cowboy seems to have taught the Indian little—or the Indian would not try to learn.

The Indian was slow to take up anything new. He clung to his old pad saddle, or his frame saddle, or rode his horse bareback. His bridle was nothing but a rawhide thong passed around the lower lip of his horse. He mounted his horse from the right side instead of the left. The right side was the natural way for anyone to mount a horse. He accepted the Westerner's firearms, but he did not want to have anything to do with the cow except to kill it for food and its hide.

From the Indian the cowboy learned his manner of gentling horses. The cowboy learned the Indian art of "reading sign" and following trails. He learned to use various Indian signals. The Navajo blanket was the best saddle blanket. The cowboy used Indian buckskin for his clothing, the Indian horsehair rope for many purposes, and the wickiup when on the range. He built his fire of buffalo chips and carried the Indian war whoop into the cow towns. See CATTLE, HORSE, SIGNALS, TRAIL (TO), WICKIUP.

**COYOTE** (ky-o'-teh). The prairie wolf, sometimes called the "barking wolf," because its bark resembles that of a dog. The Indian considered the coyote a wise animal and respected it. Coyote skin was valued by many Plains tribes for making quivers. Few tribes ate the flesh of the coyote, although the Coyoteros, a division of the Apache, are believed by some to have been given that name because they ate the flesh of the coyote. See APACHE, QUIVER.

**CRAZY HORSE.** A chief of the Oglala Sioux. Indians say his name was misunderstood by the whites and should have been translated as "His-Horse-Is-Crazy." He is supposed to have gotten this name because a wild horse dashed through the village when he was born.

Crazy Horse joined Sitting Bull when the Dakota went on the warpath in 1875 to resist white gold miners who had flocked into the Black Hills. He also led his men in the Custer battle in 1876.

Pursued later by the U.S. Cavalry, he finally surrendered with 2,000 followers in the spring of 1877. He was accused of trying to stir up another war and was imprisoned. On September 7, 1877, he tried to escape and was killed. See CUSTER'S LAST STAND, DAKOTA, DREAMS, INDIAN NAMES, SITTING BULL, SPOTTED TAIL.

**CREE** (kree). A tribe of Algonquian Indians who ranged the northern Plains. They were buffalo hunters and horsemen. Early in their history they became closely associated with the Assiniboin, a Sioux tribe which had broken away from their family group.

The Cree were friendly with the white man from their first meetings with the English and the French. Many historians have spoken of their superior qualities. They had a ceremonial pipe which the whites called a "medicine pipe." The Cree believed that this pipe guarded the welfare of their people.

They held an annual feast at which they ate the flesh of a dog. One of their customs was that when a man's wife died, he was obliged to marry her sister, if she had one.

Today the remnant of this once-powerful tribe lives with the Assiniboin on the Fort Belknap Agency and Reservation in Montana. See ASSINIBOIN.


**CREEK** (kreek). A powerful confederacy of southeastern Indians of the same family as the Seminole, Choctaw, and Chickasaw. The confederacy was built around a group of dominant tribes, called the Muskogee. While six languages were spoken in the confederacy, the Muskogee language was the most common.

The name Creek was given them because when they were first known to the Carolina colonists, and for a long time after that, the main body of Creeks lived in Alabama on the banks of the present Ocmulgee River, called by the colonists "Ocheese Creek." At first the Indians were known as those who lived on the creek, and finally the colonists got into the habit of calling them simply the Creek.

The Creek were friendly to the English and enemies of the French and the Spanish. The only time they had trouble with the Americans was during the Creek War, 1813-1814, when they were defeated by General Andrew Jackson. Previous to this they had sold the rights to their land along the Atlantic Coast to Governor James Oglethorpe for the Colony of Georgia. Between 1836 and 1840 they removed with

their slaves, as they were slaveholders, to the Indian Territory. Later they became one of the Five Civilized Tribes.

The Creek were proud, haughty, arrogant, and very brave. They liked decoration and ornament and were fond of music and ball playing. The Creek men were often more than six feet tall, but their women were described by early writers as "short in stature and well formed."

In time of war tall red poles were erected in the public squares of their towns or settlements. These poles were in charge of men known as "bearers of the red." So Creek warriors were termed "red sticks" by the white soldiers. "White towns" were known as "peace towns."

On the first day of their year a fire was built in the center of the square of each town. Four logs were placed to form a cross, each log pointing in a direction of the compass. From this fire each woman carried away her share of embers so that she might have a new hearth fire for the year.

In the center of each village, too, stood a temple, sacred to the sun, where burned an eternal fire. It was never allowed to go out.

The Creek celebrated the Festival of the Busk when the corn was ripe enough to be eaten, and drank a black drink, or *yopon*, made from a species of holly. They buried their dead under the bed where they had died. See ALIBAMU, BUSK, CROCKETT, FIRE MAKING, FIVE CIVILIZED TRIBES, GAMES, MINGO, MOUND BUILDERS, PAWNEE, RED STICKS, SEMINOLE, TATTOOING, TOMOCHICHI, TRAILS, YOPON.


CROATAN (kro'-atan). A people of mixed blood who are believed to be descendants of Raleigh's "lost colony of Croatan." They live in North Carolina, mainly in Robeson County. For many years after the Civil War they were classed as free Negroes, but refused to send their children to Negro schools. About sixty years ago they were legally given the name of Croatan Indians.

In South Carolina are found a people believed to be of similar origin. They were originally called "Red Bones." Others in Tennessee are termed "Melungeons," and some in Delaware are called "Moors." See HATTERAS, ROANOKE.

**CROCKETT, DAVID.** Famous American hunter, trapper, and Indian fighter. He was born in Green County, Tennessee, August 17, 1786. At an early age he became an expert "b'ar hunter," and had many thrilling experiences killing ferocious bears. He learned woodcraft from friendly Indians and when the Creek War started in 1813 he enlisted under General Andrew Jackson as a scout and guide.

Davy Crockett mixed in politics for a time, then finding life too dull, headed west to Texas. He joined the Texans in their fight for freedom from Mexican rule, and lost his life as one of the stanch defenders of the Alamo at San Antonio on March 6, 1836. See CREEK.

**CROW.** A dance bustle made of feathers which was worn by the Dog Soldiers of the Plains tribes. It was a badge of office and was worn only on hunts and at dances. The name is said to have come from the fact that an entire crowskin was used in making one of its important parts. However, the "crow" was usually made from feathers of whatever birds the Indians saw after a successful battle.

**CROW.** A Siouan tribe which ranged the eastern vicinity of the Rocky Mountains. They are said to have been given their name by the Cheyenne, who in first meeting them found they had a pet "medicine crow." However, their own name, *Absarokee* meant "Crow People," or "Bird People."

The Crow were at one time a part of the Hidatsa, or Gros Ventre, dwelling along the Missouri River. According to their tradition two of their chiefs had a dispute over the division of the paunch of a buffalo during a hunt, and each went his way with an equal number of followers. Those known as the Crow went farther west than the others. Because of this fight over the *ventre*, or stomach of the buffalo, they were at one time known as the Gros Ventre of the Prairies. This name, however, later was identified with the Atsina.

The Crow men were fine-looking, tall, and well-formed, although the women were said to have been small and inferior. The French called them "the handsome men." Maximilian, the German author, who wrote *Travels in the Interior of North America,* considered them the proudest of any Indians he met.

The Crow wore their hair cut in front in a bang, but when they were in full dress this portion was made to stand up by mixing it with clay and glue. The remainder of the hair was braided on both sides. In dress they wore a hooded coat made of a blanket, preferring blankets of red and white stripes.

The Crow were constantly at war with the Cheyenne, Dakota, and Arapaho. After 1876 they remained at peace with the white man and many served as army scouts in the western Indian wars. The Indian form of their name, Absarokee, appears as a place name in North Dakota, and more prominently as Absaroka, a range of mountains and a national forest in Yellowstone National Park. See FEATHERWORK, GROS VENTRE.

**CRUSTING.** A method of hunting deer and elk when the crust on the snow would bear the weight of men and dogs but not that of the larger animals. The deer and elk would break through the crust, hampering their flight and making them easy targets.

**CUSTER'S LAST STAND.** A famous battle which occurred on Sunday, June 25, 1876. General George Armstrong Custer, commanding the Seventh U.S. Cavalry, was in pursuit of the Dakota and other tribes led by Sitting Bull.

When Custer arrived at the junction of the Big Horn and Little Horn rivers in Montana on the night of June 24, he received word of what he supposed was a small force of Indians. But early next day he was surprised by some three thousand warriors. Custer and his 264 men were slaughtered to the last man. The only survivor was Custer's horse, Comanche.

Eighty-one years after the battle, a writer gave credit to Chief White Bull of the Sioux as the actual killer of General Custer. Before he died, Chief White Bull admitted that he had shot Custer in the heart, this writer said. Yet most historians believe the actual slayer of Custer will never be known. Chief Rain-in-the-Face at one time claimed he had killed Colonel Tom Custer, General Custer's brother, but he is said to have denied it later. See CHEYENNE, CRAZY HORSE, DAKOTA, GALL, RAIN-IN-THE-FACE, SITTING BULL.

**DAKOTA.** The most powerful tribe of the Sioux Indians, commonly known as the Sioux; but Dakota, Nakota, and Lakota were names used in several of their dialects.

The Dakota were divided into four main tribes: the Eastern Dakota, the Santee, the Teton, and the Yankton. The main body of the Dakota was the Teton, which, in turn, was divided into: the Blackfeet, Brûlé, Hunkpapa, Miniconjou, Oglala, Sans Arc, and Two-Kettle. Of these seven divisions the Oglala was the most prominent.

The Dakota has become the representative Indian of America. Artists, in painting or drawing an Indian, usually show him as a Dakota in full eagle headdress, fringed shirt, and elaborate beaded moccasins. The Dakota's profile has appeared on the U. S. penny and the nickel.

Associated with the Dakota are the circles of white tepees—and the Dakota gave the white man the word *tipi*, meaning dwelling—the red peace pipe, painted buffalo robes, and decorated war ponies. The Dakota was a handsome and picturesque Indian. He usually was tall with small hands and feet, but with a lithe athletic body and strong features with high cheekbones and beaked nose.

William Frederick Cody, the great "Buffalo Bill," had fought the Dakota and admired and respected them. He made them famous as the Indians of his wild west shows. People, unfamiliar with Indians, thought all of them were like Buffalo Bill's.

The Dakota were excellent fighters and were almost continually at war with the white man or their Indian neighbors. They fought with

105

the British in the War of 1812, but their most serious outbreak against the Americans occurred in Minnesota under Chief Little Crow in 1862, when about 900 settlers and 100 soldiers were killed.

There was another Sioux uprising after the discovery of gold in the Black Hills. Contrary to the provisions of the treaty the Indians had with the Government, gold prospectors flocked into Dakota territory.

The trouble led up to the great Custer battle on the Little Big Horn River, after which the Indians were relentlessly pursued by United States troops. Finally, in 1890, Sitting Bull led his men in the Ghost Dance troubles—after which there was peace.

The name of this famous tribe has been given to states, to a river, to counties in Minnesota and Nebraska, and to cities, towns, and places in Illinois, Minnesota, Wisconsin, Montana, and Iowa. The name appears as Lacota in Florida and Michigan, and as Lakota in Iowa, North Dakota, and Virginia. See AMERICAN HORSE, ASSINIBOIN, BLACKFEET SIOUX, CAMP, CODY, CONFEDERATION, COSTUME, CRAZY HORSE, CUSTER'S LAST STAND, GALL, GHOST DANCE, HEADDRESS, HOLE-IN-THE-DAY, INDIAN SCOUTS, LITTLE CROW, RAIN-IN-THE-FACE, RED CLOUD, SITTING BULL, SOUTHERN SIOUX, SPOTTED TAIL, YOUNG-MAN-AFRAID-OF-HIS-HORSES. See also illustrations, pages 104-105.


**DANCE.** Indians had a dance for almost every occasion—for war, for the hunt, to bring rain, in thanks for a good harvest, and for welcoming the seasons. Drums, rattles, and sometimes bone or reed flutes were used to aid the dancers, and there were chants and songs.

Indian dance steps were not always simple. Some were complicated and difficult to learn. In the old days men and women always danced separately and with different steps to the same dance rhythm, but later after the coming of the white man the Indians held dances where both men and women danced together. These were purely social dances, however, and their religious and ceremonial dances remained the same as in former days.

Among most tribes, when the men danced the heel and ball of the foot were lifted and brought down with force so as to produce a thud.

Among the many different steps were the toe-heel step, the toe-heel drag, the side cross-step, the hop-step, and the elk-leap step. The changes of position were slow, but the changes of attitude were rapid and sometimes violent. Dancers waved their arms in some dances, shook their weapons and gave loud whoops in others.

Women employed the shuffle, the glide, and the hop and leap. In some tribes they danced alone, to insure the safe return of their men from war. Usually dancers moved in a direction against the sun, and when dancing with men, women were on the inside circle.

Chief among Indian dances were the Buffalo Dance, Calumet Dance, Green Corn Dance, Medicine Dance, Rain Dance, Scalp Dance, Snake Dance, Sun Dance, and War Dance. See BELL, CHAPARRAL COCK, DRUM, HOPI, MAIZE, MASKS, MUSICAL INSTRUMENTS, SCALP DANCE, SCALPING, SNAKE DANCE, SONGS, SUN DANCE, WAR DANCE, WOMEN.

**DARK AND BLOODY GROUND.** Country between the Ohio and Tennessee rivers which had no home tribe, but was the hunting ground of all Indians of adjoining sections and hence the territory of many bloody battles. The name "Kentucky," which was given this territory, was erroneously said to mean "Dark and Bloody Ground." Actually, it came from the Wyandot Indian word *Kentakekowa,* which meant "the Plains," or "the Prairies." See BOONE.

**DEER.** The deer was one of the most important animals to the Indian. It provided food and clothing and its antlers and various other parts made many useful articles. Deerskin made the finest buckskin.

The American deer was found in abundance throughout the United States. The red deer was also known as the Virginia white-tailed deer. It was to be found from Maine to the Pacific Coast islands and from Canada to Florida. A full-grown buck might weigh as much as two hundred pounds. In the summer the upper parts of its body were of a reddish brown and in winter a grayish color.

The black-tailed deer, sometimes called the "mule deer" because of its long and heavy ears, was the largest of the species in this country. A full-grown buck might weigh two hundred and fifty pounds. Roaming the Plains area westward, moving north in summer and south in winter, the black-tailed deer was dark gray- or mouse-colored, its tail tipped with a tuft of black hair.

The Indian made deerskin into clothing of all types. The hair from the tail was used for ornaments and embroidery. The antlers were fashioned into tool handles and arrowheads. The hoofs provided glue and rattles. The dewclaws, or extra toes, were used for jingles on belts and for anklets. The sinews provided thread, bowstrings, and cord for snares. Needles, awls, skin-dressing tools, handles, and ornaments were made from the bone. The deer's paunch and bladder were made into bags and pouches. The brains and liver were used for dressing rawhide to make it into buckskin. See BUCKSKIN, COSTUME, DISHES, FOOD, HORN AND BONE CRAFT, RAWHIDE, STONE BOILING.

**DELAWARE.** At one time the most important confederacy of the Algonquian family. The Delaware occupied New Jersey, the basin of the Delaware River in eastern Pennsylvania and northern Delaware, western Long Island, and Manhattan and Staten Islands in New York.

They called themselves *Lenni-Lenape,* "Genuine Men," or "Original People." They comprised three powerful tribes, known by their totem symbols as the Turtle, the Turkey, and the Wolf. The latter were generally known as the Munsee, although the French termed them all *Loups,* or "Wolves."

The Delaware did not at first like the name given them by the English until it was explained to them that they and the river were named for a great and brave Englishman, Lord de la Warre, second governor of Virginia. After learning this the Delaware were much pleased.

In early history the capital of the Delaware was near what is now Germantown, Pennsylvania. William Penn had established his settlement nearby. The Delaware made their first treaty with Penn in 1682 under the famed oak tree at Shackamaxon.

The Delaware lived in small villages of rectangular bark-covered houses, dome-shaped after the Algonquian-type wigwam. They were hunters and raised corn and vegetables. Their early history is to be found in a remarkable document called the *Walam Olum,* which may or may not be authentic.

Tammany or Tamenend was their greatest chief and he won so much renown that even the whites respected him and called him St. Tammany. After the Revolutionary War the Tammany Society was organized by war veterans.

In 1720 the powerful Iroquois dominated the Delaware and forbade them to make war or sell any more of their land. They had further troubles when by 1742 the whites had pushed them westward to Wyoming, Pennsylvania. Some bands drifted farther west and made an alliance with the Huron, and being in French territory they defied the Iroquois and made war on them.

Still others of the Delaware went as far as Texas, but in 1835 most of these western bands were gathered on a reservation in Kansas. In 1867 they were removed to Indian Territory, where some occupied a corner of the Cherokee Nation.

The name Delaware has been used for post offices in Arkansas, Iowa, Kentucky, Missouri, New Jersey, Ohio, and Oklahoma, besides for the state and river. Lenape is a village in Kansas, and Lenapah one in Oklahoma. See LAPPAWINZE, PENN, TAMMANY.

**DIGGERS.** A name applied by the white man to several different tribes of Indians who lived in the desert area. They were root-eaters and also ate lizards, as well as practically every type of animal and reptile. Many ate grasshoppers. However, the name originally was given to a small tribe of Paiute Indians of southwest Utah, who practiced agriculture and for this reason were termed Diggers.

When the white man arrived in the West he began calling Indians of other tribes by the name Diggers—even those of California, Oregon, Idaho, and Nevada.

These Indians were reported to be very dirty and ill clothed and were considered the lowest form of Indian life. They lived in simple brush shelters and were too busy looking for food to engage in warfare. See FOOD, PAIUTE.

**DISHES.** Indians had many types of dishes, or vessels for the preparation and serving of food. They were made from stone, shell, ivory, horn, rawhide, bark, wood, pottery, and basketry.

Dishes, as a general rule, were not used to hold individual portions, for in most tribes Indians gathered around one large pot or dish and all ate from it. But there were small dishes to hold salt and other seasonings and for a few delicate foods. Larger dishes usually held cooked corn or vegetables, and trays and platters were used for game and bread.

Wood was the most common article from which dishes were made. For round dishes and drinking cups, burl wood, or knots on trees were utilized. The Iroquois especially made fine dishes from burl wood. The Plains Indians also made dishes from burl wood when they could get it, and they fashioned spoons from buffalo horn and made cooking pots from the stomachs of the buffalo and deer. The Paiute used dishes made from the shell of the box turtle. The Pima and Papago fashioned oblong trays and shallow platters from mesquite wood. Most of the Pueblo tribes used pottery dishes.

Dishes of birch bark were made by Woodland tribes. In the South, Indians made use of various types of gourds. Southwestern and California Indians preferred basket-type dishes. See BARK CRAFT, BASKETS, BUFFALO, DEER, HORN AND BONE CRAFT, POTTERY, RAWHIDE.

**DOG.** The only animal the Indian domesticated. Biologists have determined that the Indian brought the dog with him from Asia. Bones of dogs have been found with some of the earliest remains of American Indians.

The dog was a companion, a beast of burden, and a food. He was eaten at times as a part of a ceremonial feast and at other times when game was scarce. White dogs were sacrificed to their respective gods by the Iroquois, the Cree, the Ottawa, and related tribes.

Before the Plains Indian acquired the horse, the dog did all the hard work of transporting. With two poles, later termed *travois*, lashed to his sides a dog could trot along with forty or more pounds of baggage. The Eskimo may have been the first to use dogs for transport purposes.

Dogs usually led hard lives with little to eat. Some tribes held great feasts, but dogs were not allowed to share even scraps or bones. These were burned, since the Indians believed that if any part was given to dogs the spirits of the animals would be angry and would warn their living relatives not to let the Indian trap or kill them.

The Arapaho claimed the dog came from a cross of the coyote, the big gray wolf, and the fox. The Blackfoot, Crow, Flatheads, Nez Percé, Shoshoni, Bannock, and Ute did not eat dogs, but the Sioux,

111

Cheyenne, Arapaho, Kiowa, and Apache gave special feasts where dogmeat was the main dish.

Among the Pawnee and Arikara a Dog Dance was followed by a feast on dogmeat. Nearly every tribe on the Plains had a warrior group known as Dog Soldiers. Yet when an Indian wanted to say something to hurt a person, he said, "You dog!" See APACHE, FEASTS, HORSE, HUSKY, MYSTERY DOG, TRAVOIS.

**DOGFACE.** A modern term applied to the American soldier, possibly derived from the term "Dog Soldier" of the Cheyenne and other Plains tribes, and picked up by the United States Cavalry during the western Indian wars. See DOG SOLDIER.

**DOG SOLDIER.** A member of one of the military societies of the Plains Indians, usually chosen for his bravery and fighting ability. Among the Cheyenne, the *Hotamitaneo* or Dog Society Men, won such a reputation for their daring acts that the name was usually applied only to them.

However, other tribes had Dog Soldiers, notably the Kiowa. This group was usually formed by ten picked men, who wore a black sash around their necks and swore never to turn their faces from the enemy unless at the insistence of the entire war party. One of these men would ride ahead of the others, dismount and anchor himself to the ground by driving his lance through one end of the sash tied to his neck. He would act as cheer leader and urge the others into battle, often dying on the spot unless his companions released him. The Kiowa called them "Chief Dogs." See CHEYENNE, DOGFACE, KIOWA, LANCE, MILITARY SOCIETIES.

**DREAMS.** All Indians thought the spirits talked to them in dreams. All except the Mojave Indians believed that they must seek the dream, or induce it through some ceremony or by fasting. The Mojave thought the dream sought him.

Usually the Indian had his most powerful dreams while he was fasting at that time when he changed from a boy to a grown man. This dream influenced him through the rest of his life. Ever after, if some incident, animal, or bird which had featured in this dream, appeared in another, a special meaning was attached to it and whatever advice it gave was followed.

Those who had the most powerful dreams became medicine men, and thus leaders in all the mysterious rites and ceremonies. When a man was a leader of a war party or a hunting party great attention was paid to his dreams. Other Indians thought he had been given in his dream the proper advice on how to proceed.

Many times the Indian sought to bring on dreams by fasting, drugs, mutilating himself, or sitting for long hours in a sweat bath. He might even tie a thong of green hide around his neck, and lose consciousness as it contracted, inducing a vision or a dream in which he believed he would see just what was going to happen in the future.

The Sioux chief, Crazy Horse, a few days before he was killed was walking on the prairie and saw the body of a dead eagle. He went back to his lodge and sat down gloomily, saying he had seen his own body on the prairie. A few nights later he dreamed he was riding a white pony. He had always claimed he had a charmed life and could not be killed by a bullet and the dream evidently reassured him.

A few days later he was captured and, in trying to escape, was killed. But outside the circle of soldiers, some friends were holding a white pony to help him in his escape—just such a white pony as Crazy Horse had seen in his dream. See CRAZY HORSE, FASTING, INDIAN NAMES, MAN-BEING, MEDICINE, TOTEM.

**DRILLS.** Indians employed several forms of drills for making holes in stone, shell, pottery, bone, and wood. To drill a hole in a hard substance with his simple tools required a long time—but the Indian had plenty of time.

The simplest form of drill was similar to an awl, a sharp-pointed instrument of bone, flaked stone, or copper. To make a hole the Indian would press the instrument against the object to be drilled, turning the drill back and forth with a movement of his wrist.

Indians also used grass and bristles in drilling small holes in objects that were not too hard. The driller would twirl his tiny tool between his thumb and forefinger. The white man today uses his small pin drill in the same fashion.

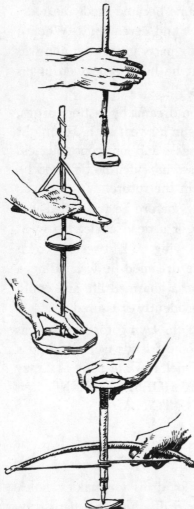

The Indian would also use a straight shaft, pointed with flaked stone, from ten inches to two feet long. This would be twirled back and forth between the palms of the hands. Or he might lay the shaft on his thigh, rolling it back and forth with his right hand while holding the object to be drilled against the point with his left hand.

The bow drill was effective. This was also used in fire making. For drilling, however, it consisted of a shaft with a hard point, a headpiece with a hollow in it to fit the top of the shaft, and a bow with a loosely fitted thong. The thong was wrapped once around the shaft and the drill was spun by drawing the bow back and forth while pressing down on the headpiece of the drill-shaft.

The best was the pump drill, still in use today by the Navajo silversmiths and other craftsmen of the Pueblo tribes. It has a long shaft which passes through a disk of stone or hard wood, and also through a crosspiece. The crosspiece is movable and is attached to the top of the shaft with thongs.

As the driller pumps up and down the thongs wind and unwind themselves around the shaft, spinning it first one way and then the other.

Some Indians employed only drills of wood without a stone point. To make a hole with these they used dry or wet sand, and it was actually the sand which cut the hole.

In making a hole through a long pipestem, the Indian usually split the wood lengthwise, removed the heart, and then glued the two pieces together. It is said that some Indians used a small wood-boring worm. The worm was placed in one end of the stem which had been hollowed out, and the hole was sealed. The end in which the worm was confined was then heated, causing the worm to bore rapidly in the opposite direction until it finally came out the other end. See FIRE MAKING, GRASSWORK.

**DRUM.** An Indian musical instrument, consisting of a round hollow part with one or both ends covered with a dried skin or hide. The drum, or tom-tom, was beaten with the hands or a stick.

Indian drums were of three kinds: the single- or double-headed hand drum; the large dance drum played by several persons; or the water drum of the Woodland tribes. To tighten the rawhide head of a drum it was held before a fire. The tone of the water drum was changed by wetting it with the water which was inside the drum.

Drums were uniformly round, except in northwestern California and on the northwest coast where square drums were used.

The drumstick was made by wrapping the end of a stick with buckskin. See DANCE, MUSICAL INSTRUMENTS, SONGS.

**DRY PAINTING.** See SAND PAINTING.

**DUGOUT.** A canoe-type boat made from a hollowed-out log, used in early days throughout America. A form known as the *pirogue* was common along the Atlantic slope south of the St. Lawrence River, while dugouts were made by Indians of the north central section of the United States, notably the Chippewa.

The dugout of the Tlingit Indians, with its high decorative prow, could carry from thirty to fifty men. Dugouts made from the giant cedar trees of the California forests were often nearly one hundred feet long.

Dugouts were made by carefully burning the wood and chipping the charred part out with stone adzes and bone chisels. When the sides were thinned down to the proper thickness, the dugout was filled with water which was heated by dropping hot stones into it. When the wood became soft the sides were bulged out by placing long sticks or thwarts inside the hollowed-out log. A high bow or stern was made from sections of logs properly shaped and fitted to the hull of the dugout with cedar ropes and pegs. See ADZE, CANOE.

**DULL KNIFE.** A noted chief of the Northern Cheyenne Indians. Dull Knife has been termed by writers one of those "admirable outlaws" against tyranny and injustice who could be compared with Rob Roy and Wallace and Bruce.

Dull Knife first came into public notice in 1868 when, as one of the representatives of his tribe, he signed the treaty of Fort Laramie. Following the Custer battle, in which the Cheyenne joined with the Dakota and other tribes, American troops attacked Dull Knife's camp and destroyed 173 lodges and captured 500 ponies. The Indians later surrendered and were placed on a reservation in Oklahoma.

With no buffalo to hunt, near starvation, and with many dying from disease, Dull Knife led his people north in September, 1878, in one of the most remarkable marches in the history of Indian warfare.

The small band, with women and children, fought its way through Kansas, outmaneuvering and outfighting hundreds of American soldiers. The Indians finally were captured and confined to Fort Robinson, Nebraska. Instead of surrendering all their arms they took their guns apart and concealed some under blankets, while children wore necklaces and bracelets of hammers, firing pins, and other small parts.

Finally, the unhappy Indians made another break for liberty, having reassembled their guns. It was a bitter cold night on January 8, 1879. Women and children were shot down by white soldiers and most of the warriors were slain. Dull Knife was among those who escaped.

Dull Knife died in 1883 and was buried on a high butte near the valley of the Rosebud River—his grave overlooking that country to which he had vainly tried to lead his people. See BRAVE, CHEYENNE, CUSTER'S LAST STAND, INDIAN NAMES.

E

**EAGLE.** The eagle was known as the "chief of all birds" to most Indians. Like the ancients, the Indian regarded the eagle as an emblem of strength and courage. They held the bird in great awe, in many instances were superstitious about it, and in other instances worshiped it. The Hopi thought of the eagle as the Sky God, and others considered it as what the white man termed the Thunderbird.

The eagle's extraordinary powers of vision, the great heights to which it soared in the sky, and the wild grandeur of the scenery where it made its home, as well as its length of life—all inspired the Indian. It filled him with hope and confidence of success and victory.

Most Indians claimed the eagle was created by their Supreme Being for its beauty, as well as to provide decoration for themselves and special charms in battle. While the bald or white-headed eagle, which became the national emblem of the United States by an act of Congress in 1782, was the most widespread, the Indian preferred the golden or mountain eagle, found chiefly in the West.

Hunting the eagle was dangerous and usually was done only by highly trained men. Those of some tribes scaled great heights and trapped the eagle in its eyrie. But among those of the Plains tribes the usual method was to trap them from covered pits. An eagle hunter would remain in a pit until an eagle came down to seize the bait placed at the edge of the pit. The hunter then grabbed the eagle's legs and overpowered it. These hunts usually were attended by solemn ceremonies.

The Pueblo Indians had eagles in captivity when Coronado first visited them.

Feathers of the golden eagle were prized as exploit feathers and for war bonnets. A complete tail of twelve eagle feathers was worth

119

a pony on the Plains. White plumes with black tips were the mos
valuable. Such feathers were fastened in the scalp lock and also in
the manes of warriors' ponies. They were used to decorate shields.

Some tribes allowed a man to wear an eagle feather only after he
had killed someone in a fight, or, in other tribes, when he had counted
coup on a live enemy. The number of feathers a warrior wore showed
the number of times he had counted coup or had slain enemies.
Among the Chippewa a man who scalped an enemy could wear two
feathers, and if he had rescued a wounded prisoner he could wear five.

Some tribes used the down, wing, and tail feathers in sacrifice.
The wings were made into fans by the Sioux and other tribes. Eagle
wing feathers were the best for feathering arrows—feathers from the
same wing always being used on an arrow to give it a revolving motion.

Bones of eagles' wings were fashioned into whistles used in ceremonies, especially in the Sun Dance of the Cheyenne. Eagle claws
were valued as good luck charms. See ARROW, FEATHERWORK,
HEADDRESS, MUSICAL INSTRUMENTS, SUN DANCE, THUN-
DERBIRD, WHISTLE.

**EARRING.** A ring or hook worn in a slit in the
ear and from which usually hung some type of
ornament. The earring denoted wealth and was a
mark of distinction. The ear-holes of both boys
and girls were bored or cut by medicine men at
special ceremonies and paid for by parents or
relatives.

Holes were not only made in the lobe of the
ear but sometimes around the rim, and the more
holes, the more honor and respect they commanded. The earrings themselves were often a
foot long and fashioned from brightly colored
shells. Many other articles were worn in the ears.
Chief Quanah Parker of the Comanche was once
described as having a brightly colored stuffed bird
in each ear as an earring. See COSTUME.

**EASTMAN, DR. CHARLES ALEXANDER.** A
Santee Dakota physician and author, born in 1858
near Redwood Falls, Minnesota. His Indian name
was *Ohiyesa,* "The Winner." He lived as a wild
Indian until he was fifteen when he entered a
mission school at Santee, Nebraska. He made such
progress that after two years he was sent to Beloit
College, Beloit, Wisconsin. He was graduated
from Dartmouth in 1887, and from the Boston
University School of Medicine three years later.

Dr. Eastman was appointed Government physician at the Pine Ridge Agency and served there
during the Ghost Dance disturbances. Later he was a traveling secretary for the Y.M.C.A. and organized forty-two Indian Y.M.C.A.'s. He
became attorney for the Sioux at Washington and in 1903 was appointed to the Bureau of Indian Affairs.

He found time to lecture, write nine books, including *Indian Boy-
hood* and *From Deep Woods to Civilization,* the story of his life, and
help organize the Boy Scouts of America and the Camp Fire Girls.
President Coolidge appointed him United States Indian Inspector in
1923. He died January 8, 1939.

**ELIOT BIBLE.** The first Bible translated into an Indian language.
John Eliot, a missionary, translated it into the Massachuset Indian
language between 1653 and 1663. Since then the Bible has been
printed in part or in its entirety in thirty-two Indian languages. See
MASSACHUSET, PRAYING INDIANS.

**ELK.** A name popularly applied to the wapiti, a large deer of the
western United States. The elk provided the Indian with food and
clothing. The Crow Indians made excellent bows from elk horn. Elk
teeth were valued as ornaments, particularly necklaces. Plains Indians
used the antlers to fashion the framework of their saddles.

There was an Elk Society among some tribes. At certain periods they performed the Elk Mystery, a ceremony in which the Indians wore masks made of skins stretched on frames, to which were added boughs to represent antlers. In their dance the Indians told the life story of the elk. See BOW.

**ERIE.** An independent tribe of the Iroquois family. In the Iroquois language the term "Erie" meant "long tail," referring to the panther, from which circumstance in the early days they were referred to as the Cat Nation. They originally lived on the south side of Lake Erie.

The Erie did not join the powerful Five Nations (later the Six Nations) of the Iroquois, and when the latter almost wiped out the Huron many of the Huron were taken in and protected by the Erie. As a result the Five Nations turned on the Erie and in 1656 killed or captured all but a few of them. These few joined with some of the Huron and fled to Wisconsin, where they later became known as the Wyandot.

The Erie will long be remembered as they not only gave their name to one of the Great Lakes, but to an important city in Pennsylvania upon its shores; to counties in New York, Ohio, and Pennsylvania, and places in Colorado, Illinois, Kansas, Michigan, North Dakota, Tennessee, Ohio, and New York; also to an important railroad and canal. See HURON, IROQUOIS.

**ESKIMAUAN** (es-ki-mo'-an) **FAMILY.** A language family which formerly occupied all the coasts and islands of Arctic America from East Greenland and the north end of Newfoundland to the westernmost Aleutian Islands.

**ESKIMO.** A group of Indians who lived on the Arctic Coast of North America. The Eskimo were divided into three divisions—the Eastern, Central, and Western Eskimo. One branch lived across the Bering Straits in Eastern Siberia.

Over this 5,000-mile spread of territory, the largest occupied by any American Indian group, customs differed in many minor respects. Basically, however, the Eskimo were a hunting and fishing people who lived on fish and sea mammals during the winter months and hunted caribou and other game inland during the summer. The Western Eskimo lived in dugouts, or pit houses, while the igloo or dome-shaped snow hut was used only by the Central Eskimo. The Eastern Eskimo lived in huts made of driftwood or whale bone.

Their name is said to have come from the Abnaki word *esquimantsic* or from the Chippewa word *ashkimeq*, both of which mean "eaters of raw flesh." They called themselves *Inuit*, which means "people." Of medium stature, the Eskimo were strong and had great endurance. They had small hands and feet, light brownish-yellow skin, and "Mongolian" eyes.

They dressed in warm skins. Excellent craftsmen, they took great pride in decorating their hunting and fishing gear, made chiefly of bone and walrus-tooth ivory. Their skin-covered kayaks were the most seaworthy boats of their kind and have been copied by the white man. The Eskimo were a cheerful, peaceable, truthful, and honest people. They lived partly on raw food, but also cooked with oil lamps. Blubber, the fat of marine mammals, was considered a delicacy, and was eaten raw.

The Eskimo of Alaska, members of the Western Eskimo group, are citizens of the United States. See ALEUT, FISHING, HUSKY, TATTOOING, TLINGIT. See also illustration, page 118.

**EXPLOIT FEATHERS.** See COUP, EAGLE, HEADDRESS.

**FASTING.** A period of doing without food. Indians fasted and prayed so that they might have dreams. Sometimes individuals fasted as boys when they reached the age of manhood, or as men when they were initiated into some society. On other occasions all members of a tribe would fast to keep off some disaster that threatened them. In most fasts the person did without water as well as food. Fasts might last from midnight to sunset, or for as long as a week or more. See DREAMS, MEDICINE, TOTEM.

**FEASTS.** In times of plenty feasts were almost daily affairs in Indian camps. An Indian was always looking for an opportunity to give a feast or to attend one. Sometimes Indians would eat for days—or until everything was gone. It did not matter if the giving of a feast meant eating all the supplies in camp. The Indian had his feast, as he believed the next day would take care of itself.

Some feasts were held at regular times. The running of the salmon among the fishing Indians, the ripening of the corn crop or the acorn crop, the building of a dwelling, the marriage of one member of a family, or the time a baby was named—all called for feasts.

Indians gave feasts for their individual gods or spirits, and even for their dead. Feasts were common after a successful hunt or victory in war. Many times a man just decided to give a feast and sent messengers to summon everyone in camp.

At some feasts women were not allowed to eat with the men. At others the bones of the animals eaten at the feast were sacrificed in the fire and dogs were not allowed to have them, as the Indians believed this would offend the living relatives of the animals.

There were some feasts known as "eat-everything-feast," and no one was allowed to leave any of his food. However, the general idea at all feasts was for the Indian to eat as much as he could. See DOG, FOOD, HUNTING, MAIZE, WOMEN.

**FEATHERWORK.** Feathers and skins of many birds were used by Indians for robes and clothing, as well as for many kinds of decoration.

The most elaborate feather robes were made in the Far West and the Southeast. In the East the Indians also cut up the skins into strips and wove them into robes. Fans were made from the wings of the larger birds, while quills of smaller birds were split and dyed and used in decoration similar to porcupine quillwork.

In California the Indians used the scalps of certain small birds as a sort of money. The calumet, shield, prayer stick, and wand all were decorated with the down and feathers of birds.

The feathers of the golden eagle were the most important to the Indian, especially for his war bonnet and his exploit feathers. Other birds whose feathers were used included the wild turkey, hawk, woodpecker, meadow lark, quail, chaparral cock, duck, bluejay, and blackbird. See CALUMET, CHAPARRAL COCK, CROW, EAGLE, HEADDRESS, PRAYER STICKS, SHIELD. See also illustration, p. 124.

**FIRE MAKING.** Fire was necessary to the Indian. He liked his food cooked, despite the common belief that he preferred it raw. It is true that certain portions of an animal were eaten raw, such as the liver and some fats, and that the Eskimo almost through necessity ate much raw food, but the common practice was to cook most foods.

The Indian needed fire also for warmth, for hardening the wooden tips of his weapons, for thickening the rawhide of his shield, for making buckskin, for felling trees and hollowing out logs for dugouts.

Fire making was a ceremony, too, among many tribes, notably

the Creek at their Busk or Green Corn Dance when a new fire was kindled for the year; the Iroquois at their White-Dog Feast, and at the New-Fire ritual of the Hopi.

There were two methods of making fire. In the East and along the northwest coast, the Indians struck together a flint and a rock which contained iron and sulphur pyrites. The sparks were made to fall in a tinder of rotted wood or shredded bark. Steel was used instead of pyrites when the Indian was able to get this metal.

The most general way of making fire, however, was by the friction of wood on wood. A drill or rod was twirled between the palms of the hands, one end resting on another piece of wood, termed the hearth. Friction caused the wood to form a hot powder or glowing coal, which was allowed to fall into a tinder. To coax this into a flame the Indian blew on it or placed it in a bunch of grass or strip of bark and swung it in the air.

An improvement of this method was using a thong of softened rawhide which was turned once around the rod and the thong pulled back and forth, spinning the rod. This was even more efficient when the thong was strung loosely on a bow, which was pulled in the same manner. The rod, or drill, was held with a stone, a piece of wood, or a clamshell to protect the hand while pressing it against the hearth.

Many tribes believed that a spark of fire slept only in certain kinds of wood, and only these could be used in kindling a flame by friction. Weathered roots of the cottonwood tree were much used by the Pueblo tribes. The Apache used the stems of the yucca. The Hupa made use of the willow root, tribes of the Northwest used cedar, and those of the East used elm and maple.

Tinder might be dried wood from decayed trees, frayed inner bark of the cedar, fungi, pounded buffalo chips, or downy feathers of the bluejay. See BUCKSKIN, CREEK, DRILLS, FOOD, HOPI, IRO-QUOIS, SHIELD.

**FIRE WATER.** Indian name for distilled spirits.

**FISHING.** Indians fished with spears, bows and arrows, nets and seines, weirs or wattlework fish traps, with the bare hand, and by drugging fish with some poison. They also caught fish with hook and line.

Fishhooks were fashioned from wood, bone, shell, copper, and certain types of cactus thorns. Some hooks were barbed. An interesting kind of hook, called a snap hook, consisted of a wooden hoop, the ends of which were held apart by a peg. This peg was loosened by the fish taking the bait and the ends of the hoop snapped together, holding the fish by the jaw. Lines were made from twisted bark and from babiche.

Not all Indians fished. Among the Navajo, Apache, and Zuñi tribes the eating of fish was forbidden by custom. But those tribes that used fish for food would utilize almost anything that came from the water, from shellfish to salmon, as well as eels.

The greatest amount of fishing was done in the Northwest. During the "salmon run," entire tribes would turn out for fishing. The fish were caught by hand, scooped into nets, clubbed, or speared. In some places they were speared from canoes and even platforms which were built out over the water. The fish were dried, pounded, and mixed with roots and berries and packed for future use.

The candlefish, caught by the northwestern Indians, was so oily that when dried and a wick placed in it, it served as a candle or lamp.

Captain John Smith, in his history of Virginia, tells that on one occasion the fish were so numerous in the water of the Potomac River that he had difficulty landing his boat. The Indians of this section used weirs, or wattlework fish traps.

Some Indians used sticks split on the end and caught fish by "pinching." In winter, holes were cut in the ice and the fish were caught when they surfaced. The Cherokee, Iroquois, and other tribes placed poisonous barks in streams to drug the fish, so that they could be easily gathered up. Some tribes used fires and torches along the shore or in canoes to attract the fish, which were then speared or taken in nets.

Salmon and herring eggs were a great delicacy. In collecting herring eggs Indians laid weighted branches under water. The herring deposited their eggs on these branches, which were then brought up and the eggs dried right on them. Later the dried eggs were scraped off and made into a kind of sausage, by stuffing them in casings made of the intestines of animals.

The Eskimo were great fishermen, and lived principally on sea mammals, particularly the seal. They had what was probably the most elaborate fishing gear of any Indians, but the harpoon was their most common fishing implement. See BA- BICHE, BARK CRAFT, BASKETS, ESKIMO, FOOD, HUNTING, ROOTS AND ROOTCRAFT.

**FIVE CIVILIZED TRIBES.** A term used for the Cherokee, Chicka- saw, Choctaw, Creek, and Seminole Indians in Oklahoma because of their advance along the "white man's road."

This group was formed some years after the five tribes were given territory west of the Mississippi River. At that time the combined population was 84,507 and the total acreage assigned them was 19,- 475,614 acres, or about 230 acres for each man, woman, and child. Their territory was as large as the state of South Carolina.

As most were slaveholding tribes they were forced to free their slaves after the Civil War. In 1907, when Oklahoma was admitted to the Union, the tribes lost their independence and the Indians became citizens of the state. See CHEROKEE, CHICKASAW, CHOCTAW, CREEK, INDIAN TERRITORY, SEMINOLE, SLAVES.

**FIVE NATIONS. See IROQUOIS.**

**FLAKING TOOL.** See FLINT

**FLATHEADS.** Curiously enough, the Indians to whom this term was applied, the so-called Salish Flatheads, never practiced the flattening of the head. They occupied the Bitterroot country in western Montana and were believed to have been of Algonquian stock, until later they were placed in a classification of their own—the Salishan family.

In the buffalo season when the Flatheads journeyed to the Plains to hunt, they lived in tepees. They were bitter enemies of the Crow and Blackfoot in whose territory they hunted.

In 1834 four chiefs of this tribe made a 2,000-mile journey to St. Louis to look for the white man's "medicine book," the Bible. One version is that some Iroquois fur hunters from New York, who lived with the Flatheads, had told them about the christening of children and of the white man's religious beliefs. The Iroquois urged the Flatheads to get a Christian teacher. As a result of their trip, the chiefs were promised a Christian teacher. Jason Lee, a Methodist, was first sent, and later Father Pierre J. de Smet, a Catholic priest, went to live among them.

With the Pend d'Oreille and some Kutenai, the Flatheads today live on a reservation in Montana. Flathead or Selish Lake, Flathead Pass, and Flathead County, all in Montana, derive their names from the Salish or Flatheads. See CHINOOK, KUTENAI, PEND D'OREILLE.

**FLINT.** A hard, dull-colored variety of quartz. True flint is found in Arkansas and Texas. The colors are dark gray or dull brown to nearly black. However, Indians used similar stones which could be shaped by flaking, and which have been called by the general name of flint.

There is a chert, found in Illinois and Missouri, which differs from true flint by being lighter in color. Another is hornstone, found in the Ohio Valley, so called because it has a peculiar hornlike characteristic of toughness. Jasper, another hard stone, which is red, yellow, and brown, is found in Pennsylvania. Other flintlike stones are agate, which is white and gray and sometimes delicately tinted, and onyx, which is a banded variety of agate.

All these stones have been termed flint and were used by the Indian in making his flaked tools, knives, and arrow- and spearheads. They were shaped by the flaking process. Some Indians used other hard stones as hammers and chipped the flint into shape, while many flaked it by pressing the edge with a piece of hard bone, or antler, shaped like an awl. In this latter method the flint was laid on a pad of buckskin and the bone point pressed against the edge to be flaked with a quick downward movement. See ARROW, CELT, KNIFE.


**FOOD.** Indians ate many varieties of vegetables and meat or fish. Food was very scarce at times, but because of their religious teachings and habits, Indians would not touch certain foods. The Navajo and Apache would not eat fish or the flesh of a bear or beaver. Some Indians would not eat turkey because they believed it was a cowardly bird and by eating its flesh they would become cowardly, too. In almost every tribe totem or clan animals could not be killed or eaten.

The most important cultivated vegetable food was maize or Indian corn. Next in importance were beans, peas, squashes, pumpkins, and melons. Wild foods, such as seeds, nuts, roots, wild rice, flowers of grasses, and leaves and parts of plants used for greens or flavorings, were gathered and eaten. In the Southwest, cactus and yucca fruits, mesquite beans, and the agave were relished. Some California Indians practically lived on acorns.

Buffalo, bear, antelope, elk, deer, and fish were most used for food. Rabbits and birds also were eaten, while the porcupine was an important food of the Montagnais. The Paiute, in season, ate grasshoppers and lizards.

In the summer the Eskimo ate caribou, musk oxen, and birds. In winter they lived principally on sea mammals, particularly seal. The Eskimo often ate his food raw, because of a lack of fuel, but other Indians, as a rule, preferred cooked food. They liked their food seasoned, too, sometimes using herbs. Some Indians used salt, but it was tabooed by the Onondaga. Salt was obtained from the evaporation of water of salt springs or the ocean, and in crystal form from salt lake beds, and by trade. Lye, as a salt substitute, was used by some southern Indians. Meat and fish were preserved by smoking, sundrying, salting, and, in winter, freezing. Some meats were preserved by a method of prolonged boiling in seasoned water. Many vegetables and fruits were dried and stored for later use. See ACORN, BEAR, BUFFALO, DEER, DIGGERS, FEASTS, FIRE MAKING, FISHING, HOMINY, JERKED MEAT, MAIZE, MESCAL, PAPER BREAD, PEMMICAN, RICE (WILD), ROOTS AND ROOTCRAFT, STONE BOILING, TOTEM.

**FOX.** See SAUK AND FOX.

**FUR COUNTRY.** Name applied to sections of Canada and the northwestern portion of the United States, known in early American history as the center of the fur trade. See FUR TRADE.

**FUR TRADE.** The exciting story of the fur trade is a preface to the history of the development and civilization of the country west of the Mississippi River, the Rocky Mountain region, and the Northwest.

The fur traders, or "mountain men," were a race apart. They were venturesome and fearless, and many operated alone, penetrating sections of Indian country no white man had ever seen before. Some married Indian women, lived with Indian tribes, and later became traders and established settlements.

The great fur companies, such as Hudson's Bay Company, the Northwest Company, the American Fur Company, and the Missouri Fur Company, served to open up much of the West and Northwest. Their forts later became towns and cities, the portages where their canoes were carried overland between bodies of water became canals, and the paths they cut through the wilderness became highways.

Furs in the old days were used as money for barter and exchange. In the north "one skin"—that of the full grown land otter or beaver— was the basic unit of trade. (Today the white man's slang for a dollar bill is a "skin.") Indians in the fur country counted their wealth in skins, just as those of the Plains counted theirs in ponies.

The fur trade established in history such picturesque characters as John Jacob Astor, Kit Carson, Joe Meek, William and Milton Sublette, Jedediah Smith, David Jackson, and Jim Bridger. See **BEAVER, CARSON, CHINOOK, FUR COUNTRY, OTTER, TRADING POSTS, TRAILS.**

G

**GALL.** A chief of the Hunkpapa Teton Sioux, who led a division of Sioux in the battle of Little Big Horn when General Custer and all his men were slain. Gall was born in South Dakota in 1840. Recognized by his people as a brave warrior, he became a leader while still a young man. He fought beside Sitting Bull as his lieutenant, fled to Canada with him, and later surrendered. He settled down as a farmer on the Standing Rock Reservation in the Dakotas. He became a friend of the whites and turned against his old chief, claiming that Sitting Bull was a coward and a fraud. See CUSTER'S LAST STAND, DAKOTA, SITTING BULL. See also illustration, page 134.

**GAMES.** The games that appealed to the Indian were those of chance, or gambling, and those where the skill of the hands was important. Among these are the strenuous ball game of *lacrosse*, and the game of *chunkey* played by the Creek and Choctaw. There were no Indian games that required deep thought, such as the white man's chess.

Usually games were played by grown men and women, while children amused themselves with top-spinning, sham battles, target-shooting, walking on stilts, playing "wolf" or "catcher," and contests where they tried to see who could hold his breath the longest.

Many games for adults were played during festivals or on religious occasions. These included guessing games, shooting the bow

135

and arrow, sliding spears or arrows on the ice or hard ground, ball games, and horse and foot racing.

The Indian game, which later became known by the French-Canadian name of *lacrosse,* was played with a small ball of deerskin stuffed with hair or moss. Each player had a netted racket with which he could drive or even carry the ball. Two goals were set up several hundred yards apart and the object was to drive the ball, without touching it with the hands, under the goal of the opposing side. Two tribes or two settlements might play against each other using from eight to several hundred players on each side.

A similar game became known in the South as "rackets." It was played with one or two bats with a sort of net on the end. In the West "shinny" was more popular. It was played with curved sticks and a ball, and was a favorite of women. "Chunkey" was played by the Creek, with a stone disk and a pole having a crook at one end. As the disk was rolled ahead, the object was to slide the pole after it in such a way that the disk would be caught on the crook of the pole. Each town had its own "chunkey yard."

In all games where a ball was used, the ball was considered a sacred object, never to be touched with the hand, since it represented the earth, the sun, or the moon.

"Hunt the button" was a favorite with some tribes, and was much like "Button, button, who's got the button?" A form of cat's cradle was popular with the Zuñi and Navajo. The bowl game, played with a kind of dice, was popular with women among the Algonquin, Iroquois, and Sioux. Marked peach or plum stones, or bone "dice" were tossed into a bowl or basket. The hand game, commonly called "hand," was a guessing game where contestants tried to guess in which hand one of them held a marked bone. The snow snake game was played with sticks called "snakes," and the object was to see which contestant could slide the stick farthest on the ice or frozen ground. See CAT'S CRADLE, CHUNKEY, CREEK, MACKINAW (FORT), WOMEN. See also illustration, page 135.

**GERONIMO** (hay-roh'-nee-mo). A famous medicine man, prophet, and chief of the Chiricahua Apache. His true name was *Goyathlay*, "One Who Yawns," but he was called Geronimo from the Spanish for Jerome.

Geronimo was born about 1834 near old Fort Tularosa at the headwaters of the Gila River in New Mexico. In 1876 he and some younger chiefs fled to Mexico with their followers when the Government wanted to move the Apache to San Carlos, Arizona.

Later Geronimo and his band were arrested and settled at San Carlos. But when the Government failed to help them irrigate their lands the Indians became discontented. Geronimo went on the warpath, but once more surrendered. Two years later, however, in 1884, he gathered a band of hostile Indians and raided white settlements in Arizona and New Mexico, as well as in Sonora and Chihuahua in Mexico. This revolt was prompted by the Government's attempts to stop the Indians from making *tiswin*, an intoxicating drink.

General George A. Crook began a campaign with instructions to capture or destroy the chief and his followers. In March, 1886, Geronimo agreed to a truce, but this was violated by the Indians and they once again fled across the border. General Nelson A. Miles now took up the fight and finally in August Geronimo surrendered. He and his entire band of 340 were sent as prisoners of war to Florida. The old chief worked at hard labor for four years until he and the other prisoners were settled at Fort Sill, Oklahoma.

Geronimo, who had raided and killed for forty years and whose history was one of blood and pillage, died peacefully, a Christian, in 1909. See APACHE.

**GHOST DANCE.** One of the last great Indian uprisings, incited by the belief that an Indian Christ would appear and return to the Indian all his lands and bring back to life all his departed friends.

The Ghost Dance craze started around 1888 when Wovoka, a young

Paiute Indian, known as Jack Wilson, was working on a ranch in Nevada and became ill with a fever. He believed he had been taken to the spirit world and claimed the "Great Spirit" told him the Indians would have their lands and dead friends back if they would sing and dance as he directed them.

While Wilson was still ill, and his prophecy was spreading like a prairie fire, there happened an eclipse of the sun. The combination of prophecy and eclipse caused great excitement and the Indians believed they had to keep dancing to remain on top of the revolving world.

Sitting Bull soon became the leader, and members of his tribe, the Dakota Sioux, joined the movement, which had grown out of a strange mixture of the Indian's and white man's religions. Indian men and women would join hands forming a large circle and dance and sing. Sometimes these dances lasted for days, Indians falling into trances and having further visions.

The situation reached a climax when Sitting Bull was killed on December 15, 1890, and Indian men, women, and children were massacred by white soldiers at Wounded Knee, South Dakota. Among certain tribes the dance is still performed, but as a social one. See AMERICAN HORSE, CHEYENNE, DAKOTA, SITTING BULL.


GLUE. Glue was used in arrow and bow making, for sealing the seams of canoes and containers of birch bark, attaching feathers to the war bonnet and for many other purposes.

The thick muscles and muscular tisues of the neck of the buffalo and bull elk were boiled for several days until a jelly-like glue resulted. Captain John Smith wrote that the Virginia Indians used the sinew and the tops of deer horns to make a glue which would not dissolve in cold water. The Hupa found glue in the gland of the lower jaw and nose of the sturgeon.

The gum resin of the mesquite tree provided glue and the California Indians used the bulb of the soap plant. Possibly the most famous glue was the *bigiu* of the Woodland Indians, made of pitch from evergreen trees. After being boiled to obtain the pure resin, it was mixed with powdered charcoal.

Glue was often colored with ocher. It was usually stored on sticks and softened for use by heating. See ARROW, BARK CRAFT, BUFFALO, CANOE.


**GRASS LODGE.** See WICHITA.


**GRASSWORK.** Grasses, like many other things in nature, were utilized by the Indian. He used various kinds for covering houses, making beds, lining caches for the storage of food; for making baskets, mats, leggings, socks, towels, belts, and headbands.

White-and yellow-stemmed grasses were interwoven into designs in baskets and sometimes used as fringes on clothing. Stiff-stemmed grasses were made into hairbrushes and brooms and used as drills for making holes in materials which were not too hard.

Grass stems were sometimes flattened and dyed and used in decoration like porcupine quills. Grass also was made into cord and rope, and some fragrant grasses were employed as perfumes. The Cheyenne burned grass and mixed the ashes with blood and tallow for paint. See DRILLS.


**GREAT SPIRIT.** A name given by the white man for what he believed was the Indian's conception of God. See MAN BEING, MANITOU, MEDICINE, ORENDA.


**GREAT SUN.** See NATCHEZ.


**GREAT WHITE FATHER.** Indian term for President of the United States.

**GROS VENTRE** (groh vawn'-tr). A name applied to two and sometimes three bands of Indians. The name meant "Big Belly" in French.

The Gros Ventre of the Prairies, the Atsina, originally were a part of the Arapaho, according to historians. They are supposed to have received their name, "Big Belly," from the fact they lived on the Big Belly River, now known as the South Saskatchewan. About 1836 smallpox wiped out more than three-fourths of the tribe and the remaining small band, continually attacked by the Sioux, fled to the protection of the Blackfoot and have been associated with them since that time.

The Gros Ventre of the Missouri (River) were of the Siouan family and called themselves the Hidatsa. They lived at one time near the Knife River, a branch of the Missouri River, in North Dakota. Some contend it was among these Indians and their neighbors, the Mandan, that the famous spreading eagle-feather headdress of the Dakota originated. They were on the Knife River at the time of the Lewis and Clark expedition and it was with this tribe that Sacajawea, the famous "Bird Woman," lived.

It is claimed by some that the Gros Ventre of the Missouri, or Hidatsa, were direct descendants of eastern Woodland tribes because of their habit of living in earthen lodges. At one time the Gros Ventre of the Missouri and the Crow Indians were grouped under the same head. It is claimed that in the latter part of the eighteenth century a quarrel arose between two chiefs over the paunch, or first stomach, of the buffalo during a hunt, and the tribe split.

As a result of the split the Crow Indians have at different times been known as the Gros Ventre of the Prairies to distinguish them from the other half of the tribe, the Gros Ventre of the Missouri. The Gros Ventre Mountains in Wyoming are named for this tribe. But the Gros Ventre of the Prairies were the Atsina, and soon the name ceased to apply to the Crow. See ARAPAHO, BLACKFOOT, CROW, HEADDRESS, MANDAN, SACAJAWEA.

GUNS. When the Indian got over his first fear of the gun, which he thought was a kind of thunderbolt hurled by the white man, he was anxious to acquire it. But even after he got the gun he attached a certain mystery to it and termed it a "medicine iron."

At first, the Indian was never without his bow and arrows, even after he had the gun. During the days of the old muzzle-loader he could shoot from six to ten arrows before his enemy could reload his gun. Then, too, bow and arrows were good to have when his powder became wet, or when he ran out of ammunition, or when his gun was in need of repair. Few Indians ever learned how to repair a gun, and they could not make powder, either, and were forced to depend on the white man for ammunition.

As soon as the Indians acquired guns they sought new enemies and new hunting grounds. In 1670 the Sauk and Fox obtained guns from the French and two years later joined the Huron in the war against the Sioux. Early history states that the Fox Indians, armed with the famous Kentucky rifle, disputed possession of certain buffalo hunting grounds with the Cheyenne and Comanche and inflicted great slaughter among them.

In many cases the guns of the Indians were superior to those of the white soldiers against whom they fought in the early Colonial Wars, the Revolutionary War, and the War of 1812. The army was always slow to adopt newer arms, and even after the Civil War while soldiers were using the single-shot Springfield rifle, the Indians already were familiar with the new Winchester repeating rifle.

The French and English both gave the Indians firearms so they could provide more furs for them. But the Indians were more anxious to use these weapons on their enemies. Indians obtained ammunition from the Department of Indian Affairs under certain treaties, which said they could use it only for hunting. See HUNTING.

141

**HAIR.** The Indian's hair was his pride and joy. Some believed, too, that hair was in some way connected with the mystery of life, and were careful to let none of their hair fall into enemy hands. It was believed that the enemy, being in possession of the hair, would have power to hurt the owner, and so all hair combings were burned.

The Indian's hair was glossy and of a bluish or brownish black. When bleached by the sun it turned a rusty hue. Indians never suffered from baldness, and what few hairs they had on their faces or bodies they pulled out.

Both men and women gave a lot of attention to their hair. Bear fat was a favorite dressing and men sometimes mixed it with soot to make the hair blacker.

Those of the eastern tribes usually cut their hair close on the sides of their heads, leaving a ridge from the forehead to the back of the neck. The top part was trimmed like a pompadour, but the scalp lock was allowed to grow long, and was braided down the back and decorated with shells, or metal or stone ornaments. The ridge on top often contained a roach of deer bristles, dyed red.

Many tribes got their names from the way they wore their hair. The Pawnee, for instance, had a ridge from the forehead to the crown, with the scalp lock separated in a small circle, and this hair was parted off and stiffened with paint and fat. It stood up like a horn, and so the tribe got its name from an Indian word meaning "horn."

The Dakota, like other Plains Indians, parted their hair in the middle, back to a circle forming the scalp lock on the crown of the head, and then down the back from the scalp lock to the nape of the neck. The scalp lock was braided. The rest of the hair was braided separately on both sides and wrapped with beaver or otter skin and allowed to hang down on the chest. The line or part was painted red.

The Nez Percé and other far western tribes usually wore their hair long and unbraided. The Pueblo men cut theirs in "bangs," and in some ceremonies wore wigs of black wool and bangs of dyed horsehair.

Indian women wore their hair differently from men. They took pride in their long hair and some of them did their hair up in the back in the shape of a beaver's tail. Many changed the way of wearing their hair after marriage. For instance, before marriage Hopi girls dressed their hair in big circles on each side, in the form of the squash flower. After marriage they wore it in a single braid.

In mourning for the dead, Indians sometimes wore their hair unbraided and other times cut it off. The Crow, Assiniboin, Mandan, Mojave, and Yuma often wore false hair. See BEAR, HOPI, IROQUOIS, PAINT, SCALP LOCK, WOMEN.

**HAIR PIPE.** See BEADS, BREASTPLATE.

**HAIRWORK.** Indians used the hair of various animals for many things. They braided the hair from the tail and mane of the horse and the forelock of the buffalo into ropes. They also learned from the early Spanish to make horsehair headstalls and other horse gear, as well as belts and handle coverings. This type of work was known as "Spanish hitching." White hairs were dyed various colors, which enabled the craftsmen to work out patterns and fancy designs.

Besides that of the horse and buffalo, Indians used the hair of the dog, mountain sheep, mountain goat, moose, deer, elk, antelope, opossum, rabbit, beaver, otter, mountain lion, and sometimes even human hair.

Hair was used to stuff pillows, balls, drumsticks, dolls, pad saddles, and many other things, while tufts of hair were employed as decora-

144

tion on clothes, pouches, horse gear, ceremonial pipes, and such. The hair of the otter was believed to possess a powerful charm. See CALUMET, COSTUME, HORSE, LARIAT, OTTER, RABBITSKIN WEAVING, SADDLE, SCALP LOCK.

**HALF-BREED.** A western term meaning a person of mixed Indian and white blood. In the Gulf States such a person was called a *mustee*, from the Spanish form *mestizo*. In the northern sections he was called a *metís*, from the French-Canadian word meaning mixture.

A fraction or less than one-eighth white blood is considered a full blood by the United States Indian Service, which lists 60.5 per cent of all Indians today as full bloods. But it is impossible to tell the amount of Indian blood in the veins of the present white population, or the amount of white blood in the so-called Indian. Some writers have gone so far as to say no pure-breed Indians exist today, but this is undoubtedly untrue.

The mixture of white and Indian blood dates back to the earliest colonial days. The first English colonists were in favor of marriage with Indians. The most noted of such marriages was that of Pocahontas and John Rolfe. The early fur trappers married Indian women and lived with their wives' tribes. The Five Civilized Tribes of Oklahoma have much white blood, some dating back to the squaw-men of the West and some to the British and French fur traders before the Revolution.

There is a tribe of Indians known as Half-Breeds, of the Red River section—a mixture of white and Algonquian blood. These people live as Indians when with Indians and as whites in a white community.

The old idea that people of mixed blood had few of the good points of either parent, but all of the bad points, has long since been discarded in America. The opposite has been found true, especially with Indians and whites. There have been many cases of prominent men in this country who were justly proud of their Indian blood.

Many famous chiefs were of mixed Indian and white blood. See BRANT, CORNPLANTER, KEOKUK, LOGAN, OSCEOLA, PARKER (QUANAH), SEQUOYA, SQUAW MAN.

**HAPPY HUNTING GROUNDS.** The white man's term for what he believed was the Indian's idea of a future life after death. The Comanche Indians thought they went to a country in the West after death. The Flatheads, Crow, and others, believed they went east. The Sioux believed they went south. The Blackfoot and the Gros Ventre of the Prairies, to the north. The Caddo and others, inside the earth. The Cheyenne, to the zenith.

Northern Indians expected to go to a nice warm climate. Southern Indians hoped for a comfortable, cool climate. Indians had no idea of a place of punishment after death. One chief, when told of the white man's hell, said: "Indians won't be bothered with white men in the hereafter—all white men I know will go to their hell." See APACHE MOON.

**HATCHET.** See TOMAHAWK.

**HATTERAS.** A tribe of Indians who lived on the sand banks around Cape Hatteras, North Carolina. They were of Algonquian stock, but claimed their ancestors were white. Some think they may have been the same as the Croatan Indians with whom Sir Walter Raleigh's colonists are believed to have taken refuge on Roanoke Island. See CROATAN.

**HEADDRESS.** Formerly a sure way of telling an Indian's tribe was by his headdress. Each tribe had a distinct type of headgear, which varied from the famous eagle-feather war bonnet of the Dakota Sioux to the turban of the Iroquois.

The headdress of the Woodland Indians had no tail, and turkey, crane, and heron feathers were used, as well as those of the eagle.

The most picturesque headdress was that of the Dakota Sioux, which probably originated among the early Chippewa. Each feather in the Dakota headdress had a meaning and was known to the white man as

146

an "exploit feather." For instance, a feather with a red spot on the top was for killing an enemy. If the feather was cut off at the top it meant the enemy's throat had been cut. Notches in various parts of the feather showed whether the warrior had been second, third, or fourth in counting coup on an enemy, while cut edges of the feather meant he had been fifth. A split feather showed he had been wounded in battle—his "Purple Heart."

Among the Hidatsa, or the Gros Ventre of the Missouri, the first man to touch and kill an enemy wore a feather with a horsehair tuft; the second to strike the enemy wore a feather with one red bar; the third to strike, two red bars; and the fourth to strike, three red bars. Wounded men wore feathers with a band of quillwork.

The Omaha wore a roach made of a deer's tail and turkey-neck hair, dyed red, to designate one who had won first honors. The Sauk and Fox also had a deer-tail roach headdress. The Cheyenne wore a buffalo-horn bonnet during certain ceremonies.

The Blackfoot and other northern Indians wore a fur cap in winter, made from the pelt of the coyote, otter, or badger. Such a cap also was worn by the Omaha, Osage, and Ponca, and was decorated with quillwork.

The eastern Indians, chiefly the Iroquois, wore headdresses of animal skins, turbans of buckskin, and feathered headbands. One feathered cap, called *gustoweh*, or "real hat," had overlapping circles of smaller feathers on top, with one eagle feather in the center. See COSTUME, COUP, DAKOTA, EAGLE, FEATHERWORK, GROS VENTRE, IROQUOIS.

147

**HIAWATHA.** Both a name and title of chieftainship which was passed on from father to son in the Tortoise Clan of the Mohawk Indians.

The first known Indian to bear the name Hiawatha lived during the middle of the sixteenth century. He was famed as a reformer, a legislator, a statesman, and a magician, and was founder of the League of the Iroquois, first known as the Five Nations.

Hiawatha, as a reformer, sought to banish murder, the eating of human flesh, and to bring about peace among the Indian tribes of the same family. One of his ideas was that when a man was killed in a blood feud, his relatives should receive ten strings of wampum, each the length of the forearm. This was the value he placed on human life.

Apparently Hiawatha's ideas were so radical that he was banished by his own tribe. He went up and down the Mohawk Valley preaching for a brotherly feeling among tribes, and a strong union of relatives for war and defense. Finally the Oneida consented to such a union if Hiawatha's own tribe would join. The Mohawks later agreed and so the Five Nations was formed.

The hero of Longfellow's poem *Hiawatha* is drawn from the writings of Henry R. Schoolcraft, who had confused the real Hiawatha with a Chippewa deity. As a result nothing in Longfellow's poem relates in any way to the great Iroquois reformer and statesman. See IROQUOIS, LONGFELLOW, MOHAWK, SCHOOLCRAFT, TORTURE.

**HIDATSA.** See CROW, GROS VENTRE.

**HOGAN.** The earth house of the Navajo. The name comes from the Navajo word *goghán*. See NAVAJO, TEPEE, WIGWAM.

**HOLE-IN-THE-DAY.** A famous Chippewa chief, who fought the Dakota over possession of the fisheries and hunting grounds of the Lake Superior region. His Indian name actually meant "Rift in the Sky," or "Rift in the Clouds," and was given him by his mother because he was born when a ray of hope came to her after a troubled time.

Hole-in-the-Day was recognized as a chief by the United States Government for his bravery and loyalty to the Americans during the War of 1812, but he did not become a chief of his people until 1825, on the death of Chief Curlyhead.

He finally drove the Dakota across the Mississippi River and would have pursued them to the western Plains had not the Government compelled the warlike tribes to make peace at Prairie du Chien.

He died in 1846, and was succeeded by his son of the same name. See CHIPPEWA, DAKOTA, INDIAN NAMES.

**HOMINY.** A dish prepared from Indian corn, pounded or cracked and boiled. Sometimes the kernels were merely hulled by steeping them in lye or ashes, and then boiled. The word comes from the Algonquian dialects of New England and Virginia. See FOOD, MAIZE.

**HOPI.** A group of pueblo or village Indians who have remained in the same territory they occupied when first seen by Coronado's troops in 1540. They spoke a Shoshonean dialect.

Many of their ancient pueblos found in the northeastern area of Arizona are in ruins. In the Hopi village of Oraibi is a dwelling with timbers which are known to have been cut around 1370 A.D.

The Hopi depended on maize and other vegetables, and game for food. They were potters and raised cotton. When the Spaniards came the Hopi were reported to have been wearing cotton "towels." They domesticated the turkey and hunted the rabbit with a type of boomerang.

In their villages are structures, known as *kivas*, built partly underground, and entered through the roof by ladders. These kivas are used for ceremonial purposes.

Among the many dances of the Hopi is the Snake Dance, or Snake Ceremony, in which live snakes are carried about in the mouths of the dancers. This dance is usually held every two years around August 20th, and is primarily a prayer ceremony for rain. The Snake Dance, formerly alternated with the Flute Ceremonies, is now a tourist attraction.

Hopi men wore a breechcloth, hair band, and moccasins. Later they adopted the calico shirt. The women dressed in a blue cotton blanket, tied with an embroidered belt, a calico shawl, moccasins, and leggings. Some Hopi men dressed as women and did women's work.

Murder and theft were almost unknown among them and one of the worst crimes was telling a falsehood. The Hopi are said to have made more progress toward civilization than any other tribe of the Shoshonean group. They developed pottery-making to an art.

Today the Hopi occupy six pueblos in northeast Arizona. See BAKING STONES, BAT HOUSE, CORONADO, DANCE, FIRE MAKING, HAIR, KACHINA, MASKS, PUEBLO INDIANS, RABBIT STICK, SAND PAINTING, SNAKE DANCE, TRAILS.

**HORN AND BONE CRAFT.** Many of the Indian's most useful and decorative implements and objects were made from horn and bone and related material from birds and animals.

Horn was the most easily worked because when heated it could be flattened and made into any shape desired. Two pieces could be welded by first heating them and then pressing them firmly together. Horn was made into spoons, ladles, dishes, and containers.

From bone the Indian made tools, arrow- and spearheads, knives, buttons, and many other useful things. Antlers, which were bone and not horn, were fashioned into bows, flaking tools, and awls. Some of the larger and flatter bones of animals were used as hoes by the farming Indians. The wingbones of certain birds were used as whistles, and were thought to produce the same note as the bird's cry.

The hoofs and dewclaws of animals and the shells of turtles were made into rattles. Beaks of birds were used for decoration; teeth of bears for necklaces; and elk teeth were sewed on buckskin clothing.

The Indian had only crude stone tools to fashion his bone and horn articles. See ARROW, BOW, COSTUME, DEER, DISHES.


HORSE. The Indians of the Southwest were the first to obtain the horse.

When he first saw the horse the Indian was frightened. He thought the horse and its rider were one animal. Some considered it sacred. When the Hopi first saw this animal they spread scarfs on the ground for it to walk on. The Dakota termed the horse the "mystery dog."

After the Indian had overcome his superstition and fear, he captured and stole horses or traded for them, and then he felt himself as powerful as the Spaniard.

Previously the Indian had only the dog as a transport animal. His life and habits quickly changed with the acquisition of the horse. He could travel greater distances, take more baggage, hunt buffalo more efficiently, and put his unmounted enemy at a disadvantage in war.

There had been horses in America thousands of years ago. Fossil bones show them to have been very small. It is believed the early Indians considered the horse only as a food animal, and that these horses were killed off, finally becoming extinct.

The horses brought to America by the Spaniards increased rapidly. After a time they roamed the territory from the Rio Grande to what is now the Canadian border.

The Ute, Apache, Comanche, Kiowa, and Caddo were among the

first to acquire horses. Comancheros, unscrupulous half-breed traders, bartered for horses with the Plains Indians and then carried them to far-off tribes. By the middle of the eighteenth century no band of buffalo-hunting Indians was unmounted.

While many students of the "horse culture" of the Indians believe that the horses which stocked the Plains had been left behind by Coronado, others contend that all his "five hundred and fifty-eight horses, two of them mares," were accounted for in his muster roll. These latter authorities believe that horses came from stock-raising settlements in the Southwest, particularly those in the neighborhood of Santa Fé, New Mexico. Many of them spread northward through the normal channels of trade, although Indians acquired many by raids on ranches and settlements.

The English first brought horses into Virginia in 1620. The Spanish introduced them into the Southeast, where in 1650 they had seventy-nine missions, eight large towns, and two royal ranches. Attacks by the English and Indians scattered these horses and they increased and multiplied in the wild state.

The French brought the first horses into Canada in 1635. Indians marveled at these animals and called them the "moose of France." In 1735 the Iroquois were raising these French horses.

Indians at first rode bareback or with only a pad saddle of skin. Their bridles were thongs looped around the horses' lower jaws. An Indian would keep a long neck rope dragging so that if he were unseated he could grab the rope and stop his horse.

The Indian broke his horse by a system all his own. Sometimes it was by what cowboys termed "injun gentling," where he spent days becoming on friendly terms with his horse. Other times he employed the "Indian blanket act," where by the use of a blanket he was enabled to "hypnotize" his horse. "Injun gentled" horses were prized by cowboys. They were tough and easily managed.

The Indian mounted his horse from the right side, instead of the left side as did the cowboy. Horsemen today mount from the left side because in the old days cavalrymen and others who carried swords on the left side were forced to do so. The custom was carried down through the ages—but the Indian was not bound by such custom and mounted in the way that seemed natural to him.

The Indian's horsemanship was excellent. He could slip to the side of a speeding horse and shoot from beneath the animal's neck. He guided by pressure of his legs. He tethered his horse on the prairie by using a bone at the end of his tie-rope and burying it in the ground, or he would hitch the rope to a tuft of grass.

The pinto pony and the gray horse were favored by most Indians. These blended better with the landscape and also took war paint better than other horses. Indians had different ways of painting their ponies. The Blackfoot favored red paint. If a horseman ran over an enemy in battle, he could paint a hand on both shoulders of his pony. War ponies were decorated not only with paint, but with cloth streamers tied to their manes and tails, and human scalps to their bridles.

The war pony and the buffalo pony were considered the most valuable. Horses were used in barter and trade and a suitor might pay twenty horses for a bride. A medicine man might charge five horses as a fee for expelling some disease. Among the Sioux and Cheyenne a good horse was worth the plumage of two eagles.

Some Indians ate horses, drank the melted fat, and rubbed the blood in their hair, because they believed this would give them the strength of the horse. They used the hair of the mane and tail to braid into ropes and for decoration. A dead warrior's horse often was killed at the burial place, so the brave's spirit would be properly mounted in the hereafter. See CHEYENNE, COMANCHE, COMANCHERO, CORONADO, COSTUME, COWBOY, DOG, HAIRWORK, HORSE INDIANS, MYSTERY DOG, PAINT, QUIRT, SADDLE, SCALPING, SHOSHONI, TRAVOIS. See also illustration, page 142.

**HORSE INDIANS.** Term originally applied to the Cheyenne, Comanche, and Shoshoni. See CHEYENNE, COMANCHE, HORSE, SHOSHONI.

**HOUSE BURIAL.** See BURIAL.

**HOW.** Word of greeting used by Indians, who had no expressions for "good morning," "good day," or "good evening." While westerners claim it came from the word "Howdy," some authorities say it came from the Indian word *Hau*, or *Hao*, meaning "good" or "satisfactory."

**HUDSON'S BAY COMPANY.**
See FUR TRADE.

**HUNTING.** All but a few Indians lived by hunting. One estimate is that nine-tenths of the American Indians hunted. Schoolcraft, the great Indian authority, estimated that it required 8,000 acres of land, kept in a wilderness state, to support a single Indian by the chase. This meant 40,000 acres to keep the average family in food.

The Indian hunted much as the white man goes to war. He used strategy and tactics. His strategy consisted in capturing animals by traps, pitfalls, and nets. He employed tactics in stalking his game, in using the proper weapons, and sometimes by the use of fire, when he smoked out his quarry.

The Indian regulated his life to the habits of the animals upon which he depended for food. He lived as close to them as possible, and if they were roving animals like the buffalo, he followed them.

Hunting was done by the men of the tribe, but the game was usually left for the women to skin and cut up.

Stalking was a necessary art. The hunter tried to get as close as possible, especially if using a bow and arrow, for the average arrow was only effective at fifty yards or less. When he saw a group of animals he wanted to kill as many as he could. One writer says that on such occasions the Indian became very nervous, pointing his weapon at first one animal and then another before he could decide which to shoot first. If using a gun he tried for a "pot shot," or one which would kill several animals at once—or more for the pot.

Hunting was regulated by tribal rules and sometimes took on a religious aspect. See ARROW, BOW, BUFFALO, FEASTS, FISHING, GUNS.

**HUPA** (hoo'-pah). A tribe of Indians who lived in the Hupa (or Hoopa) Valley on the Trinity River in California. A village in Humboldt County, California, preserves the name Hupa. See TATTOOING.

**HURON** (hu'-ron). A once-powerful federation of four highly organized tribes of the Iroquois. The Huron remained outside the league of the Five Nations, and became bitter enemies of the Iroquois. In 1649 a large portion of the Huron were slain by the Iroquois.

The Huron survivors fled to the Erie Indians for protection, pursued by the Five Nations. The few remaining Huron and Erie found refuge with the Algonquian in Wisconsin. They became known as the Wyandot.

Some of the Huron joined the Dakota Sioux. The Huron had guns, and ridiculed the Dakota for using bows and arrows, until finally the Dakota expelled them. See ERIE, IROQUOIS, LEATHERLIPS, TARHE.

**HUSKY.** The wolflike dog of both the white man and Indian used in Alaska and the Arctic region. See DOG, ESKIMO.

**IDAHO.** Name of a state taken from the Shoshoni Indian word for "Salmon Eaters." The name has been misrepresented to mean "Sunrise Mountain," and "Gem of the Mountain."

**ILLINOIS.** A confederacy of several Algonquian tribes, formerly living in Illinois, southern Wisconsin, and parts of Iowa and Missouri. They were first visited by Père Marquette when he journeyed down the Mississippi River in 1673.

Their name was a combination of Indian and French—the Algonquian *inini* or *illini* meaning "man," with the French termination *ois*.

It was one of their number, a Kaskaskia Indian, who murdered the great chief, Pontiac, in 1769, which caused the Great Lakes tribes to make war on them. The Illinois were almost wiped out.

The Illinois gave their name to a state, and river in that state. There are also rivers named Illinois in Arkansas, Oklahoma, and Oregon; an Illinois Bayou in Arkansas; Illinois Peak in Idaho and Montana; Illinois City and Illiopolis, Illinois. There is a Kaskaskia River in Illinois, and there are towns in Illinois, Arizona, and Mississippi named for the Peoria tribe of the Illinois. See KASKASKIA, PONTIAC.

**INDIAN.** The name Columbus gave to the natives of America, a name which has survived to this day and has passed into the languages of the civilized world, including that of India. The early French called the natives *sauvages* (savages) and *peaux-rouges* (redskins), and the early English termed them "Americans."

The attempt to rename them "Amerind," a combination of "American" and "Indian" proved unpopular.

Congress has never given a general definition of an Indian in its legislation, nor have the courts ever interpreted the term. In 1879 certain rights were denied the Ponca Indians on the ground that they were "not persons within the meaning of the law." But in the same year Judge Dundy rendered his famous decision that "an Indian is a person within the meaning of the law of the United States."

Indians had no general name for themselves as a race, and their own tribal names usually meant simply "people," or "men." Most tribal names, as we know them, were given by other tribes or by the white man. See AMERICAN, AMERIND, BRIGHT EYES, COLUMBUS, RED MAN, SAUVAGE, STANDING BEAR.


**INDIANA.** The name of a state from the word "Indian." There is a county and a town by that name in Pennsylvania, and an Indianapolis in Indiana and Oklahoma.


**INDIAN FILE.** Single file, one behind the other. The term came from the way Indians march.


**INDIAN GIFT.** A gift which is demanded back. It comes from the Indian custom of expecting a more valuable gift than the one given, and if not satisfied, of demanding back the original gift.


**INDIAN IRON.** Term for rawhide. See RAWHIDE.

**INDIAN LADDER.** A ladder made by trimming off the branches of a tree and leaving some for steps at proper places along the trunk.

**INDIAN LANGUAGE.** Indians north of Mexico had more than ten totally unrelated "language families." These, in turn, were divided into more than two hundred separate languages, none of which could be understood by the others. Some Indian languages utilized many vowels and were smooth: for example, the Dakota Sioux; while others, such as the Chinook, were filled with consonants and were harsh. Indians had no written records by which to preserve or standardize the family language.

Because of their independent nature, many Indians would not take the trouble to learn the language of other tribes. The Cheyenne and Arapaho lived together for centuries and neither would learn the language of the other, but communicated by the sign language.

Besides the sign language, some Indians of different sections communicated with each other by what were known as "trade languages," such as the Chinook Jargon in the Northwest; the Choctaw, Chickasaw, or Mobile language in the South; and the Comanche in the Southwest.

It had been thought at one time that Indian languages had no formal structure, but it has now been determined that all of them have a complete and systematic grammatical structure, capable of expressing any thought.

Indian grammar is complicated, and the vocabularies of most languages are large. In a survey of three languages it was found that one had 7,000 words, another had 11,000 words, and the third had 19,000 words. While the English language has more than 130,000 words, an English-speaking person rarely uses more than 10,000 of them.

In speaking, Indians often combined a number of ideas into one word. Sometimes one word was an entire sentence. Some verbs, too, could be used to form hundreds of different expressions.

In some tribes there were no personal pronouns, so an Indian in speaking English might well call his wife "he." Sometimes there were "male" and "female" words. Other languages had several plurals, such as one meaning a pile of things and the other, things scattered around. The Eskimo had a dozen different words for "seal." The Papago would be puzzled if asked his word for arrow. He would want to know whether hunting arrow or war arrow was meant.

Some students claim that Indians used a private language in council, adding syllables to words, in the manner of English pig-Latin; also that medicine men frequently used a language of their own in their chants, which could not be understood by others. Women, too, occasionally had different ways of saying words.

It is true that in some California tribes the speech of men and women differed. Men spoke this "woman's talk" only when conversing with women. The difference was not great, but women usually shortened the words used by men, saying *ya* for *yana* meaning "person," or *ha* for *hana* meaning "water."

Many Indians had poetic ways of expressing abstract terms such as love, truth, spirit, or soul. They spoke of the "heart being warm," meaning it was glad. A man with a "big heart" was a brave man. The white man's written words were called "hearing with the eye," "painted speech," or "the paper that talks."

Of about 250 languages and dialects spoken today, Navajo and Sioux have become written languages, as did Cherokee with Sequoya's alphabet. See BIG HEART, CHINOOK JARGON, COMANCHE, INTERPRETER, MOBILE, ORATORS, PICTURE WRITING, SEQUOYA, SIGN LANGUAGE, WOMEN.

**INDIAN MONUMENTS.** For monuments erected in memory of famous Indians, see BLACK HAWK, BRANT, CORNPLANTER, CORNSTALK, JOSEPH, KEOKUK, LEATHERLIPS, LOGAN, MIANTONOMO, PARKER (QUANAH), POKAGON, RED JACKET, SACAJAWEA, SEATTLE, SHABONEE, TEKAKWITHA, TOMOCHICHI, UNCAS.

**INDIAN NAMES.** Indians did not have family names handed down from father to son or daughter. Each Indian had his individual name.

An Indian might take his name from something he saw in a dream, and he might change it many times if he felt the name he had was unlucky. He might change his name, too, after some notable deed, and if he did nothing more notable later he would keep the name for life.

The Cheyenne did not name a boy until he had gone to war and "counted coup" on an enemy. Then he was often named for something that happened on his journey, some animal killed, or some bird he had seen which he thought had helped him overcome his enemy.

In some tribes certain names were taboo. For instance, the Bannock would not name anyone after a fox, dog, coyote, or wolf. In other tribes it was customary not to speak the name of any animal whose name a dead man had borne.

Girls usually got their names from flowers and from attractive things in nature. Some received their names from frogs.

It was common in many tribes to carry on the name of a famous warrior or brave man after his death. When a certain time had elapsed after the man's death, his relatives would assemble and decide who should bear the name. If the man who was chosen agreed to assume the name, he was also expected to assume all the dead man's former duties. If the dead man had been a chief, he became a chief. He considered all the dead man's enemies his own enemies. He became the dead man's widow's husband and the father of his children. His former name was passed on to some one of his own relatives.

This act was known as bringing the dead back to life. Indians were superstitious about speaking the name of a dead man until that name had been given to a living person. They thought the very mention of the name would disturb the spirit of the departed. Thus the old chief, Seattle, of the tribes around Puget Sound, insisted on payment when the white men named the City of Seattle for him. He felt that this payment of tribute would make it easier on his spirit, which would be disturbed when the white man spoke his name after he had died. Names, too, were personal property and could be bought and sold.

Often it was considered improper for an Indian to mention his own name, and personal names were not used by husbands and wives when speaking to each other.

Indian names which described some incident in the life of their bearers are to be found in such as Chief Twelve O'Clock, Chief Crazy Horse, Chief Rain-in-the-Face, Chief Dull Knife, Chief Woman's Shirt, Chief Hole-in-the-Day, and others. There was a Chief Stinking Saddle Blanket, who got his name because he had been too busy fighting his enemies to change his sweaty saddle blanket.

When named for a living person, an Indian changed the name slightly, Big Wolf becoming Little Wolf, etc. See CAPTIVES, COUP, CRAZY HORSE, DREAMS, DULL KNIFE, HOLE-IN-THE-DAY, RAIN-IN-THE-FACE, SEATTLE, WHITE MAN, WOMEN.

**INDIAN REORGANIZATION ACT.** An act passed by Congress in 1934 authorizing Indian tribes to establish and conduct their own governments and form business corporations. The I.R.A. abolished the old Allotment Act, authorized the Secretary of the Interior to return to the tribes all "surplus lands," and prohibited the sale of Indian lands to non-Indians. More lands were to be purchased for Indian tribes.

The I.R.A. restored to the Indian the right to practice his own religion and tribal ceremonies. All restrictions on the use of his language were abolished. An Arts and Crafts Board was established to encourage the production of Indian art and handicraft and to promote the sale of such work. Indian teachers speaking native languages were employed in grade schools. A scholarship fund was established from which Indians could borrow for college or special training, and a revolving loan fund was set up for incorporated tribal enterprises.

After passage of the act, tribes were given two years to decide whether to go on as they had before, or to accept the conditions of the I.R.A. In 1936, 195 out of the 258 eligible "tribes" accepted. Others, who felt that their reservations and treaty rights might be affected, did not accept the act in full, but many have taken advantage of certain provisions of the act, such as the revolving loan fund. See ALLOTMENT ACT, ASSOCIATION OF AMERICAN INDIAN AFFAIRS, BUREAU OF INDIAN AFFAIRS, INDIAN RESERVATION, INDIAN SCHOOLS.

**INDIAN RESERVATION.** A tract of land reserved by the Government for Indians. The Government adopted this policy in 1786, when it became necessary to settle boundary disputes between Indians and colonists. Some tribes were given ownership of the land by treaties and could dispose of it as they saw fit.

Today there are over 300 separate and distinct areas of land in the United States which are occupied by Indian groups and held in Federal trusteeship for the use and benefit of the Indians. The largest reservation is that of the Navajo in Arizona, Utah, and New Mexico, with 25,000 square miles, while in California there are some reservations of only a square mile or two. The Pueblo Indians live on reservations given under nineteen Spanish grants.

There are some small state reservations in Maine, New York, Virginia, and South Carolina. See BUREAU OF INDIAN AFFAIRS, INDIAN REORGANIZATION ACT, INDIAN TERRITORY, OKLAHOMA.

**INDIAN RIGHTS ASSOCIATION.** The oldest welfare group devoted entirely to Indian affairs. It was formed in 1882 as a nonpartisan, nonsectarian organization for promoting the civilization of the Indian and for securing his natural and political rights. Toward this end it collects data, principally through personal investigation by its officers and agents, regarding the Indian's relations with the Government and the white race; his progress in industry and education; and his present and future needs. It also exposes wrongs and aids in the progressive program of legislation. The Indian Rights Association has its headquarters in Philadelphia.

**INDIAN SCHOOLS.** The Bureau of Indian Affairs operates 365 Federal schools in the United States and Alaska, with a total enrollment of over 43,000 Indian children. Of these, 265 are day schools ranging in size from one-room rural schools to consolidated elementary and high schools enrolling from 400 to 500 children. Sixteen others are non-reservation schools, and sixty-nine are reservation boarding schools. In eleven localities dormitory care is provided for children enrolled in local public schools.

The Bureau does not operate colleges for Indians. The graduates of Federal high schools who wish to go to college are encouraged to enroll in state and private colleges. The Bureau operates a scholarship program, as do many private and tribal organizations, to aid Indian students to gain higher education. The Indian Reorganization Act also provides a scholarship fund from which Indians can borrow for college or special training. See BUREAU OF INDIAN AFFAIRS, CARLISLE, INDIAN REORGANIZATION ACT.

**INDIAN SCOUTS.** A term applied both to white men and Indians who acted as guides or scouts for army troops and for pioneers.

The most famous of the Indian army scouts were the Pawnee. This tribe boasted it had never been at war with the white man. Pawnee scouts wore uniforms on parade but when they went into battle they discarded practically all their clothing. These scouts gained many honors for their work with the United States Army during the Indian wars between 1865 and 1885. Major Frank North was leader of the Pawnee Scouts.

Among the white scouts the most famous included Buffalo Bill Cody, Kit Carson, Frank Grouard, and Jim Bridger. See CARSON, DAKOTA, PAWNEE.

**INDIAN SIGN.** A term meaning to put a hoodoo on anyone or bring him bad luck. White men spoke of giving someone the Indian sign. Indian sign also meant certain traces of Indians in a vicinity as indicated by some mark or sign. See TRAIL (TO).

**INDIAN SUMMER.** A short season of pleasant weather, usually coming in the middle of November.

**INDIAN TERRITORY.** Former territory of the United States, originally part of the Louisiana Purchase. It was set aside by Congress in 1829, to be used by Indians who were to be transferred from east of the Mississippi River to the West. The Five Civilized Tribes first occupied it. In 1890 the area was cut down one-half by the creation of Oklahoma Territory. In 1907 both Indian and Oklahoma territories became the state of Oklahoma. See FIVE CIVILIZED TRIBES, INDIAN RESERVATION, OKLAHOMA.

**INDIAN WARS.** The War Department has made up the following official list of Indian Wars in the United States:

1790–1795—War with the Northwest tribes: Mingo, Miami, Wyandot, Delaware, Potawatomi, Shawnee, Chippewa, and Ottawa, which included Harmar's and St. Clair's bloody defeats, and Wayne's victory at Fallen Timbers, which brought peace.

1811–1813—War with the Northwest tribes, which included General Harrison's victory at Tippecanoe, Indiana, and later the defeat of Tecumseh's forces at the Battle of the Thames in Canada, when the great Shawnee chief was killed.

1812—The Florida or Seminole War when Spanish Florida was invaded by the Georgia Militia under General Newman, and the Seminole under King Wayne were defeated.

1813—Peoria Indian war in Illinois.

1813–1814—Creek War in Alabama when General Andrew Jackson defeated the Creek Indians in a series of bloody battles.

1817–1818—Seminole War in Georgia and Florida when General Jackson took possession of the Spanish territory, and brought the Indians to terms.

1823—Campaign against the Blackfoot and Arikara Indians on the Upper Missouri River.

1827—Winnebago expedition, or La Fevre Indian War, in Wisconsin.

1831—Sauk and Fox Indian War in Illinois.

1832—The Black Hawk War, which ended in the surrender of Chief Black Hawk at Prairie du Chien.

1834—Pawnee expedition in Indian Territory.

1835–1842—The Toledo War, or Ohio-Michigan boundary dispute.

1835–1842—The Seminole War in Florida. Osceola defeated.

1835–1837—Creek uprising in Alabama.

1836–1838—Cherokee disturbances which ended in the removal of the Cherokee Indians to Indian Territory.

1836—Indian troubles on the Missouri and Iowa line.

1837—Osage Indian disturbance in Missouri.

1849–1863—Navajo disturbances in New Mexico. Kit Carson rounded up 8,000 Navajos and held them prisoner.

1849–1861—More than ten years of continuous troubles with the Comanche, Cheyenne, Lipan, and Kickapoo Indians in Texas.

1850—The Pitt River expedition in California.

1851–1853—Utah Indian disturbances.

1855—Expedition against the Snake Indians in Oregon.

1855–1856—Sioux expedition in Nebraska Territory.

1855—The Yakima expedition which failed, but the following year the Indian allies were defeated and peace was made.

1855–1856—Cheyenne and Arapaho troubles.

1855–1858—Seminole War in Florida.

1857—Sioux Indian disturbances in Minnesota and Iowa.

1858—Expedition against the northern Indians in Washington Territory.

1858—Spokane, Coeur d'Alêne, and Palouse Indian disturbances.

1858—Navajo expedition in New Mexico.

1858–1859—Wichita expedition in Indian Territory.

1859—Colorado River expedition in California.

1859—Pecos expedition in Texas.

1860—Kiowa and Comanche expedition in Indian Territory.

1860–1861—Navajo expedition in New Mexico.

1862–1867—The Sioux War in Minnesota led by Chief Little Crow, which ended in the defeat of the Indians and the removal of the Minnesota Sioux to Dakota.

1863–1869 War against the Cheyenne, Arapaho, Kiowa, and Comanche Indians in Kansas, Nebraska, Colorado, and Indian Territory.

1865–1868—Indian wars in southern Oregon and Idaho and northern California and Nevada.

1867–1881—Campaigns against the Lipan, Kiowa, Kickapoo, and Comanche Indians, and troubles along the Mexican border.

1874–1875—Campaigns against the Kiowa, Cheyenne, and Comanche Indians in Indian Territory.

1874—Sioux expedition in Wyoming and Nebraska.

1875—Expedition against the Indians in eastern Nevada.

1876–1877—Big Horn and Yellowstone expeditions against the Sioux, during which General Custer and his entire command were killed.

1876–1879—War with the Northern Cheyenne and Sioux in Indian Territory, Kansas, Wyoming, Dakota, Nebraska, and Montana.

1877—The Nez Percé campaign in which Chief Joseph was defeated.

1878—The Bannock and Paiute campaign.

1878—The Ute expedition in Colorado.

1878–1887—Apache wars in which Chiefs Victorio and Geronimo led their warriors.

1879—The Snake or Sheepeater troubles in Idaho.

1890—Sioux Ghost Dance troubles and the death of Sitting Bull. Also the Battle of Wounded Knee.

1913—The Navajo War in New Mexico.

1915—The Paiute War in Colorado.

**INTERPRETER.** One who was a go-between for two or more people who could not understand each other's language. The Indians said interpreters were those "who handed words from one to the other."

Interpreters were important in the understanding of the Indian and the white man, and the lack of honest and efficient interpreters was one of the greatest causes of trouble and even wars.

In explaining Indian talk to a white man and the white man's talk to the Indian, the interpreter had to know more than the language of each—he had to know the customs, laws, habits, and many other things as well. Interpreters sometimes purposely translated incorrectly.

An excerpt from the official report of the Board of Indian Commissioners for 1870, when Chief Dull Knife, of the Cheyenne, appeared at Fort Laramie, reads: "The interpretation of the interview was carried on through 'Cheyenne Bob,' a full-blooded Indian, who interpreted the Cheyenne dialect into the Sioux tongue to Leon Pallarday, the Sioux and English interpreter temporarily employed for the occasion." Pallarday in turn interpreted it into English. See INDIAN LANGUAGE.

**IOWA.** See SOUTHERN SIOUX.

**IROQUOIAN FAMILY.** A powerful language family composed of thirteen tribes, including those of the Six Nations.

**IROQUOIS.** A powerful confederation of Iroquoian tribes, usually spoken of by historians as the Iroquois. First known as the Five Nations, the league was composed of the Cayuga, Mohawk, Oneida, Onondaga, and Seneca. But they became known as the Six Nations when in 1722 the Tuscarora were adopted into the confederacy. The name Iroquois is from an Algonquian word meaning "real adders," with the French suffix -ois.

The Delaware called them Mingwe, or Mingos, a name familiar in early colonial history. They called themselves *Ongwanonsionni,* or "We of the Extended Lodge." Thus the French also named the confederacy the "Long House." In their long house the Seneca were guardians of the "western door," the Mohawks of the "eastern door," while the Onondaga, in the center, were keepers of the council fire and wampum belt treaties.

The League of the Iroquois, or the original Five Nations, was formed in the late 1500's by the great Mohawk chief, Hiawatha, who advocated many reforms. Each tribe was to keep its independence, but was to act with the others for the common good. There was to be no war until all tribes voted for it. The "constitution" of the Iroquois was not written, but it was greatly admired by the colonists. Many claim that this confederacy served as a pattern for the Constitution in providing the sovereign rights of states.

The Iroquois were ruthless in war and wiped out their relatives, the Huron, and later the Erie. They began to expand their territory, but were stopped in the west by the Chippewa, in the south by the Cherokee, and in the north by the French. But at one time they were masters of all territory from the Ottawa River to the Tennessee River and from the Kennebec River to the Illinois River and Lake Michigan.

On one of his early expeditions, the French explorer Champlain joined a party of Canadian Indians against the Iroquois, which made the latter bitter enemies of the French, and caused them to side with the English in the early colonial wars. When the Revolutionary War started, the Iroquois league agreed to allow each individual tribe to decide whether or not to enter the conflict. All the tribes, except the Oneida and about half of the Tuscarora, joined the English.

Although citizens of the United States, the Iroquois still consider themselves an independent nation. When the United States declared war on Germany in 1917, the Iroquois sent a runner in full war regalia to Washington with a message that the Iroquois Nation also had declared war. However, when war was declared in 1941, the Iroquois sent no declaration. They had never made peace with Germany, so this second war was to them a renewal of hostilities.

The name Iroquois has been given to a river, county, and town in Illinois, and to a village in South Dakota. The names of each of the other tribes of the confederation have been widely used. See BARK CRAFT, CONFEDERATION, CORNPLANTER, COSTUME, ERIE, FIRE MAKING, HAIR, HEADDRESS, HIAWATHA, HURON, LOGAN, LONG HOUSE, MASKS, MINGO, MOHAWK, PAWNEE, RED JACKET, TRAILS, WAMPUM.

**JERKED MEAT.** Thin strips of the meat of buffalo, elk, deer, or other animal, dried on racks in the sun. The term "jerked meat" or "jerkie," came from the South American Indian word *charqui* (tchar'-key). See BUFFALO, FOOD, MORTAR, PEMMICAN.

**JESUITS.** Priests of a Roman Catholic order. French Jesuits were among the first to come in contact with the northern tribes of American Indians. They lived among the Indians, observing them at first hand and reporting on Indian life to their superiors in Paris. Their writings, assembled in the *Jesuit Relations*, are one of the best reference sources on the early Indian.

**JICARILLA** (hee-kah-ree'-ya). Indians of the Apache buffalo-hunting group. See APACHE.

**JOSEPH.** A chief of the Nez Percé Indians. He was handsome and learned, noted for his wisdom and oratory, and much admired and respected by white men.

Joseph's father was a Cayuse and his mother a Nez Percé. He was named Joseph by his white teacher, a missionary. His Indian name was *Hinmaton-yalatkit,* meaning "Thunder Coming from the Water over the Land."

Because his tribe, friendly to the whites, revolted after the treaty of 1863 which allowed white settlers to gain possession of the Wallowa Valley, they were ordered on a reservation. The Indians put off moving and in 1877 the Indian agent insisted on their going to their new home near Fort Lapwai, Idaho.

Joseph refused and with a part of his tribe made a stand at White Bird Canyon, near the Salmon River in Idaho. Here on June 6, 1877, he was defeated by white soldiers, but most of the Indians escaped. Joseph led his tribe toward Canada and for two months, traveling almost 2,000 miles of mountain roughness, he outfought and out-maneuvered hundreds of white soldiers. But finally, on October 5, within a day's journey of Canada, he was forced to surrender in the Bear Paw Mountains in Montana.

Joseph was taken as a prisoner to Oklahoma. Later he and his faithful followers were allowed to go to the Colville Reservation in the state of Washington, where he died on September 21, 1904. A monument of white marble was erected to him in the cemetery at Nespelim, Washington, where the remains of the great chief were buried. See APPALOOSA, CAYUSE, NEZ PERCÉ, ORATORS. See illustration, page 170.

# K

**KACHINA** (kah-chee'-na). Kachinas were believed by the Pueblo Indians to be supernatural spirits or gods which inhabited the mountains, and during ceremonial dances these gods were supposed to visit the village in spirit. The dancers themselves, with masked faces, represented the gods. Wooden dolls, with masked faces and bright-colored garments, representing the kachinas, were used in instructing the children. There were more than one hundred kachinas, each with a name, a distinct form, and an individual type of dress. See HOPI, MASKS. See also illustration above.

**KANSA.** See SOUTHERN SIOUX.

**KANSAS.** A state named for the Kansa Indians. The name in the language of the Kansa Indians means "South Wind." See ARKANSAS, SOUTHERN SIOUX.

**KASKASKIA.** A town in Randolph County, Illinois, at the mouth of the Kaskaskia River. It is believed to be the oldest town in the Mississippi Valley, and was founded in 1683 by the French under La Salle.

173

Kaskaskia, which obtained its name from the Kaskaskia Indians, was the capital of the Illinois Territory until Illinois was admitted to the Union in 1818. See ILLINOIS.

**KATO.** A small tribe of Indians who lived on the uppermost course of the South Fork of the Eel River in California. A few still live in California.

**KENTUCKY.** See DARK AND BLOODY GROUND.

**KEOKUK** (ke′-o-kuk). A Sauk Indian leader, born on the Rock River in Illinois, around 1770. His mother was said to have been French. Keokuk, whose name meant "Watchful Fox," was not a chief by birth, but rose to that position through skillful leadership, force of character, and brilliant oratory.

He was one of the few Indians more honored by Americans for his wisdom and gift of speech than for his fighting ability.

During the War of 1812, when Chief Black Hawk with part of the Sauk and Fox joined the British against the Americans, Keokuk and his followers remained loyal to the Government, but did not fight in its support. He wanted to be a leader in peace and not in war, and refused to take part in the Black Hawk War of 1832.

Keokuk won his greatest fame in a debate in Washington with leaders of the Sioux and other tribes, before Government officials, when he established the claim of the Sauk and Fox to that territory which is now known as the state of Iowa.

He died in Kansas in 1848. In 1883 his bones were removed to Keokuk, Iowa, where they were reburied, and a monument was erected to his memory. Later a bronze bust of Keokuk was placed in the marble room of the United States Senate, and a likeness of him was printed on an issue of paper money. See BLACK HAWK, HALF-BREED, ORATORS, SAUK AND FOX.

**KERESAN** (kcr'-c-san) **PUEBLO.** Indians of an independent stock, having no connection with any other. They are generally called Pueblo Indians. The Keresan lived and still live on the Rio Grande, in north-central New Mexico, between the Rio de los Frijoles and the Rio Jemez, and on the latter stream from the pueblo of Sia to its mouth. There are seven pueblos: Acoma, Cochiti, Laguna, San Felipe, Santa Ana, Santo Domingo, and Sia. See ACOMA, PUEBLO INDIANS.

**KERN RIVER TRIBES.** Several small groups of Indians who lived in the upper valley of the Kern River in California. Some survivors still live in that section.

**KICKAPOO** (kik'-ah-poo). A tribe of Algonquian Indians who formerly roamed what is now the state of Wisconsin. They were allied with the Sauk and Fox from early history, and in 1712 entered into a plot with the Fox to burn the fort at Detroit. They joined with Tecumseh in the War of 1812, and some of them fought under Black Hawk in 1832.

At one time a large group journeyed west and became known as the Mexican Kickapoo. They were troublesome along the border. The eastern band, which claimed the central portion of Illinois, ceded this to the Government in 1819 and moved west. The Kickapoo have given their name to a river in Wisconsin, creeks in Illinois and Texas, and small places in these states and Kansas. See BLACK HAWK, SAUK AND FOX, TECUMSEH.

**KING PHILIP.** A famous chief of the Wampanoag Indians, son of Massasoit. While known as *Metacom* to his tribesmen, the British named him Philip of Pokanoket, or King Philip.

King Philip undoubtedly was the most remarkable of the New England chiefs. Historians have said that had he succeeded in driving the colonists from the shores of America, he would have established himself as a powerful ruler.

He is best known as the leader of King Philip's War which raged during the years 1675 and 1676. It was the most destructive war in the history of the New England colonists and the most disastrous to the Indians. The decisive battle was fought August 12, 1676, when the Indians attacked a swamp fortress in Rhode Island. The Indians were defeated and King Philip was slain.

Like such later chiefs as Pontiac, Tecumseh, Black Hawk, and Sitting Bull, King Philip vainly sought to federate the tribes to resist the inroads of the white man. See BLACK HAWK, NARRAGANSET, ORATORS, PONTIAC, PRAYING INDIANS, SITTING BULL, TECUMSEH.

**KINNIKINNICK** (kin-i-ki-nik'). An Algonquian term originally applied to a mixture of bearberry leaves and tobacco. Because of the early scarcity of tobacco, or because he liked this mixture, the Indian rarely smoked pure tobacco. The name actually came from the Cree and Chippewa dialects and meant "what is mixed." The term later covered mixtures of Indian tobacco and leaves of the sumac, laurel, mansanita, squaw bush, and the inner barks of the red willow, dogwood, cherry, arrowwood, poplar, birch, etc. See BARK CRAFT, TOBACCO.

**KIOWA** (ki'-o-wa). A warlike tribe that formerly ranged the area

around the upper Arkansas and Canadian rivers in Colorado and Oklahoma. Associated with the Comanche and Shoshoni, members of all
three tribes were sometimes called Snakes. The Kiowa joined the
Comanche, Kiowa Apache, and Cheyenne in the general outbreak in
1874 and 1875.

The Kiowa, dark-skinned and heavy-set, were horse Indians and buffalo hunters. One of their claims to fame is the fact that they are believed to have killed more white people in proportion to their numbers
than any other tribe.

Today they are on the Kiowa Reservation in Oklahoma with the
Kiowa Apache and the Comanche. The name Kiowa has been given
to counties in Colorado and Kansas; to a stream in Colorado; and to
places in Kansas, Oklahoma, and Colorado. See CAMP, CHEYENNE,
COMANCHE, DOG SOLDIERS, KIOWA APACHE, MILITARY
SOCIETIES, SHOSHONI.


**KIOWA APACHE.** A small orphan group of Apache who became
friends of the Kiowa at an early period. The popular name for them
was the Prairie Apache. While they lived with the Kiowa and fought
with them, they still clung to their original language and customs.

It was less than a century ago that these people learned of their
kinship to the Apache. The Kiowa gave them the name of "Thieves,"
but this could have been a praiseworthy one, for in the old days a smart
thief was a highly respected Indian. See COMANCHE, KIOWA.


**KIVA** (kee'-va). See HOPI.


**KLAMATH** (klam'-ath). A tribe in southwest Oregon closely connected
with the Modoc. The Klamath were called "People of the Lakes," because their principal villages were on Upper Klamath Lake. They were
a hardy people and unlike their kinsmen, the Modoc, always lived in

peace with the white people. They took no part in the fierce Modoc War of 1872–1873. It is said their contemptuous treatment of the Modoc was the main cause of the latter's leaving the Klamath Reservation and returning to their former stamping grounds along the California boundary, which brought on the troubles with the whites. See MODOC.

**KLICKITAT** (klik'-i-tat). A tribe of Indians, noted as traders, who formerly lived south of the Columbia River in Washington. Today a few live on the Yakima Reservation in the state of Washington.

**KNIFE.** A cutting instrument which Indians fashioned from many materials, including hard wood, stone, metal, shells, and even the teeth of animals.

The most common of the early knives was made from flint. The edges were beveled by flaking. Where copper was to be had, some Indians made their knives from this metal. However, after the white man came, Indians used knives of tempered steel. A butcher knife was highly prized and the Indian would sharpen this on one side of the blade only so that the cutting edge was made from the hardest, or outer part of the steel. Such a knife made an ideal scalping knife.

Some Indians made a "crooked knife," on which the end was curved, for use in carving and gouging. Many of these were fashioned from old discarded files.

In eating, the Indian held his meat with his left hand and teeth and cut off a bite by an upward sweep of his knife. He was adept at just missing his nose. See FLINT, METALWORK, SCALPING.

**KNIFE SHEATH.** A protective covering usually made of rawhide, enclosed in buckskin which was highly decorated with beadwork or quillwork. The knife and sheath were worn hung from a belt. See BEADS, QUILLWORK.

**KNOTS.** Knots were used on bowstrings, spearhead and arrowhead lashings, snowshoes, and for a variety of other things.

The bowstring was usually fastened with a simple honda knot, or with an ordinary slipknot secured by a half hitch.

The Pueblo Indians kept a calendar by means of knotted strings, much like the famous *quipu* of the Peruvian Inca. The California Indians, who sold blankets to the missions, would send a salesman who was provided by each blanket-maker with two strings or cords. Every time the salesman received a *real*, or Spanish coin, he made one knot in the cord; when he received ten *reals*, or one dollar, he made a double knot. In the second cord he would make a knot each time he sold a blanket. In this way he could make an accounting to his clients.

Knots were made in rawhide by splitting and drawing the ends through. Loops, handle or strap knots were made in this fashion. This type of knot is known as a slit-braid.

Grass and bark were tied together by two simple overhand knots, which when drawn together would jam and make a secure fastening.

For covering articles with horsehair, the Indian employed "Spanish hitching," which he learned from the early Spaniards.

**KOASATI** (ko-a-sa'-ti). A tribe of Indians of Alabama, who are believed to have been related to the Alibamu Indians.

**KUTENAI** (koo'-te-na). A tribe of Indians, one division of which was known as the Flatbows, who roamed northwestern Montana into Canada, northwestern Washington, and the northern tip of Idaho. They have given their name to the Kootenay or Kootenai River, also called the Flat Bow River, which flows through Montana and Idaho; to the Kootenai Mountains and Kootenai Falls in Montana; and to a county and village in Idaho. See FLATHEADS.

**LACROSSE. See GAMES, MACKINAW.**

**LADY REBECCA. See POCAHONTAS.**

**LA FLESCHE, SUSETTE. See BRIGHT EYES.**

**LAKOTA. See DAKOTA.**

**LANCE.** A long shaft with a sharp head of bone, flint, or metal used for thrusting or throwing both in war and in the hunt. The lance, or spear, was used in some form by almost all Indians.

Early Indians employed a throwing stick in hurling the lance. The Plains Indians, in using the lance in hunting buffalo, hugged it beneath the arm as they thrust it into the side of the animal. Hunting lances usually were heavier and shorter than those used in war. There were other types of lances, some highly decorated with feathers and used only during ceremonies.

Among some of the Plains tribes there were special lances used by members of societies composed of the bravest warriors, such as the Dog Soldiers of the Cheyenne and Kiowa. Among the Dakota such men were known as "Strong Hearts," and there were two men of this society known as sash-wearers. Sitting Bull was a sash-wearer of such a society.

During battle the sash-wearers advanced toward the enemy, dismounted, and pinned their sashes to the ground with the lance. The other end of the sash was around their necks. They had to remain in the spot and fight until killed or until a brother warrior released them. Such lances as those used by sash-wearers were decorated with skins, feathers, and horsehair.

There were also lances known as "medicine lances," which were carried as "good medicine," or for good luck. See DOG SOLDIER, MEDICINE, MILITARY SOCIETIES, SHIELD, SITTING BULL, THROWING STICK. See also illustration, page 181.


**LAPPAWINZE** (lap'-pah-win-ze). A Delaware Indian chief noted as the signer of the "Walking Purchase Treaty" at Philadelphia in 1737. This treaty granted the whites land extending from Neshaming Creek in Pennsylvania as far as a man could walk in a day and a half. The Pennsylvania governor had a road built inland and employed a trained runner, which the Delaware considered a fraud. See DELAWARE.


**LARIAT.** Lariats or throw ropes were made of both rawhide and hair from the buffalo or horse. The early Indian buffalo or elk hide lariats usually were about twenty feet long. Most were merely strings or thongs of rawhide, unbraided, about two fingers wide. A slit in one end formed the honda, or eye through which the rope ran to make the noose.

Some ropes were braided from three rawhide strings in the "hair braid," or flat braid, with a small loop on one end. After a lariat had been braided from the damp rawhide strings, it was stretched on the ground until dry and then greased with tallow and softened by drawing it back and forth around a tree trunk or post.

Later, Indians made better lariats by using four strings in a round braid, an art they learned from the Mexicans.

Buffalo hair or horsehair throw ropes were braided from the neck hair of the buffalo and the mane and tail of the horse. They were much used by Plains Indians, but mainly as stake ropes or tie ropes, because they were liable to kink and were much lighter and could not be thrown as far as the rawhide lariat. See HAIRWORK, RAWHIDE, SADDLE.

**LEATHERLIPS.** A Huron (Wyandot) chief of the Sandusky tribe or Ohio, who was sentenced to death by Tecumseh because of his friend ship for the whites. Leatherlips, whose Indian name was *Shateiaronhi* (Two Clouds of Equal Size), had aroused the jealousy of Tecumseh, because of his honorable character and loyalty to the Americans.

Tecumseh termed him a wizard and sent Leatherlips' own brother to him with a piece of bark on which had been drawn a tomahawk as the token of his death sentence. Another Huron chief, Roundhead, was ordered to carry out the execution.

The execution took place on the Scioto River near Columbus, Ohio, in the summer of 1810. A number of white men, including a justice of the peace, made an effort to save the friendly chief, but without success. Leatherlips was tomahawked as he knelt beside his open grave, chanting his death song.

In 1888 the Wyandot Club of Columbus, Ohio, erected a granite monument to the memory of Leatherlips in a park surrounded by a stone wall, encompassing the spot where he died. See HURON, TECUMSEH.

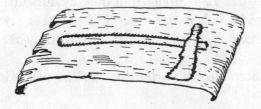

**LEGGINGS.** Cloth or skin coverings for the legs. Leggings were worn by both Indian men and women of most tribes. Men's leggings reached from the ankles to the hips, while those of women usually reached only to the knee.

Men's leggings were open both in front and back and were fastened to a belt by thongs. They were worn with a breechcloth. The cloth or skin of the leggings of the western tribes projected beyond the seam on the outer side and were cut either into a triangular flap or into fringe. In the leggings of the eastern tribes the seam was up the front and had no triangular flap or fringe.

The leggings of men were loose and much like the cowboy's *chaparejos,* or "chaps."

Those of women were close-fitting, either wrapped or buttoned. In some tribes, such as the Ute and Apache, women's leggings were fastened to the moccasins and formed a part of them.

Leggings were decorated with quillwork or beadwork or with painted designs. See COSTUME.

**LEWIS, CAPTAIN MERIWETHER.** Famous explorer and leader of the Lewis and Clark Expedition from the Missouri River to the Pacific Coast. Lewis and Clark found many Indian tribes never before seen by white men and they made valuable scientific collections and observations.

Lewis was born near Charlottesville, Virginia, August 18, 1774.

He served with "Mad Anthony" Wayne in the Indian campaigns and in 1797 was commissioned a captain. While private secretary to President Thomas Jefferson, he was chosen in 1803 to head an exploring party authorized by Congress for the development of trade with the Indians of the Missouri River Valley. At that time this area was held by Spain and owned by France, but before Lewis started out France sold the Louisiana Territory to the United States.

Lewis selected an old friend and army comrade, Lieutenant William Clark, as his companion. On May 14, 1804, with twenty-four army men and an additional sixteen persons who were to accompany them part of the way, they left St. Louis, Missouri. They ascended the Missouri River in three boats and arrived at the present site of Bismarck, North Dakota, on November 2.

They spent the winter among the Mandan and Hidatsa Indians. It was among the Hidatsa that they found *Sacajawea*, the "Bird Woman," who was to act as their guide for the remainder of the journey.

In the spring of 1805 the party made its way up the Jefferson River to what is now Montana, where they received aid and horses from Sacajawea's people, the Shoshoni. They crossed the Rockies in the fall and reached the Columbia River on October 7. They followed the river to its mouth, arriving November 5, being the first white explorers to cross the continent north of Mexico.

Lewis and Clark spent the winter on the Pacific Coast and started their return journey early in the spring of 1806. After crossing the Great Divide, the party split and Lewis explored Maria's River and Clark the Yellowstone. They met at the juncture of the Yellowstone and Missouri rivers and proceeded to St. Louis, where they arrived September 6, 1806. One person died and another deserted during the trip.

Lewis later was made governor of the northern part of the Louisiana Territory. On October 11, 1809, while on his way to Washington, he committed suicide near Nashville, Tennessee. See MANDAN, NEZ PERCÉ, SACAJAWEA, SHOSHONI. See also illustration, page 180.

**LILY OF THE MOHAWKS.** See TEKAKWITHA.

**LIPAN APACHE.** See APACHE.

**LITTLE CROW.** A Santee-Dakota Sioux chief who was noted as the leader of the bloodiest massacre of whites in the history of the West. Little Crow, or *Taoya-Teduta* (His People Are Red), had signed the treaty at Mendota, Minnesota, in 1851, by which the Dakota gave most of their lands in Minnesota to the United States.

Little Crow became a Christian convert and a devout member of the congregation of a little church near Fort Ridgely, Minnesota, and was known as a sincere friend of the settlers. However, when the promised food and other supplies were delayed in 1862, the Dakota went on the warpath. Little Crow led them in a reign of terror over 200 miles of the frontier, killing more than 1,000 white men, women, and children.

He was defeated in an attack on Fort Ridgely and with 300 followers fled to the protection of the Sioux of the Plains. He was killed by a settler on July 3, 1863, near Hutchinson, Minnesota. See DAKOTA.

**LITTLE TURTLE.** A famous chief of the Miami Indians. He was born in 1752 at what became known later as Little Turtle's Village on the Eel River, and what is known now as Fort Wayne, Indiana. His father was a Miami chief and his mother was a Mahican.

Little Turtle became a chief at an early age and was the principal leader of the Indians who defeated General Harmar on the Miami River in the fall of 1780. Five years later, after being defeated by General Wayne's army, Little Turtle signed a treaty of peace. At the time, he said: "I am the last to sign it and I will be the last to break it." He kept his word and when the War of 1812 started he refused to join Tecumseh.

In 1797 Little Turtle made a memorable trip to Washington. Here he met, among others, General Kosciusko, the Polish general who had fought with the Americans in the War of Independence. General Kosciusko gave Little Turtle his own pair of handsome pistols. During this trip, too, Gilbert Stuart, the famed artist who had painted George Washington, made a portrait of the chief.

Little Turtle died in 1812 at Little Turtle's Village. See MIAMI, TECUMSEH.

**LO.** A poetical name for the Indian, which came from Alexander Pope's lines: "Lo, the poor Indian! whose untutored mind/Sees God in the clouds and hears him in the wind." The Indian was sometimes called "Poor Lo," a name he was perfectly right in not liking.

**LODGE.** A general term applied to Indian dwellings, including tepees, wigwams, grass and earth houses, and wickiups. However, a lodge usually meant a permanent dwelling such as the earth lodge of the Pawnee, or the grass lodge of the Omaha.

Many times the term was used to designate the population of an Indian camp or village, it being said that such and such a tribe consisted of so many lodges. As it was estimated that an average of five persons lived in a dwelling, a camp of 100 lodges would consist of 500 men, women, and children. See CAMP, TEPEE, WICKIUP, WIGWAM.

**LOGAN, JOHN.** A famous Iroquois chief and noted Indian orator. He was born in 1725 near Shamokin, Pennsylvania. His father was said to have been a Frenchman, who had been captured as a child by the Oneida and who later became a chief.

Logan, whose Indian name was *Tahgahjute* (His Eyelashes Stick Out or Above) took the name by which he became known to history from that of his friend, James Logan, secretary to William Penn and for a time acting governor of Pennsylvania.

Logan has come down in history because of the much-quoted speech he made in 1744 under an elm tree still standing in Circleville, Ohio. His speech was delivered after white men had murdered some of his followers, including members of his family. It was then that he went to war against the colonists.

Logan was killed in 1780 by a nephew. A monument stands today in his honor in the Fort Hill Cemetery, near Auburn, New York. See HALF-BREED, IROQUOIS, ORATORS.

**LONGFELLOW, HENRY WADSWORTH** (1807–1882). An American poet born in Portland, Maine. He was best known for his poem, *Hiawatha,* written in 1855, which was founded on traditions and legends of the American Indians. See CHIPPEWA, HIAWATHA, SCHOOLCRAFT.

**LONG HOUSE.** A name applied to the Iroquois Confederacy as well as to their type of dwelling. Sometimes written as one word, longhouse. See IROQUOIS.

**LONG KNIVES.** An early Indian term for American colonists. The Indians also called them "Big Knives." They called the Englishmen "Coat Men." See WHITE MAN.

**LONG WALK, THE.** Term used by the Navajo Indians after their surrender to Kit Carson, for their journey from their homeland along the Arizona-New Mexico border to Bosque Redondo in eastern New Mexico. See CARSON, NAVAJO.

# M

**MACKINAW** (mack´-i-nô), **FORT.** A famous trading post, situated on Mackinac Island—or Michilimackinac (Big Turtle) as it was formerly called—between Lakes Huron and Michigan. In 1764 Fort Mackinaw was captured for the English from the French by Indian allies who used a ruse of following a lacrosse ball into the fort.

The term mackinaw, which is from the Chippewa word meaning "turtle," is applied to several things in English. A mackinaw is a kind of bateau or flatboat used by traders. A heavy blanket is known as a mackinaw blanket, and there is a hat by the name. A species of lake trout is termed Mackinac trout. See BLANKET, GAMES.

**MAHICAN** (ma-he´-kan). A one-time powerful Algonquian tribe that occupied both sides of the upper Hudson River, extending north almost to Lake Champlain. Their name means "wolf." They are not to be confused with the Mohegan Indians of Connecticut.

James Fenimore Cooper made this tribe famous by his book, *Last of the Mohicans*. The hero, Uncas, however, was a Mohegan in real life.

With the coming of the colonists the Mahicans gradually began to lose their territory and shortly after the Revolutionary War most of them dropped from sight.

But the Mahican did not entirely disappear. One band was gathered into a mission near Stockbridge, Massachusetts, and became known as the Stockbridge Indians.

Later, for one reason or another, they lived in various places, and finally settled in Wisconsin, where today on the Stockbridge Reservation, west of Shawano, these "last of the Mohicans" number with the Munsee Indians around 500. There is a Mohican River and town in Ohio. See COOPER, MOHEGAN, UNCAS.

**MAIZE** (mays). A tall hardy grass now cultivated both for its grain and as forage for cattle. Maize, which comes from the Haitian word *mahis* or *mahiz*, is usually designated as "Indian corn," or simply "corn."

The early explorers found this grain under cultivation from Canada to Chile, and the Spaniards introduced it into Europe whence it spread all over the world. It is estimated today that more people throughout the world are nourished by corn than by any other grain, except rice.

Columbus spoke of the Indians making an intoxicating drink from maize. Champlain left the first record of the cultivation of corn in New England. The Pilgrims, soon after landing, were taught to cultivate it by Chief Massassoit.

The Indians have many legends about the origin of corn. Some believed it was the gift of their gods. Some termed it "Mother Corn," the "Giver of Life." The Pawnee believed that Corn had visited the earth first as a beautiful, fair-haired young woman, whose locks were preserved in the corn silk. The Six Nations held a Corn Festival each year. The Creek held a Green Corn Dance.

The time of planting, ripening, and harvesting corn were times of festivities among many tribes. Corn has long been used as food. Recent excavations in New Mexico have shown that corn was grown in that area several centuries before the birth of Christ.

From the Indians the white man got his ashcake, hoecake (Algonquian *nokake*), samp, hominy, roasting ears, and popcorn. Even the farmer's corn cribs, elevated on posts, are patterned after those of the southern Indians. See DANCE, FEASTS, FOOD, HOMINY, MAPLE SUGAR, METATE, PAPER BREAD, PARCHED CORN, PAWNEE.

**MAN-BEING.** Term for one of the many wise men some Indians believed came before everything else and created the earth and the gods. In most tribes this belief forms the basis of their mythology.

It would appear from the many legends that this once-powerful race of man-beings lived in a region above the sky. They all existed in peace and harmony in the beginning. However, these beings were not alike. Each one, as time ripened, became transformed more and more into what he later was to become. He had his own magic power by which he would perform his duties after the changing of all things.

Naturally these changing man-beings began to think differently, and unrest and discord arose among them. Then after commotion, collision, and strife the great change came about. The transformed man-beings were banished from their sky home to the earth where they assumed their proper forms. Some became trees, others plants, fish, rocks, animals, mountains—in fact they took the shapes of all things, even man.

The worlds were grouped into seven forms—a magic number among Indians. There was the east, west, north, south, upper world, lower world, and midworld. All these worlds were inhabited by man-beings in the forms of wind, sun, stars, the moon, and even storms. Winter, summer, fall, and spring—all were man-beings.

As all man-beings had magic powers, the Indian believed that mere man could not exist without the aid of man-beings around him. And, as some man-beings were good and others bad, the Indian thought it wise not to offend the bad ones.

Without knowing the Indian's belief in man-beings, the white man was at a loss to understand the Indian's religion. For each Indian selected his own man-beings to aid him in overcoming difficulties, after seeing them in dreams or visions, and often entire tribes would worship one or more man-beings.

The Mandan, for instance, placed a piece of cloth around one of the poles of his lodge as a gift to the God of Timber, believing it would keep this god from being angry at him for cutting down a tree to make a pole. The Navajo was always apologetic to the Earth when he removed clay to make pottery. The Menominee would not cultivate wild rice because in doing so he would have to disturb Mother Earth. See DREAMS, GREAT SPIRIT, MANITOU, MASKS, MEDICINE, MENOMINEE, ORENDA, SACRED BUNDLES, STARS.

**MANDAN** (man'-dan). An important division of the Sioux Indians, who originally lived in the neighborhood of what is now Bismarck, North Dakota. The artist, Catlin, who spent much time among them, made them famous on canvas and in literature. Lewis and Clark spent the winter with them in 1804–1805.

The Mandan had among them a type which inherited gray hair, often at an early age. Since gray hair was unusual among Indians, the tribe was often referred to as being composed of "white Indians." Some thought their hair was blonde and it was speculated that the Mandan might be descendants of the Welsh believed to have been brought into Canada by King Madoc of Wales—the so-called "Lost Welsh Colony."

The Mandan practiced tattooing to a certain extent—the chiefs decorating their left arms and breasts with black parallel stripes and a few figures.

The Mandan were rarely in trouble with the whites. Smallpox was their worst enemy. In 1837 the disease almost wiped them out, leaving only 31 survivors out of 1,600, according to one report. These few joined with the Hidatsa and have been with them ever since. Mandan is the name of a city in North Dakota. See ARIKARA, CATLIN, GROS VENTRE, LEWIS, TATTOOING.

**MANHATTAN.** The island of Manhattan, which is the heart of Greater New York City. It was bought from the Manhattan Indians on May 6, 1626, by Peter Minuit for 60 guilders' (about $24.00) worth of trinkets. In 1609 these Indians attacked Henry Hudson, while he was returning down the river which bears his name. While the word "Manhattan" is said to come from the Indian words *manah*, meaning island, and *atin*, meaning hill—Hill Island—a few claim that it came from the word *manhachtanick*, or "the-place-where-we-all-got-drunk," after Hudson had given the Indians some liquor.

**MANITOU** (man'-i-too). A term used by Algonquian Indians to mean the mysterious and unknown powers of life of the universe. The white man narrowed down the meaning of the word to that of "spirit," good or bad. Thus the Indian was supposed to have a Great or Good Spirit and an Evil or Bad Spirit. However, Indians had many manitous. See GREAT SPIRIT, MAN-BEING, MASKS, MEDICINE, ORENDA.

**MANUELITO.** A war chief of the Navajo, who led the lawless element of his tribe for many years. Colonel D. G. Miles punished this group of troublesome Navajo in 1859 and when they finally settled down on reservations, Manuelito was elected commander of the Indian police force. He died in 1893. See NAVAJO.

**MAPLE SUGAR.** A sugar obtained from the sap of the sugar maple tree. Maple syrup was first made by the Indians, chiefly those of the Algonquian tribes. Later they were taught by the French to render the syrup into sugar.

Indians drank the sap both fresh and fermented. They poured the syrup over popcorn and this "sugar snowball," as the French called it, was the forerunner of the present-day crackerjack. Today the making of maple sugar and maple syrup is a major industry in some eastern states and parts of Canada. See MAIZE.

**MASKS.** The false faces of the Indians. Many Indians wore masks during ceremonies, but sometimes young people wore them during certain festivities.

The wearing of masks had definite meanings at all times. Masks

represented some sort of animal, or some one of the Indian's manitous, man-beings, or gods. Whenever an Indian put on a mask he believed he was assuming the character of the animal or being while he wore it.

Masks were made from wood, basketwork, pottery, or hides, and were carved, painted, and decorated with shells, fibers, hair, or feathers. Some masks were male and others female.

The Iroquois carved their masks from wood, first cutting it out on the tree itself, and then removing it. The mask was supposed to contain the spirit of the tree. If the tree died after the operation, the mask was not used.

The Hopi made little dolls to represent their *kachinas*, or gods, and also masks which gave the wearer the identity of the *kachina*. Thus when a person wore one of these masks he was for the time being transformed into the god the mask represented. See DANCE, HOPI, IROQUOIS, KACHINA, MAN-BEING, MANITOU.

**MASSACHUSET** (mas-a-choo'-set). An early tribe of Algonquian Indians who occupied the site of the present city of Boston. They are mentioned by Captain John Smith in 1614 as having eleven villages on the coast. They caused the early colonists little trouble. When disease had almost wiped them out, the remaining few joined the "Praying Indians," or Christian converts, at Natick, Nonantum, and Ponkapog where they were no longer known by their tribal name.

Crispus Attucks, of mixed Negro-Massachuset ancestry, who was killed in the Boston Massacre, is believed to have been the first victim of the Revolutionary War. The name of the tribe has been preserved in that of the state of Massachusetts and of Massachusetts Bay. See ELIOT BIBLE, PRAYING INDIANS.

**MATACHIAS** (ma-ta'-chee-as). Little ornaments of beads, porcupine quills, or braided strings, which the Indians of Maine used on the cradles of their papooses. See PAPOOSE.

**MEDICINE.** Something that is used as a cure or remedy. But medicine was more than this among the American Indians. It was a bond with the supernatural world. To some tribes the term "medicine" meant "mystery," while among others there were two kinds of medicine: one dealing with magic and one with the actual curing of diseases or illness by its use. At other times medicine meant an object or objects which were believed to have mysterious powers to protect the owner.

The term "medicine" as used by the white man in connection with the Indian might have come from the name of the Midewiwin Society, a secret society of the Chippewa, Menominee, and Potawatomi. *Midewiwin* was translated as Grand Medicine Society, and its members received instruction which increased their spiritual insight and power and taught them to cure diseases, mostly by secret methods.

Indians believed in both good and bad medicine. Good medicine was something that brought them good luck. Bad medicine was something that brought them bad luck. A person, animal, or object might be spoken of as good or bad medicine.

One of the first things a young Indian did when he reached manhood was to obtain his medicine. He might do this through a dream or vision. Or he might select certain things which had brought him luck. All these various charms were placed in a little bag which he carried at all times. Sometimes this bag or container might be a huge affair and he would have to carry it strapped on his back.

Once he had his medicine, the Indian believed nothing could harm him. He would purposely test its potency by exposing himself to the enemies' arrows or bullets. He had complete faith in the power of protection his own medicine gave.

General Richard I. Dodge, a close observer of the Plains Indians, said in his book, *Our Wild Indians:* "According to the best authorities and to tradition, it was the custom thirty or forty years ago for an Indian to select the special ingredient of his 'medicine' but once in his life, sticking to it and believing in it through all the subsequent years of good or ill fortune. This is changed at the present time [1882], and an Indian who has an unusually long or severe turn of bad luck, attributes his misfortune to the failure of his 'medicine,' and going off alone will starve himself into a trance in the hope of having a new and more efficacious ingredient revealed to him."

There were occasions when an Indian would "make medicine." He would not commence anything, or undertake a hunt or a journey without first making medicine. Earth or sands of different colors, ashes of plants or of bones, or portions of birds, animals, or reptiles, and other things about which he might be superstitious would be mixed in a shallow dish, kept for this purpose, and stirred gently with a stick. From the combination of colors, or some other peculiarity developed by the process, the Indian could "read" the outcome of his project.

Should such medicine be good, off he would go on his hunt or undertake his journey. If bad he would probably stay home.

A medicine man would make medicine for the entire tribe before some great event, such as going to war. It was said, but never proved, that during the Custer Battle, Sitting Bull, who was a medicine man as well as a chief, was off in the hills "making medicine."

Tribes had sacred bundles containing the "tribal medicine," which were closely guarded.

Indians used roots, leaves, and bark of certain plants, as well as specified animal and mineral substances as remedies. Some of them have been found valuable by the white man, and he has adopted cinchona, jalapa, hydrastis, ginseng, and others.

Indians often thought that like cured like. A plant with a worm-like stem would be used in getting rid of worms. The Hopi treated baldness by using hairlike plants. Southwestern tribes treated snake-

bite by applying a part of the snake's belly to the wound. When a person was burned it was thought that fire would draw out the pain, and the Hopi blew charcoal, ashes, and other products of fire on the burned part. See DREAMS, FASTING, GREAT SPIRIT, LANCE, MAN-BEING, MANITOU, MEDICINE MAN, ROOTS AND ROOTCRAFT, SACRED BUNDLES, SAGE, SECRET SOCIETIES, TOTEM.

**MEDICINE IRON.** See GUNS.

**MEDICINE MAN.** A person who gained his power of healing the sick through some secret means. This power usually came to the Indian medicine man through dreams or visions. Most of the healers claimed they could communicate with the spirit world and many of them were expert conjurors and magicians.

Some medicine men would build themselves a special hut and go inside it for a session with the spirits. Soon the hut would shake and strange sounds would come forth. Often the medicine man would be found in a trance and when he came to, he would tell what the spirits had said. Usually these spirits had told him how to cure diseases and what might be expected in the future.

It was common for medicine men on visiting sick persons to beat tom-toms, make noises with rattles, and sing. Some would place their mouths on certain portions of sick persons' bodies and claim to suck out the object which had caused all the trouble. After showing this object they would immediately destroy it.

Most medicine men did not practice surgery. But there are cases on record, such as the one where a medicine man bored two holes in a patient's chest so that he could blow out the evil spirit. This was a cure for asthma. There was another case of a woman who had brain fever and a hole was bored in her skull to let the evil spirit escape.

Most medicine men were feared and respected. Some rose to great power, notably Sitting Bull and Black Hawk. See BLACK HAWK, MEDICINE, SITTING BULL. See also illustration, page 190.

199

**MEDICINE PIPE.** See CALUMET.

**MEKADEWAGAMITIGWEYAWININIWAK.** Probably the Indians with the longest and most unpronounceable name. They were a small band of Chippewa formerly living on the Black River in southeast Michigan and their name meant "People of the Black Water River." Thus the Black River was named for them, after a fashion.

**MENOMINEE** (me-nom'-i-nee). A tribe of Algonquian Indians who have lived in almost the same locality in Wisconsin since they first came in contact with the white man in 1634. They have given the whites little trouble. The beliefs and rituals of these Indians are almost the same as those of the Chippewa. Their chief vegetable food is wild rice, and their name means "Wild Rice Men." But they refuse to cultivate wild rice for fear of wounding "Mother Earth." They live today on the Menominee Reservation near the head of the Wolf River in Wisconsin.

Some years ago this tribe won a $9,500,000 lawsuit against the Government on a charge of mismanagement of tribal affairs. The money was placed in a trust fund. In 1954 the first payment was made, each of the 3,254 adult Menominee on the tribal rolls receiving $1,500—a total of $4,881,000. When the final payment was made in 1959 these Indians were freed from Government control.

The name Menominee was given to a Michigan county and towns in Michigan and Illinois. In the form of Menomonee it has been applied to a river and falls in Wisconsin, and as Menomonie to a city in the same state. See CHIPPEWA, MAN-BEING, RICE (WILD).

**MERRIMAC** (mer'-i-mak). A Chippewa chief who signed a treaty between his tribe and the Government in 1805 on the St. Mary's River. Merrimac is also another name for the Pennacook Indians. See PENNACOOK.

**MESCAL** (mes-kal'). A plant of the agave family, the fleshy bases of whose leaves and trunk were used as a food by the Indians of the Southwest. A pit was made and lined with stones. A fire was built over the stones and when they became hot, the coals were raked out and the mescal placed in the pit and covered with grass. After two days' steaming the food was ready to eat. When the crops of the whites failed at El Paso, Texas, more than half a century ago, the entire population lived for six months on mescal. Mexicans make a fermented drink from the plant. The Mescalero, a tribe of Apache, got their name from the custom of eating mescal. See APACHE, FOOD.

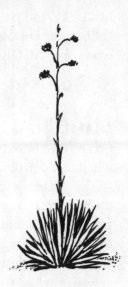

**METALWORK.** Using crude tools of bone and rock, the early Indians were able to work with copper, which appears to have been the only metal actually mined by them. There is no evidence that the Indians extracted the metal from the ore by smelting, but some did use heat in making the metal more workable. Indians usually fashioned their copper objects by cold-hammering and grinding.

After the white man introduced silver, this became a very popular metal with the Indians. The Navajo and Pueblo Indians were the most expert silversmiths.

Indians quickly learned to use iron and steel. They made arrowheads from hoop iron and converted old files into knives. See ARROW, BELL, KNIFE.

**METATE** (may-tah'-tay). A flat and slightly hollowed stone used by Indians for crushing or grinding maize, acorns, seeds, chile, and other foods. See ACORN, MAIZE, MORTAR.

**MIAMI.** A tribe of Algonquian Indians who roamed the central portion of the United States. They termed themselves *Twightwees*, a name which came from the cry of the crane.

The Miami joined Pontiac, the great Ottawa chief, in 1763 at the unsuccessful sieges of Detroit and Pittsburgh. They took part in all regional wars until the end of the War of 1812, and were noted as one of those tribes which offered steady resistance to the westward movement of the white people. Their greatest chief was Little Turtle.

The Miami worshiped the sun and thunder, lived in cabins covered with rush mats, were slow spoken and polite. They cut off a woman's nose when she was unfaithful to her husband.

By 1827 the Miami had sold all their lands in Indiana and Ohio and drifted to Kansas. To kill the buffalo here they set fire to grass on three sides of a herd, and shot the animals when they rushed out the open side. Later they went to a reservation in Oklahoma. Their name has been given to three rivers in Ohio, the Great Miami, Little Miami, and Maumee (another way of spelling the name); to counties in Indiana, Kansas, and Ohio; and to places in Ohio, Indiana, California, Oklahoma, Missouri, and Texas; and a creek in-Missouri. The names of Miami, Miami Beach, and Miami Springs, all in Florida, have a different origin. See LITTLE TURTLE, PONTIAC.

**MIANTONOMO** (mi-an-to'-no-mo). A noted chief of the Narranganset Indians who aided the English colonists against the Pequot. After Miantonomo had signed a three-way treaty between the English of Connecticut, the Narraganset, and the Mohegan, his tribe and the

Mohegan became involved in a bitter war. Miantonomo was defeated and Chief Uncas of the Mohegan delivered him to the English, who tried him and condemned him to death.

Uncas was selected to kill Miantonomo. But Uncas did not choose to take the chief's life, as he did not believe he had conspired against the English, as charged. So Uncas' brother executed him.

Miantonomo was buried a mile east of Norwich, Connecticut, on the spot where he died. For many years members of his tribe made visits to his grave, and each added a stone to a pile until a considerable monument was raised to his memory. The settlers became impressed with the reverence of the Indians for their dead chief, and began to doubt the justice of his execution.

As time went on the respect for Miantonomo grew and finally in 1841 a monument was erected at the grave, and the site was called "Sachem's Plains." It was the first monument erected by the whites to an Indian. See NARRAGANSET, PEQUOT, UNCAS.

**MICHIGAN.** A state and one of the great inland lakes. The name came from *Majiigan*, an Algonquian word meaning "A Clearing." It has also been claimed that the name was derived from the Chippewa word *Michigamea*, meaning "Big Water."

**MICMAC** (mik'-mak). An Algonquian tribe of Indians believed to have been the first on the northeast coast of America to have been encountered by the white man. It is thought the Norse voyagers met them around 1000 A.D. In 1497 Sebastian Cabot visited them and carried three of the tribe back to England. Among their closest relatives were the Abnaki. The Micmac today are in Canada. See ABNAKI.

**MIDEWIWIN** (mi-da'-wi-win). The Great Medicine Society. See SECRET SOCIETIES.

**MILITARY SOCIETIES.** Bands of picked warriors of the Plains tribes. These war groups usually took their names from animals, and each society had its own dances, songs, costumes, and insignia. At all tribal meetings, ceremonial hunts, or war expeditions they assumed charge and were not only participants, but police and guards as well.

The Dog Soldiers among the Cheyenne were considered among the bravest of the warrior bands, and won such a reputation that all societies of other tribes became known to the white man by this name. But these societies are believed to have started among the Crow Indians, who had from four to twelve warriors groups. The Kiowa had six, including one known as the Rabbits, composed of boys from ten to twelve, who were trained in the future duties of warriors. The Rabbits had a dance that resembled the hop of the rabbit. See CHEYENNE, DOG SOLDIER, KIOWA, LANCE, SECRET SOCIETIES.

**MILLY.** The story of Captain John Smith and Pocahontas was relived in that of an American named Duncan McKrimmon and Milly, beautiful daughter of a Seminole chief.

McKrimmon was captured in 1817 and ordered burned to death, but as the fire was lit, Milly fell on her knees before her father, Hillis Hadjo, and begged for the white man's life. She threatened to throw herself into the flames unless her request was granted.

Old Hadjo ordered McKrimmon released and then sold him as a slave to the Spaniards, who gave him his liberty. Later Milly was captured by American soldiers and McKrimmon offered to marry her. But Milly felt he did this only out of gratitude, and refused. When freed she married an Indian. See WOMEN.

**MINGO.** A term the Delaware Indians gave the Six Nations, or Iroquois proper. Chiefs of the Chickasaw were also called *mingos*. A Creek chief was called a *mico* or *miko*. See CHICKASAW, CREEK, IROQUOIS.


**MINICONJOU** (mi-ni-con'-jou). See DAKOTA.


**MINNEHAHA** (min-e-ha'-ha). The heroine of Longfellow's *Song of Hiawatha*. The name Minnehaha was first mentioned in the *Life and Legends of the Sioux*, by Mrs. Mary Eastman in 1849, and it was from this book that Longfellow took some of the incidents for his poem. Between Fort Snelling and the Falls of St. Anthony in Minnesota are the Little Falls, forty feet in height, called by the Indians *Minnehaha*, or "Water Falls." See WOMEN.


**MINNESOTA.** The state and river which get their name from the word in the Dakota dialect which means "cloudy water." Some claim the word means "sky-blue water."


**MIRROR SIGNALS.** See SIGNALS.


**MISSION INDIANS.** Indians of California brought together under that name by the Catholic Order of Franciscan Fathers. Some of these Indians were of Shoshonean stock. The Mission of San Diego, established in 1769, was the first white settlement in those parts and friendly Indians were drawn around it.

205

**MISSISSIPPI.** The river which received its name from the Algonquian words *misi,* or "great," and *sipi,* or "river." The state was named for the river.

**MISSOURI.** A tribe of Siouan Indians who roamed the Missouri River area near the mouth of the Grand River. Warfare and disease nearly wiped them out. Today the few remaining are classified as Oto and live on what the Government calls the Otoe Reservation in Oklahoma. The name Missouri means "People Having Dugout Canoes." As the Missouri River was sometimes called "The Big Muddy," it was believed for a long time that this was the meaning of the word. The state of Missouri also is named for this tribe. See SOUTHERN SIOUX.

**MIWOK** (me-wuk'). A tribe of California Indians one group of which lived north of the Golden Gate area and others along the Sacramento River.

**MOBILE.** A Muskhogean tribe who lived near Choctaw Bluff in Alabama on the Alabama River. Later a corrupted Choctaw jargon, used for intertribal communication from Florida to Louisiana, and as far north on the Mississippi River as the mouth of the Ohio River, was called the Mobile language. This language also was termed Chickasaw.

Their greatest chief was Tuscaloosa, a very tall and commanding Indian. Tuscaloosa inspired them to attack the invading Spaniards, and a bloody battle was fought in the fall of 1540 for the possession of one of their fortified towns, Mabila. The Spaniards won with heavy losses, while 2,500 Indians were killed or wounded. The survivors appear to have been absorbed by the Choctaw Nation. The city, county, bay, and river in Alabama are named for the Mobile, and Tuscaloosa, Alabama, is named for their chief. There is also a Mobile, Arizona. See CHICKASAW, CHINOOK JARGON, CHOCTAW, INDIAN LANGUAGE, TRADING LANGUAGE.

**MOCCASIN** (mok'-a-sin). The skin foot-wear of all American Indians, except a few along the Mexican border and on the Pacific Coast who went barefoot or wore sandals. The Indian moccasin is one of the most widespread articles of Indian clothing. The word is from the Algonquian *mockasin*.

Moccasins are divided roughly into two general classes: those of the Plains Indians with hard rawhide soles sewed to a soft buckskin upper, and those of the Woodland Indians where the sole and upper consisted of one piece of thick soft leather, sewed together at the instep and heel. The latter sometimes had a small vamp on top to which the sole was sewed by puckering it.

Moccasins were ornamented with dyes, quills, beads, cloth, buttons, fur, and fringe. Types of decoration differed among tribes, and the tribe to which an Indian belonged usually could be told by the cut and decoration of his moccasins.

Moccasin tracks, too, would reveal the T-shaped seam at the toe and heel of the northern Athapascan; the hard flat soles of the Plains Indian; the soft rounded soles of the Woodland Indian; or the seam along the side from the great toe to the heel of the Nez Percé. The Cheyenne always left a little "tail" of leather at the back of the moccasin heel. The trail of a moccasin worn by a warrior who had gained honors might reveal that he wore tails of small animals at the heels.

The boot or legging-moccasin, worn from Alaska to New Mexico and Arizona, was common as part of a woman's costume.

The women of the tribe made the moccasins and a man on a journey or hunt usually carried several pairs with him. See BAREFOOT INDIANS, BEADS, BEAR, BUCKSKIN, COSTUME, QUILLWORK, RAWHIDE, TRAIL (TO), WOMEN.

**MOCCASIN TELEGRAPH.** Frontier term for information sent by an Indian runner. Also a term for gossip.

**MODOC** (mo'-dok). A small tribe of Indians, closely related to the Klamath, who formerly lived in southwest Oregon. Although they came in contact with the white men later than did most Indians, they acquired an unfortunate reputation because of the frequent conflicts with the white immigrants and the atrocities committed on both sides.

They are mainly noted for their remarkable defensive action in the so-called Modoc War. This was a war fought among the lava beds on the California frontier in 1872 and 1873 when United States troops tried to round up a band of Modoc Indians and return them to their reservation. The Modoc, led by Chief Kintpuash, known to the whites as Captain Jack, were endeavoring to reach their former homes in the Lost River Valley, Oregon.

Between January and April, 1873, a small band of Modoc, entrenched in the lava beds, fought off a superior force of soldiers. Finally a group of peace commissioners found their way into the Modoc camp, but General E. S. Canby and another white man were treacherously slain. One commissioner's life was saved by an Indian girl, Toby Riddle.

After the Indians' defeat, Kintpuash and five others were hanged.

A California county is named for them and places called Modoc are to be found in Arkansas, Georgia, Louisiana, Ohio, South Carolina, Illinois, and Indiana. There is a Modoc Point in Oregon and Kansas, and the Modoc Lava Beds in California. See KLAMATH, RIDDLE.

**MOHAWK** (mo'-hok). A powerful tribe of the Iroquois, formerly occupying the territory of the Mohawk Valley between Utica and Albany, New York. The Mohawk were members of the Five Nations, the great Iroquois Confederacy, which was founded by one of their chiefs, Hiawatha.

They were a warlike tribe and killed and ate their captives, according to the *Jesuit Relations*. In fact, their name was given them by the Narraganset and meant "man-eaters."

During the Revolutionary War they sided with the British under the leadership of Joseph Brant. See BRANT, HIAWATHA, IROQUOIS, MOHOCK.

**MOHEGAN** (mo-he'-gan). An Algonquian tribe which formerly occupied most of the valley of the Thames River in Connecticut. They are not to be confused with the Mahican, or Mohican, who lived farther west near the upper Hudson River. However, it is believed that the two tribes are related. The name of each means "wolf" in the different dialects. The noted chief of the Mohegan was Uncas.

Some are said to survive as mixed bloods in their old town of Mohegan, Connecticut. There is also a town named for their chief, Uncasville, on the Thames River in Connecticut. There is a Mohegan in West Virginia, and a Mohegan Lake in New York, although the latter is said actually to be named for the Mahican. See COOPER, MAHICAN, NARRAGANSET, PEQUOT, UNCAS.

**MOHOCK** (mo'-hok). Slang term of the colonists meaning a "tough" or "ruffian." It was derived from Mohawk, because of the evil reputation of the members of this tribe. See MOHAWK.

209

**MOJAVE** (mo-hah′-veh). A tribe of Indians who lived on both sides of the Colorado River in California, Nevada, and Arizona. Their chief claim to fame is that they gave their name to the great Mojave Desert in California, as well as to a river and town in the same state, and to Mohave County, Arizona. See PIMA.

**MOLALA** (mo-la′-la). A tribe of Indians formerly living in Oregon, believed to have been associated with the Cayuse Indians, whose language is related to their own. A few are thought to be still living in Oregon.

**MONEY.** See BLANKET, FUR TRADE, HORSE, SEWAN, WAMPUM.

**MONGOLIAN SPOT.** Now and then Indians are born with one or more purple spots on the skin of the back. These are known as "Mongolian spots," as similar spots occur on the backs of Japanese and other Mongolians. The appearance of such spots on Indians is believed to be an important clue to their origin.

**MONO TRIBES.** A general term applied to the Shoshonean tribes of southeast California.

**MONTEZUMA** (mon-te-zoo′-mah), **DR. CARLOS.** A full-blood Apache who, like other Indians born in a wild state and given proper opportunities, achieved a notable success in the white man's world. He was known as *Wasajah* (Beckoning) to his people.

At the age of five, Wasajah was seized with a dozen other children, including two sisters, when the Pima Indians raided the camp of his band in Arizona in the fall of 1871. The captives were taken to the Pima rancheria on the Gila River, and a week later Wasajah was sold to Charles Gentile, a prospector, for $30, or the price of a horse.

Gentile took the boy to Chicago. He gave him the name of Carlos Montezuma—Carlos, as the Spanish of his own name, and Montezuma from the so-called *Casa de Montezuma,* a historic ruin on the Gila River erroneously believed to have been built by the Aztec. Carlos was placed in the Chicago public schools and later the University of Illinois, and finally was graduated from the Chicago Medical School.

He served as physician at the Western Shoshone Agency in Nevada, the Colville Agency in Washington, and the Carlisle Indian School. Later he practiced medicine in Chicago and taught in the College of Physicians and Surgeons and in the Postgraduate Medical School in Chicago. During his career he sought to arouse interest in his people through his writings. He died January 31, 1923.


**MOON.** See CALENDAR.


**MOOSE.** The American form of elk. This animal, a member of the deer family noted for its great spread of flattened antlers, at one time roamed most of the northeastern section of North America. The average moose was seven feet high and weighed 1,000 pounds.

The moose was to the Indians of the northeastern part of the United States what the buffalo was to those of the Plains. It provided them with both food and clothing.

The name of this animal came into the American language almost directly from the Algonquian dialects, *mus* or *moos,* meaning "he strips," or "eats off," signifying an animal that ate the young bark and twigs of trees.

**MORACHE** (mo-rah'-tche). Ceremonial scraping stick of the southwest Indians, sometimes called *guayos* (goo-ah'-jos). The notched morache was scraped with another stick and was commonly used with a gourd to give it more sound and tone quality. See MUSICAL INSTRUMENTS.

**MORTAR.** Utensil of wood or stone used by Indians to grind grain, paint, or other substances. The mortar was hollowed out and the grain which was placed in it was pounded with a rock or stick. Plains Indians sometimes used mortars of rawhide in which to pound jerked meat for pemmican. See JERKED MEAT, METATE, PEMMICAN.

**MOTHER-IN-LAW TABOO.** A custom in some Indian tribes of forbidding a man to speak to his wife's mother or look upon her face. Nor could he enter the same house his mother-in-law was in. Among the Navajo, the mother-in-law wore small bell earrings which tinkled a warning to her son-in-law. The mother-in-law taboo is still preserved on some Indian reservations, and it is a practice found in many parts of the world. See BELL, WOMEN.

**MOUND BUILDERS.** Once believed to have been an ancient and mysterious people whose mounds, fortifications, and monumental structures are to be found in the northern lake section of Wisconsin, the Ohio Valley, and in the Gulf region.

Skeletons of the Mound Builders show that they did not differ from those of the modern Indian, and articles of European manufacture found in mounds indicate that many mounds were built after the arrival of Columbus.

Modern archeological work has demonstrated that there were a number of types of mounds built by many different groups of Indians over a period of two thousand years.

The earliest Mound Builders are known as the Burial Mound People. Their mounds were evidently an aspect of a Cult of the Dead which moved into the Ohio Valley. Much later another mound building culture came into the area and their mounds were known as Temple Mounds. These mounds in general are larger than those of the Burial Mound People and were erected as substructures for their wooden temples. Such mounds continued to be built until the beginning of the seventeenth century. Many of the tribes visited by DeSoto were Mound Builders.

The largest mound in the United States is the Cahokia mound in Madison County, Illinois. It is 100 feet high and the base covers 16 acres. Emerald Mound in Mississippi is another large mound.

The Great Serpent Mound in Adams County, Ohio, is 500 feet in length. There is a "platform mound" in Missouri 150 feet long and 25 feet high. Two "bird mounds," said to represent birds, are in Georgia, and a mound with a moat and encircling wall and another fashioned in the form of an oblong enclosure are in West Virginia. See BASKETS, CALUMET, CHEROKEE, CHOCTAW, CREEK, NATCHEZ, QUAPAW, SERPENT MOUND.

**MOUNTAIN LION.** A catlike animal of reddish tawny color, which lives in mountainous regions. Also known as cougar, painter, American panther, catamount, and puma. The skin of this animal was highly prized by Indians of many tribes for making quivers for their arrows. The Ute were fond of such a skin as a kind of riding pad, which they threw loosely over the pony's back. See QUIVER, UTE.

**MOUNTAIN MEN.** Name applied to white fur trappers. See FUR TRADE.

**MUGWUMP** (mug'-wump). An Algonquian Indian word meaning "big man" or "chief." Today it is used in politics to mean an independent voter or one who "straddles the fence" in politics. It was first used in this sense in 1884 when a group of Republicans left their party in a national election. They were charged with thinking themselves superior to their party, hence "big men" or "mugwumps."

**MUNSEE** (mun-see'). See DELAWARE.

**MUSICAL INSTRUMENTS.** The musical instruments of the Indians were crude and consisted mainly of drums, rattles, or notched sticks used to establish rhythm or make noise.

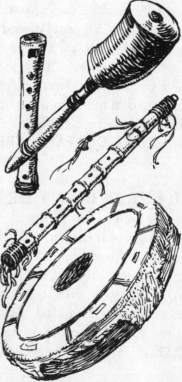

Drums were of many types, but usually were made of skins stretched over frames. On the northwest coast a plank or box might serve as a drum. Noise was made on notched sticks by rubbing them with other sticks. Whistles were ordinarily made from the wingbones of birds, as the Indians believed the sound that was produced by them was like the cry of the bird whose wingbone had been used. But there were whistles of wood and of pottery. The Omaha had a type of flute with five holes and the Pueblo used a flageolet to accompany songs in certain ceremonies. These flageolets were used, too, by young men during courtship.

Bells were used on the ankles and legs of dancers.

Rattles of different kinds were made from animal hoofs, dewclaws, horns, and turtle shells. However, rattles were not ordinarily used in dances, but were considered sacred objects to be employed in rituals, religious festivals, and by medicine men.

The only stringed instrument known among the early Indians was the musical bow, on which notes were produced by stroking a thong stretched on a bow.

While the chief idea of the Indian's music was to make noise and produce rhythm, he might dance to one rhythm and sing to another at the same time. See BELL, BULL-ROARER, DANCE, DRUM, EAGLE, MORACHE, SONGS, WHISTLE.

**MUSKHOGEAN** (mus-ko'-ge-an) **FAMILY.** A language family of Indians confined chiefly to the Gulf states east of the Mississippi River. They occupied almost all of what is now Mississippi and Alabama, and parts of Tennessee, Georgia, Florida, and South Carolina.

**MUSKOGEE** (mus-ko'-gee). See CREEK.

**MYSTERY DOG.** Dakota name for the horse. As dogs had been used as pack animals before the horse, when the Indians first saw horses they believed them to be a large, strange type of dog. The Siksika called them "elk dogs," and the Cree termed them "big dogs." See DOG, HORSE.

**NARRAGANSET.** A tribe of Algonquian Indians, at one time the most powerful of southern New England, who occupied the present state of Rhode Island in that section west of Narragansett Bay. Their name meant "People of the Small Point."

In the early part of the seventeenth century the Narraganset were friendly with the English colonists and aided them in the Pequot War. In 1636 Roger Williams settled among them and through their favor was enabled to lay the foundations of the state of Rhode Island. Later, the Narraganset fought the Mohegan and were defeated. Their chief, Miantonomo, was executed for conspiring against the English.

The Narraganset later fought in King Philip's War, and in the celebrated swamp fight at Kingston, Rhode Island, on August 12, 1676, they lost almost 1,000 in killed, wounded, and prisoners. This was the end of the tribe, as the survivors were forced to abandon their territory and join scattered bands of other tribes to the north and west.

Their sachem, Canonchet, was believed by many historians to have ranked with King Philip. He was captured by the English and shot and his head sent as a trophy to the magistrates of Hartford, Connecticut.

They gave their name to Narragansett Bay, the town of Narragansett, and to Narragansett Pier, the well-known summer resort, all in Rhode Island. See CANONICUS, KING PHILIP, MIANTONOMO, MOHEGAN, ORATORS, PEQUOT, UNCAS.

**NATCHEZ** (nach'-ez). A tribe of Indians related to the great Muskhogean family, who were the largest and strongest on the lower Mississippi River at the time Louisiana was settled by the French. The Natchez were noted for their type of government, being ruled over by a chief called the "Great Sun," who actually was a sort of king, as he had the power of life and death over his subjects. When the "Great Sun" died all his wives were executed.

Unlike most tribes, in which the government was democratic and each Indian cherished his independence, the Natchez had a king, so to speak, and "nobles" and "common people." The nobles were grouped after the Great Sun as "Suns," then "Nobles," and then "Honored People," or aristocrats. The common people were termed "Stinkers."

An early French writer, in telling of the Great Sun, said:

"Every morning as soon as the sun appears, the great chief comes to the door of his cabin, turns himself to the east, and howls three times, bowing to the earth. Then they bring him a calumet, which serves only for this purpose. He smokes, and blows the smoke of his tobacco toward the sun; then he does the same thing toward the other three parts of the world. He acknowledges no superior but the sun, from which he pretends to derive his origin. He exercises an unlimited power over his subjects, can dispose of their goods and lives, and for whatever labors he requires of them they cannot demand any recompense."

The Natchez were Mound Builders when first encountered by the French. The center of their nation was near the great Emerald Mound in Mississippi. This tribe was first mentioned in narratives of La Salle's descent of the Mississippi River in 1682, when it was located a little east of the present city of Natchez.

Relations between the French and the Natchez were hostile for a time and then peace was made. But in 1729 the Indians attacked a French settlement and massacred 200 persons. The French and the Choctaw campaigned against the Natchez, and drove them from their homes. Some joined the Creek, others the Cherokee. Today a few are identified with these tribes in Oklahoma. Their name has been preserved in that of Natchez, Mississippi, and in villages in Alabama, Louisiana, and Indiana. See CHIEF, MOUND BUILDERS, SACHEM, SLAVES, TAENSA, TUNICA.

NAVAJO (nav'-ah-ho). A tribe of southwestern Indians, known to the early Spaniards as *Apaches de Navajó—Navajó* being the name for a large area of cultivated land in what is now Arizona and New Mexico. The Navajo called themselves *Diné,* which meant simply "People."

In the early days they were much like the Apache, and were a war-like people, raiding pueblos and Spanish settlements. Even after New Mexico became a possession of the United States, the Navajo were un-tamed according to the white man's idea, and it was not until Colonel Kit Carson rounded up some 8,000 of them and kept them captives from 1863 to 1867 that they became peaceful.

The Navajo were noted for their blankets, or rugs; their jewelry; and their sand painting. They raised their own sheep and goats, sheared them, washed the wool, prepared it for spinning, dyed the yarn, and wove their blankets. No two blanket designs ever are the same. Their jewelry, with its familiar "squash blossom beads," and their silver conchas are equally well known.

The Navajo believed that corn or maize was a living child of the gods. They lived in hogans, or earth-covered lodges, scattered through-out their territory, and seldom in villages. A hogan where a person had died was called a "devil house" and was destroyed by fire. Because of their long association with Mexicans, many of them spoke Spanish.

The Navajo held their first election under the white man's system in March, 1951, in which 75 per cent of the eligible voters cast ballots. They cling to their old customs, however, and resent the intrusion of the white man. When the Office of Price Administration met at Phoenix, Arizona, in World War II and sought to ration beef on the Navajo reservation, one old chief replied:

"In no part of the Treaty of Guadalupe is the Office of Price Administration mentioned. Neither is there said anything that the white man can investigate the eating habits of the Indians. The territory reserved for the Navajo is vast and the narrow mountain passes are treacherous for feet unfamiliar with them. It would not be impossible that investigators of the Office of Price Administration would frequently throw themselves headlong down one of these steep canyons."

There was no rationing of meat in the Navajo country. It is a vast area and their reservation is as large as Massachusetts, New Hampshire, and Vermont put together, spreading out in Arizona, New

Mexico, and southeast Utah. Today they are the largest tribe in the United States. Their name has been given a county, creek, village, and spring in Arizona; a village in Montana, and there is a Navajoe in Oklahoma. See BLANKET, CARSON, HOGAN, LONG WALK (THE), MANUELITO, PRAYER STICKS, SAND PAINTING. See also illustration, page 216.

**NEBRASKA.** Name of the state, from the Omaha Indian word which means "flat or broad water."

**NETS.** See FISHING, KNOTS.

**NEUTRALS.** A tribe of Iroquois Indians who were given the name "Neutrals" by the French because they refused to take part in the wars between the Iroquois and Huron. Their chief claim to fame is that one of their bands, the Ongniaahra, gave its name in the form of Niagara to Niagara Falls. See NIAGARA.

**NEW MEXICO.** Name of the state which derives its name from Mexico. Mexico, in turn, is said to mean "the home of Mexitli, the Aztec god of war."

**NEZ PERCÉ** (nay per-say'). A powerful Indian tribe that roamed the territory between the Blue Mountains in Oregon and the Bitter Root Mountains in Idaho. The name Nez Percé (Pierced Nose), was given them by the French, although they are said never to have practiced the custom of piercing their noses. One of their own names for themselves meant "The People."

When Lewis and Clark met them in 1805 they had been horse Indians for more than a century, breeding their famous war ponies, which the white man called the Appaloosa. They formerly fished for salmon in the tributaries of the Columbia River, but after obtaining horses they became buffalo hunters and lived in tepees during the hunting season. At other times they lived in underground lodges, or dugouts. They made fine baskets in which they could boil water by dropping hot stones in them.

They were friendly to the whites, with one exception. In 1877 their famous chief, Joseph, headed a revolt, which proved disastrous to the tribe. From this tribe Nez Perce County and a village, Nezperce, both in Idaho, derive their names. See APPALOOSA, CAYUSE, JOSEPH, LEWIS, PALOUSE.

**NIAGARA.** The name of the falls and the river which is derived from the Ongniaahra, a band of the Iroquois Neutrals. See NEUTRALS.

**OGLALA** (og-la′-la). Principal division of the Teton Sioux. See DAKOTA.

**OHIO.** The Iroquois name for "Beautiful River," which was given to the river and state as well as to various counties in the United States. The French called the Ohio River *La Belle*, meaning "The Beautiful."

**OJIBWA** (o-jib′-wa). See CHIPPEWA.

**OKLAHOMA.** Choctaw term meaning "Red People." It was coined by the Reverend Allen White, a missionary to the Choctaw Indians. See INDIAN RESERVATION, INDIAN TERRITORY.

**OMAHA.** See SOUTHERN SIOUX.

223

**ONEIDA** (o-ni'-da). See IROQUOIS.


**ONONDAGA** (on-on-dah'-ga). See IROQUOIS.


**ONTARIO.** One of the great inland lakes which derived its name from the Iroquois word *oniatara,* meaning "lake," with the ending *io,* meaning "great." It has been translated as "great lake" or "beautiful lake."


**ORATORS.** There have been many great Indian orators. While deeds in time of war were important to the standing of the Indian in his community, most of the important chiefs ruled only through their persuasive oratory.

Since early days the white man has been impressed by the ability of Indian leaders to express themselves. Even when the colonists could not understand the language, they were struck by the poise and dignity and delivery of the Indian speaker. When translated many of these speeches were masterpieces of oratory and have found their way into literature and textbooks.

Logan's speech is one of these. After white men had murdered some of his followers, including members of his family, he spoke as follows:

"I appeal to any white man to say if he ever entered Logan's cabin hungry, and he gave him not meat; if he ever came cold and naked, and he clothed him not. During the course of the last long and bloody war, Logan remained idle in his cabin, an advocate of peace.

"Such was my love for the white man that my countrymen pointed as they passed, and said: 'Logan is the friend of the white man.' I have even thought to have lived with you, but for the injuries of one man, Colonel Cressap, who last spring, in cold blood and unprovoked, murdered all the relations of Logan, not even sparing my women and children.

"There runs not a drop of my blood in the veins of any living creature. This called on me for revenge. I have sought it; I have killed many; I have fully glutted my vengeance.

"For my countrymen I rejoice at the beams of peace. But do not harbor a thought that mine is the joy of fear. Logan never felt fear! He will not turn on his heel to save his life. Who is there to mourn for Logan? Not one."

The Indian spoke simply and drew on his knowledge of nature in making his comparisons. He was familiar with the birds and beasts, the forests and the plains, and the winds and the storms—and he seemed to know how men felt in their hearts. He took advantage of everything around him to illustrate the point he was making.

One Indian, a Wichita chief, after listening to the arguments of some white commissioners, reached down and took up a handful of dust and threw it into the air. As it blew away in thousands of particles, he said: "There are as many ways to cheat the Indian."

Canonchet, the Narraganset chief, an ally of King Philip, when sentenced to death said proudly: "I like it well, for I shall die before my heart is soft, or I have spoken anything unworthy of myself."

Red Bear, a Sioux chief, on a visit to New York spoke thus: "The Great Spirit told me when a chief, 'If you get strong and become rich, you cannot take your riches with you when you die.' He must have told a different thing to the white man, who is so grasping, and who piles up his money. He must have told him, 'When you die, you can take all into the next world.'" Another time he said: "When the Great Father sent out men to our people, I was poor and thin; now I am large and stout and fat. It is because so many liars have been sent out here, and I have been stuffed full of lies."

Red Cloud, the great Sioux chief, speaking at Washington said: "You promise us many things, but you do not perform them. You take away everything, yet if you live forty or fifty years in this world, and then die, you cannot take all your goods with you. . . . The Great Spirit raised me naked and gave me no weapons. This is the way I was raised (pulling aside his blanket, and exposing his bare shoulder). . . . I do not ask my Great Father to give me anything. I came naked, and will go away naked."

Chief Joseph of the Nez Percé, one of the greatest Indian orators, said when he surrendered after the Nez Percé outbreak of 1877:

"I am tired of fighting. Our chiefs are killed. Looking Glass is dead. Toolhulhulsote is dead. The old men are all dead. It is the young men who say yes or no. He who led on the young men is dead. It is cold and we have no blankets. The little children are freezing to death. My people, some of them, have run away to the hills and have no blankets, no food. No one knows where they are—perhaps freezing to death.

"I want to have time to look for my children and see how many of them I can find. Maybe I shall find them among the dead. Hear me, my chiefs. I am tired. My heart is sick and sad. I will fight no more forever."

Chief Washakie, of the Shoshoni, spoke at a conference in this fashion: "The white man, who possesses this whole vast country from sea to sea, who roams over it at pleasure and lives where he likes, cannot know the cramp we feel in this little spot, with the undying remembrance of the fact, which you know as well as we, that every foot of what you proudly call America not very long ago belonged to the Red Man. The Great Spirit gave it to us. There was room enough for all his tribes, and all were happy in their freedom.

"But the white man had, in ways we know not of, learned some things we had not learned; among them how to make more superior tools and terrible weapons, better for war than bows and arrows; and there seemed no end to the hordes of men that followed them from other lands beyond the sea.

"And so, at last, our fathers were steadily driven out, or killed, and we, their sons, but sorry remnants of tribes once mighty, are cornered in little spots of the earth, all ours by right—cornered like guilty prisoners and watched by men with guns who are more than anxious to kill us off."

There were many great Indian orators. See CORNPLANTER, INDIAN LANGUAGE, JOSEPH, KEOKUK, KING PHILIP, LOGAN, NARRAGANSET, RED CLOUD, RED JACKET. See also illustration, page 222.


**ORENDA** (o-ren'-da). The spirit or magic power which the Iroquois believed was to be found in all things in the world. The Orenda was a sacred or divine essence that connected all the elements of the world, one to the other, including man. The white man believed this was the Indian's "Great Spirit," but to the Iroquois the Orenda was made up of thousands of spirits, as they believed that every object was alive and was possessed of this spirit. See GREAT SPIRIT, MAN-BEING, MANITOU.

**OSAGE** (o-saj'). See SOUTHERN SIOUX.

**OSAGE ORANGE.** See BOW.

**OSCEOLA** (os-e-o'-la). One of the great chiefs of the Seminole Indians. He was described as having been tall, slender, and straight, with a pleasing countenance, though of melancholy cast.

Osceola was born about 1803 on the Tallapoosa River in the Creek country. He was part white, as his grandfather on his father's side was a Scotchman. After his father's death his mother married a white man named Powell, and Osceola was sometimes called Powell.

He was not a chief by descent, but at the age of thirty-two he took his place as the leader of his people and commander of the warriors when the United States tried to round up the Seminole and place them on a reservation in Oklahoma.

Osceola, fighting in the Florida Everglades, outwitted the Government troops. Finally peace negotiations were started, and when Osceola appeared under a flag of truce he was knocked on the head, bound, and thrown into a dungeon. This treachery was condemned throughout the country, but the young chief died, brokenhearted, a prisoner at Fort Moultrie, Florida, in January, 1838.

His name has been preserved by towns in Arkansas, Indiana, Iowa, Missouri, Nebraska, Pennsylvania, Texas, and Wisconsin; by counties in Florida, Michigan, and Iowa; and by Osceola Mills, Pennsylvania. See HALF-BREED, SEMINOLE.

**OTHERDAY, JOHN.** A Wahpeton Sioux who became noted for his friendship to the whites, and who even aided them in the great Sioux outbreak of 1862. Otherday was born at Swan Lake, Minnesota, in 1801, and at an early age showed his desire to follow the "white man's road." He adopted the white man's dress, later married a white woman, and became a Christian.

In 1857 John Otherday rode into a hostile Sioux camp and, single-handed, rescued a white woman captive, Miss Abigail Gardner. When the Sioux went on the warpath five years later, Otherday gathered together sixty-two whites and guided them to safety. He then donned a pure white suit, as was his custom, and went into battle against his own people. An account of him reads:

"He was often in their midst [the Sioux] and so far in advance of our own men that they fired many shots at him, believing he was one of the foe. He was clothed entirely in white; a belt around his waist, in which was placed his knife; a handkerchief was knotted around his head, and in his hand he lightly grasped his rifle."

Congress later granted him $2,500 with which he bought a farm. In time he sold the farm and moved to the Sisseton Reservation in South Dakota, where the agent built a house for him. He died there in 1871.

**OTO** (o'-to). See SOUTHERN SIOUX.

**OTTAWA** (ot'-a-wa). A tribe of Algonquian Indians formerly inhabiting the Great Lakes region, particularly the shores of Lake Huron from Saginaw to Detroit. They were Woodland Indians and in the early days were known as traders and barterers, dealing in corn meal, sunflower oil, skins and furs, rugs, tobacco, and healing roots and herbs. In fact, their name came from the Cree word *adawe*, meaning to buy and sell.

The Ottawa were warlike and cruel, and during the days of the colonists, sided with the French against the English. Before their westward movement, they joined with the Chippewa and Potawatomi and the confederation was known as the "Three Fires."

Pontiac, the celebrated chief, was a member of the tribe, and Pontiac's War of 1763, fought mainly around Detroit, is an important part of their history. They were active in all Indian wars up to and through the War of 1812.

In 1833 all Ottawa lands along the west shore of Lake Michigan were ceded to the Government in the Chicago Treaty. Many of the Ottawa moved west and today they have a small reservation in Oklahoma. Others are scattered among the Chippewa in Michigan.

They have given their name to the most important branch of the St. Lawrence River, as well as to the city on its banks which became the capital of the Dominion of Canada. Their name also is borne by counties in Kansas, Michigan, and Ohio, and the province of Quebec; by important cities in Illinois and Kansas; and by smaller places and streams in Kentucky, Wisconsin, Minnesota, Ohio, and Virginia; and by Ottawa Beach and Ottawa Lake in Michigan. See ALGONKIN, CHIPPEWA, PONTIAC, POTAWATOMI.

**OTTER.** A weasel-like, web-footed animal with dark brown fur, found in streams and lakes. The skin of the otter was highly prized by some Indian tribes, and in many cases such magical qualities were attached to certain skins that they were passed down for generations from father to son.

Nearly all Plains Indians, and some of the mountain tribes, especially the Ute, wore strips of otter skin around their wrists or other parts of the body. Some braided it into the hair to hang down over both shoulders in the front. Others twisted it in the scalp lock. Portions of the skin were attached to quivers.

Among the Arapaho so great was the superstition surrounding the skin of the otter that all warriors wore it in some fashion and believed it would protect them from harm. Otter skins became a valuable article of trade, not only among the Indians, but with the whites. See ARAPAHO, COSTUME, COUP STICK, FUR TRADE, HAIRWORK, QUIVER, UTE.

**OURAY** (oo-ray'). A chief of the Ute Indians, noted for his friendship with the whites. Ouray was born in Colorado in 1820, and after he became chief of his tribe, he always kept faith with the white man.

In 1863, while fighting against the Sioux, his only son was captured and every effort was made by the United States Government to restore the boy to his father. In 1873 Ouray visited the Indian commissioner at Cheyenne, Wyoming, and said he had learned through a Mexican woman, who lived with the Sioux, that his boy was still alive, and had passed into the hands of the Southern Arapaho. The boy was never found. Ouray, still mourning his son, died in 1880. There is a county, town and mountain peak named for him in Colorado, and a town in Utah. See UTE.

**PAD SADDLE.** See SADDLE.

**PAINT.** Indians found many things in nature from which they could make paint. They used fine clays containing different oxides of iron. These they mixed with bear grease or buffalo tallow. The hard, yellow substance in the gall bladder of the buffalo was prized as a medicine paint. The Sioux used bullberries, a plant like sumac. Flowers, barks, and other vegetable matter also provided paints and colorings.

Usually the Indian applied the paint with his fingers. But sometimes he made brushes from sticks which were chewed or beaten on the ends. Plains Indians employed a spongy bone from the knee joint of the buffalo which held paint as the modern fountain pen does ink.

The Indian painted himself to be admired or to strike fear in his enemy. Sometimes he painted as a disguise and other times merely to protect his skin from insects and the wind and the sun. He also painted for dances and other ceremonies.

Without a doubt Indians were first called Red Men because of their use of red paints in decorating their faces and bodies. Red was a sacred color with all Indians and usually stood for strength and success. For this reason red was the favorite color for painting the face and body for dance and warpath, and for painting the war pony, lance, and other articles of war and ceremony.

While it might appear that the Indian's colors and designs were often put on merely to satisfy his own whims, the fact was he commonly followed a definite pattern and each design and color had a meaning. However, when an Indian found a certain color had proved lucky, or had been "good medicine," he might continue its use regardless of any meaning that others might give it.

The meaning of certain colors varied among tribes. War paint among the Plains Indians, for instance, might be an excessive use of any color. White stood for mourning, black for joy, and red for happiness and beauty. The Cheyenne used rings and stripes of different colors when going to war, and on returning they used only black to indicate their joy at arriving back safely. The Cherokee, on the other hand, used red for success, blue for defeat or trouble; black meant death, and white, peace and happiness.

Women beautified themselves with paint. It was used to decorate lodges, totem poles, parfleche bags, robes, and for ceremonial pictures. Red paint might be daubed on stones, trees, or other objects to which the Indian wanted to show respect. Ponies were painted for war, and in historical paintings men were shown with blood-red wounds. See BEAR, BLANKET, BUFFALO, COSTUME, HAIR, HORSE, PARFLECHE, PICTURE WRITING, RED MAN, RED STICKS, SAND PAINTING, TATTOOING, TEPEE, TOTEM POLES, WOMEN. See also illustration, page 233

PAIUTE (py-ut'). A group of the Shoshonean branch of Indians, whose name is said to mean "Water Ute" and "True Ute." They have been divided into the Northern and Southern Paiute, and students of the Indian are not sure that either group can properly be termed a tribe.

The so-called Northern Paiute lived in western Nevada, southeastern Oregon, and a strip of California, while the Southern Paiute occupied territory in western Utah, northwestern Arizona, southeastern Nevada, and southeastern California. The Southern Paiute usually were termed "Diggers."

The name Paiute has been applied at various times to most of the Shoshonean tribes of west Utah, north Arizona, south Idaho, east Oregon, Nevada, and east and south California. There is a Paiute County in Utah. See CHEMEHUEVI, DIGGERS, UTE.

**PALOUSE** (pah-loose'). A tribe of Indians closely related to the Nez Percé, who formerly lived in the valley of the Palouse River in Washington and Idaho. They were included in a treaty in 1855, but refused to recognize the treaty, and have refused to live on a reservation. A small number live in the state of Washington. See NEZ PERCÉ.

**PAPAGO** (pah'-pa-go). See PIMA.

**PAPER BREAD.** A type of bread made by Pueblo women from corn meal. Wood lye was added to the meal and it was spread in a thin layer over a flat cooking stone. The bread was termed *piki* or *bunjabe,* and the meal was usually made from the kernels of the blue corn. It had a taste like that of popcorn and was commonly carried on long journeys. It was also known as wafer bread. See BAKING STONES, FOOD, MAIZE.

**PAPOOSE** (pa-poose'). A term now applied to any Indian baby. The word is said to have come from the Narraganset Indian infant's way of saying *papu* for father. Students of languages have found that the first words of babies throughout the world are much like the English "papa" and "mama."

The Narraganset added *es* meaning "little" to the word *papu,* and thus obtained *papues.* The white man pronounced it "papoose" and the word has been adopted by practically all Indian tribes today.

The papoose of almost all tribes spent

its younger days in some form of cradle. In Alaska these cradles were made of bark and decorated with quillwork. However, in winter the mother might carry the baby in the hood of her fur parka. And in some tribes the infant was gathered in a blanket and slung on the mother's back.

On the Plains, especially among the Kiowa, Comanche, and others, cradles made of dressed skins were lashed on a framework or lattice of flat sticks. Many tribes borrowed this idea. The cradle was highly decorated and the frame was supported and carried on the mother's back or swung from the pommel of a saddle by bands attached to the rear of the lattice frame.

Among the Algonquian and the Iroquoian tribes of the East, a thin long board took the place of the latticework of the Plains. On the Pacific Coast basket cradles and even dugout cradles—made after the fashion of dugout canoes—were used. In tribes that practiced head flattening, cradles were made so that there was continuous pressure on the infant's skull.

In many tribes scented herbs were placed in the infant's bedding. In others rattles of various kinds dangled from the cradle to amuse and occupy the child. A new cradle was made for each child among some Indians, but the Pueblo considered the cradle a sacred object and it was handed down in the family. Every time a new child occupied it a notch was cut in the frame.

Indians in general were fond of children. They rarely killed a captive child of another tribe or even a white one, but adopted it into the tribe. They loved their own and the grief of a mother on the death of her infant was intensely pathetic.

Indian girls of all tribes played with dolls and cradles. See BEADS, CAPTIVES, QUILLWORK, MATACHIAS.

**PARCHED-CORN INDIANS.** An old colonial term for Indians who were more or less civilized, according to the white man's standards, and who used corn or maize for bread. See MAIZE.

**PARFLECHE** (par'-flesh). Term applied both to the rawhide and to the container made from it. The parfleche was the suitcase or trunk of the Plains and Rocky Mountain tribes. It was made in various sizes from rawhide molded into shape and lashed together while damp.

Parfleches were used for storing food such as pemmican, and clothing, and other articles. They were usually about two feet by three feet in size. Smaller ones, more like large envelopes, were used for paints, mirrors, and personal effects. The parfleche was painted with a design and sometimes had fringed edges.

The most probable derivation is from the French *par* meaning "for," and *fleche*, meaning "arrow"—as Indians often made quivers in the same fashion. Some believe it came from the French *parer*, "to ward off," or "parry," and *fleche*, "arrow," or a rawhide shield for warding off arrows. See BAGS AND POUCHES, PAINT, PEMMICAN, QUIVER, RAWHIDE.

**PARKER, GENERAL ELI SAMUEL.** A mixed-blood Seneca, grandson of the celebrated Chief Red Jacket, who rose to the rank of brigadier-general in the United States Army and later was appointed by President Ulysses S. Grant as Commissioner of Indian Affairs. General Parker had the distinction, as General Grant's secretary, of drawing up the articles of General Robert E. Lee's surrender at Appomattox Courthouse.

General Parker was born on the Tonawanda Reservation in New York in 1826. He later became an "eighth chief" of the Seneca Indians.

After his education in the common schools he studied civil engineering and at the start of the Civil War was employed as an engineer on a government project at Galena, Illinois, then the home of General Grant. He and Grant became fast friends and joined the Union Army together. Grant made him a member of his staff, after Parker had distinguished himself at Vicksburg.

Following the war Parker was appointed Commissioner of Indian Affairs, a position he held for three years. He practiced his profession at Fairfield, Connecticut, until his death on August 21, 1895. With his friend, Lewis H. Morgan, he wrote *The League of the Iroquois,* a work of value, as Parker, a sachem of his tribe, had full knowledge of the institutions of his people. See RED JACKET.

**PARKER, QUANAH** (kwa-nah'). One of the most warlike chiefs of the Comanche. He was born in 1845, son of the leader of the *Kwahadi,* the most savage division of the tribe, and a white woman, Cynthia Ann Parker.

As a girl of twelve, Cynthia Ann had been captured in 1835 in a raid on Parker's Fort, on the Navasota River in east Texas. Many years later she was rescued and brought back to Texas, but both she and an infant daughter she had with her died, the mother being unable to adapt herself to the ways of her people, and mourning her husband and other children.

Quanah Parker became chief of the Comanche after the death of his father and in 1874, at the head of seven hundred warriors of allied tribes, attacked Adobe Walls in the Texas Panhandle in an attempt to drive out the white buffalo hunters. Although he was defeated in this battle, the war continued along the whole of the south border of Kansas.

When United States troops entered the conflict, Quanah Parker kept his band out on the Staked Plain in Texas for two years, but finally surrendered.

From that time on he became a powerful influence in leading his people along the "white man's road." He encouraged education, house building, and agriculture. He died at his home near Fort Sill, Oklahoma, on February 23, 1911.

This last chief of the Comanche was buried on the bank of Cache Creek at Lawton, Oklahoma, beside the grave of his white mother. A monument, authorized under an act of Congress, was erected over his grave in 1926. In 1956 the United States Army decided to take over the land to extend the firing range at Fort Sill. A year later the bodies of both Quanah Parker and his mother were removed to the historic military cemetery at Fort Sill. See ADOBE WALLS, BURIAL, COMANCHE, HALF-BREED.

**PASSAMAQUODDY** (pas-a-ma-kwod'-i). The easternmost body of Indians in the United States. They gave their name to Passamaquoddy Bay, which forms a part of the eastern boundary of Maine. See ABNAKI, PENOBSCOT.

**PAWNEE.** A powerful confederacy of the Caddoan language family. This group, like the Iroquois League and the Creek Confederacy, at one time had reached a high state of governmental organization.

The Pawnee Confederacy consisted of four tribes: the Chaui or Grand Pawnee, the Kitkehahki or Republican Pawnee, the Pitahauerat or Tapage Pawnee, and the Skidi or Skiri Pawnee.

The Pawnee had an unusual scalp lock in which the hair was stiffened with paint and fat and curved back like a horn. From this they obtained from other tribes their name Pawnee, or "horn." They called themselves "Men of Men."

The Pawnee formerly inhabited Nebraska along the Platte River, but at one time raided east of the Mississippi River. Here they were driven out by the powerful Five Nations, who sent a force of 1,000 warriors to avenge the raiding by the Pawnee of an Illinois village.

A Pawnee, El Turco (The Turk), acted as a guide to Coronado's army and led it on a wild-goose chase through Kansas. The Pawnee never fought the whites and many times sided with them against hostile Indians. The Pawnee Scouts, under Major Frank North, became famous during the Indian wars between 1865 and 1885.

In battle Pawnee warriors fought with as few clothes as possible. They usually stripped down to the breechcloth, not wishing any piece of cloth or skin to be carried into a wound by an arrow or bullet. Even when a scout for the U. S. Army, the Pawnee warrior would cast off his uniform when he started fighting.

The tribal unit of the Pawnee was the village and the chief of each village was a member of the tribal council. The council in turn was represented in the Pawnee Confederacy.

The Pawnee were considered mystery men by members of other tribes because of their strange rituals and ceremonies. They worshiped the Morning Star and the Evening Star, and professed to be experts on all stars. By the stars they were able to determine the proper time for planting corn. The wind, thunder, and lightning they thought of as messengers of the heavenly bodies.

One group of Pawnee each year killed a virgin as a human sacrifice to the Morning Star, until this practice was stopped by a great reformer, Chief Petalesharo.

As a strange kind of reward for their friendliness to the whites, the Pawnee were forced to leave their country and move to a reservation. When Petalesharo II, their chief, protested, he was killed by one of his own men.

Though they numbered more than 10,000 about a century ago, today this mighty tribe has dwindled to around 1,100. They live in Oklahoma, where a city has been named for them. They have also given their name to counties in Oklahoma, Kansas, and Nebraska; streams in Colorado and Kansas; places in Colorado, Indiana, and Illinois; to Pawnee City in Nebraska; Pawnee Rock and Pawnee Station, both in Kansas; and Pawnee Buttes in northeastern Colorado. See ARIKARA, CREEK, INDIAN SCOUTS, IROQUOIS, MAIZE, PETALESHARO, SLAVES, STARS, TURK.

**PEACE PIPE.** See CALUMET.

**PECAN.** A thin-shelled, smooth, olive-shaped nut with a superior flavor, the fruit of a large hickory tree. It is found in the river bottoms of southern Indiana, southern Illinois, and in Iowa, Louisiana, and Texas. The word is from the Algonquian *pakan, pukan,* or *pagan,* meaning a "hard-shelled nut." It is sometimes called the "Illinois nut," and was highly prized by the Illinois Indians.

**PECOS** (pay'-kos). A tribe of Indians who occupied the largest and most populous of the pueblos of New Mexico in historic times, situated on the upper branch of the Pecos River, thirty miles southeast of Santa Fé. At the time of Coronado's visit in 1540 the population was estimated as more than 2,000. Raids by the Apache and Comanche resulted in the death of practically all the inhabitants, and in 1838 the last seventeen fled to the Jemez Pueblo, where their survivors still live. Their name has been preserved in the Pecos River, largest branch

241

of the Rio Grande; a county and town in Texas; and a town in New Mexico near the ruins of the ancient pueblo.

**PEMMICAN** (pem'-i-kan). An Indian food made from jerked meat or dried meat pounded to a powder and mixed with melted fat. The word is from the Cree *pimikan,* meaning "manufactured grease."

Stored in parfleche bags and kept dry, this food could be preserved for several years. Some Indians mixed berries with the dried meat and fat. Others made pemmican from powdered dried fish, which was mixed with sturgeon oil.

Indians carried pemmican on long overland trips and also depended on it during seasons when game was scarce. Early trappers and frontiersmen made a soup from it called *robbiboe.*

Peter Pond, a Connecticut Yankee, is said to have learned to make and use pemmican from Indians he met as one of the traders of the North West Fur Company. It was after spending the winter of 1788–1789 with old Peter Pond, that Sir Alexander Mackenzie, the Scottish explorer, using pemmican as a food, went on northward to the Arctic Ocean, traveling the river which now bears his name.

Admiral Robert E. Peary took along pemmican on his trek to the North Pole in April of 1909. It was the same as Indian pemmican, except that he mixed in dried raisins instead of berries. Peary said this was the only food a man could eat twice a day for 365 days and still relish it to the last mouthful. See BUFFALO, FOOD, JERKED MEAT, MORTAR, PARFLECHE, ROBBIBOE.

**PEND D'OREILLE** (pahn do-ray'). A tribe of Indians whose native name was Kalispel, but who were called Pend d'Oreille because when they were first encountered by Europeans they wore large shell earrings. The term means "earring" in French. They formerly lived in Idaho on the Pend Oreille River and Lake. See FLATHEADS.

**PENN, WILLIAM.** An English Quaker who founded the colony of Pennsylvania. Penn, who had been in prison because of his disrespect to the king, sailed for America in 1682 and in October of that year made his famous treaty with the Delaware Indians. William Penn planned and named the city of Philadelphia. See DELAWARE, TAMMANY.

**PENNACOOK** (pen'-a-kook). A tribe of northeastern Indians, related to the Abnaki, who lived in parts of New Hampshire, Massachusetts, and Maine. They were also known as the Merrimac, from the river of that name. Some still live in Maine with what are known as the St. Francis Indians, remnants of many New England tribes. The town of Penacook and Lake Penacook, both in Merrimack County, New Hampshire, are named for them, as is a branch station of the Concord post office. Their name also appears in Whittier's poem *The Bridal of Pennacook*. See ABNAKI, MERRIMAC.

**PENOBSCOT** (pe-nob'-skot). A tribe of the Abnaki Confederacy, who lived in Maine. In the latter part of the sixteenth and early part of the seventeenth centuries European mapmakers believed these Indians had established a fabulous city and that their king, Bashaba, ruled over a large "kingdom" which extended as far south as Virginia. Early maps showed this city on the banks of the Norumbega River (the Penobscot River). Later exploration, however, showed the "city" to be but a small village of Penobscot Indians, the "kingdom" did not exist, and Bashaba was only an ordinary chief.

The Penobscot have remained in their old country to the present day, and several hundred live on Oldtown Island, off the coast of Maine. With the Passamaquoddy they have a representative at the Maine State Legislature, privileged to speak on tribal matters only. They have given their name to a bay, river, county, and town in Maine. See ABNAKI, PASSAMAQUODDY.

**PENUTIAN** (pe-noo'-ti-an) **FAMILY.** A fairly recent name under which several small language families of Indians in California and the Northwest are grouped. The name is a combination of the term *pene*, which means "two" in the language of several of these related families, and the term *uti*, which also means "two" in the language of several other families.

**PEQUOT** (pe'-kwot). An Algonquian tribe, believed to have been an eastern division of the Mohegan, who lived in what is today the state of Connecticut. They were the most dreaded of the southern New England Indians until their defeat by the English.

The Pequot War began in 1637 after these Indians had killed a white trader and committed several other hostile acts. The colonists killed some 600 Indian men, women, and children, and captured others who were sold into slavery. The remainder were distributed among other tribes under the authority of the Mohegan chief, Uncas, and forbidden to ever call themselves Pequot.

Today there are believed to be a few Pequot-Mohegan living in the vicinity of Norwich, Connecticut. The name of this tribe exists only as that of two small villages, one in Minnesota and one in Connecticut. See MIANTONOMO, MOHEGAN, NARRAGANSET.

**PERSIMMON.** An orange-red or yellow plumlike fruit of an American tree of the ebony family, found from Connecticut to Florida and from Ohio to Texas. The tree is sometimes called date-plum or possumwood.

Captain John Smith wrote that the persimmon "draws a man's mouth awry with much torment" until ripened by the frost, when it is sweet and fine-flavored.

The Virginia Indians preserved the fruit by drying it on mats. The Algonquian tribes used the hard flat seeds in playing a dice game. The Natchez Indians made a famous persimmon bread.

**PETALESHARO** (pe-tal'-e-sha-ro). A chief of the Pawnee Indians who is given credit for stopping the practice of sacrificing a virgin each year to the Morning Star. The girl to be killed on the altar was always a captive from another tribe.

Petalesharo carried away a Sioux maiden, who had been prepared for sacrifice, and sent her back to her own people. When his fellow tribesmen found no harm came to Petalesharo through wrath of the Morning Star, they discontinued their custom of human sacrifice. See PAWNEE, STARS.

**PETUN** (pe-toon'). An Indian word for tobacco. The white man uses the term today in medical science. See TOBACCO.

**PICTURE WRITING.** A system by which some Indians kept a record of time and important events by drawing or painting crude pictures or symbols on skins, bark, or stone. Picture writing was in a way a permanent record of the sign language, for the Indian made his drawings in a fashion that brought to mind the idea or thing he wanted to express or tell about.

As time went on the Indian became more skillful and artistic and his pictures became symbols, and by a few lines he was able to convey an idea that formerly had required a more complete picture. Colors, too, stood for certain ideas and by the arrangement of colors the Indian could tell a story. Tattooing was a type of picture writing in certain tribes, and the lines and marks on a man's body told a story.

The Indian called the white man's writing "painted speech," for it was in this manner he considered his own picture writing. But when the white man came the Indian had not reached that stage where he had, like the white man, a written sound language—where a symbol like that for a letter meant a certain sound. Many believe, however, that the Indian's picture writing was leading to this and had the white man not come he would have had such an alphabet eventually.

There are some notable examples of picture writing records left by Indians. Among these are the *Walum Opum* of the Delaware; Sitting Bull's story of his life painted on a buffalo hide; records of the Midewiwin Society, or the Great Medicine Society of the Algonquian; and the Kiowa and Dakota calendars. See CALENDAR, INDIAN LANGUAGE, PAINT, SEQUOYA, SIGN LANGUAGE, SITTING BULL, TATTOOING.

**PIEGAN** (pee′-gan). See BLACKFOOT.

**PIESKARET** (pees-ka′-ret). A famous chief of the Adirondack Indians who was noted for his daring deeds. His tribe joined with the French in the early 1600's and drove the powerful Iroquois out of Canada into the United States. It was during this war that Pieskaret distinguished himself. On one occasion he ventured alone within the Iroquois domain and, coming to one of their villages, hid himself during the day and for three successive nights stole into the village, scalping the members of a lodge each night. He was later killed when he encountered a large band of Iroquois. See ADIRONDACK.

**PILGRIMS.** English colonists who in 1620 settled in Plymouth, Massachusetts. The first group of 102 men, women, and children came over on the *Mayflower,* and having lost their course at sea, landed on Cape Cod instead of that section of Virginia to which a grant had been given them by King James I of England. They were met by an English-speaking Indian, Samoset.

Many years ago, Rufus Choate, a lawyer famous for his wit and after-dinner speeches, remarked that the Pilgrims upon reaching America, "First fell on their knees and then on the aborigines." See CANONICUS, MASSASOIT, SAMOSET, SQUANTO, STANDISH.

**PIMA** (pee'-mah). A tribe belonging to the Uto-Aztecan family, inhabiting the valleys of the Gila and Salt rivers in Arizona. Their name means "No" in the dialect of their Mexican relatives, but they called themselves *Aatam,* or "The People."

The Pima were closely allied with the Papago (Bean People), and more than a century ago were joined by the Maricopa, a tribe of an entirely different language family, who had been driven out of their territory by their relatives, the Mojave. The Maricopa have lived with the Pima ever since.

The Pima have known for centuries how to irrigate their lands and they raised beans, corn, pumpkins, and other vegetables. In later years wheat was their main crop, and they also raised cattle.

By frequent attacks and raids hostile tribes, especially the Apache, caused the decline of the Pima at an early date. Though a peaceful people, they proved themselves courageous when attacked. They never took Apache men prisoners, always killing them on the spot, but spared the lives of Apache women and children and took them into the tribe. It is notable that they never scalped an enemy, and considered all enemies, especially the Apache, possessed of evil spirits and would not touch one after death.

The Pima formerly lived in adobe houses, grouped in pueblos. But when their pueblos were destroyed they began erecting dome-shaped dwellings of pliable poles covered with thatch and mud. They considered these safer, and the Pima, Papago, and Maricopa use such lodges today. Pima women were, and still are, expert basket-makers. The Pima were among the last of the Indians to discard the bow and arrow in favor of the white man's gun.

This tribe came under the jurisdiction of the United States after the Mexican War in 1846-1848. Today with the Papago and Maricopa they live on reservations in Arizona. A county and town in Arizona preserve the name Pima. One of the marines who raised the American flag on Iwo Jima in World War II, the late Ira Hays, was a Pima Indian. See APACHE, MOJAVE, PUEBLO, SCALPING.

**PIPESTONE.** See CALUMET, CATLIN.

**PISÉ** (pee-say'). A type of adobe work in which the adobe mixture is poured between frames made of poles, interwoven with reeds. Some pisé walls are three to four feet thick. This wall was used by the Pueblo Indians in building their famed Casa Grande (Big House), the principal structure of a large prehistoric ruined pueblo on the Gila River, near Florence, Arizona. See ADOBE, PUEBLO INDIANS.

**PLAINS INDIANS.** A term applied to Indians inhabiting the Plains country between the Mississippi River and the Rocky Mountains. In 1882 it was estimated that sixty Plains tribes, broken up into innumerable bands, comprised more than half the Indian population of the United States.

**POCAHONTAS** (po-kah-hon'-tas). An Indian "princess," daughter of the chief Powhatan, and one of the most famous women in American history. She was credited with having saved the life of Captain John Smith.

Pocahontas' Indian name was *Matoaka*, meaning "to play," because of her fondness for playthings. Her father called her *Pokahantes*, which had much the same meaning. She was given the title "princess" by the English, who believed that all rulers and their kin were members of royalty.

After Captain Smith left America and sailed for England in 1609, faith was not kept with the Indians, as had been promised, and Pocahontas was decoyed on board the ship of Captain Argall in the Potomac River, and carried off to Jamestown.

Here Pocahontas was held as a hostage for English prisoners in the hands of her father, Powhatan. But while on board the ship she met John Rolfe, an Englishman, and the two fell in love. With the permission of Powhatan and the governor of Virginia, they were married in April, 1614. Pocahontas was converted to Christianity and baptized under the name of "Lady Rebecca."

The marriage brought about peace with the Indians. The young couple with several members of Pocahontas' tribe sailed for England two years later. The king and queen received Pocahontas as a princess. The following year she started back to America but was taken ill at Gravesend, England, where she died and was buried.

Pocahontas and Rolfe had one son, Thomas Rolfe, who settled in Virginia, and from whom many prominent Virginians claimed descent, among them John Randolph of Roanoke. Pocahontas' name is preserved in that of towns in Virginia, Arkansas, Illinois, Iowa, and Tennessee; and counties in Iowa and West Virginia. See POWHATAN, SMITH, SQUAW MAN, WOMEN.

**PODUNK** (po-dunk'). A small tribe of Algonquian Indians who lived on the Podunk River in Connecticut. Their principal village, at the mouth of the river, was also called Podunk. They joined the hostile Indians in King Philip's War and never returned. The name has been applied ironically by American writers and others to an imaginary small town—a typically dull, placid, and unprogressive community.

**POKAGON** (po-kag′-on), **SIMON.** The last chief of the Pokagon band of the Potawatomi Indians, and son of Chief Leopold Pokagon, who owned the land upon which the city of Chicago now stands. Simon, who was born in 1830 in Michigan, was sent to school at the age of fourteen at Notre Dame in Indiana, and later to Oberlin College in Ohio.

As a man he spoke four or five languages and was noted as the most educated Indian of his time. He wrote numerous articles for leading magazines, and during the Columbian Exposition at Chicago in 1893 published a book, printed on birch bark, called *The Red Man's Greeting*. For forty-three years he ably managed the affairs of his tribe and enriched them when he collected a Potawatomi claim for $150,000 from the Government.

He died in 1899 in Michigan and was buried in an Indian cemetery near Watervliet. A monument was erected to him and his father in Chicago's Jackson Park. See POTAWATOMI.

**POMO** (po′-mo). A group of Indians living in north-central California. They are famed as the world's best basket-makers.

**PONCA** (pong′-ka). See SOUTHERN SIOUX.

**PONTIAC.** A great chief of the Ottawa Indians and leader of the confederacy of tribes of the Ohio Valley and the Great Lakes region when these Indians sought to drive out the English in 1763–1765. Described as patient, subtle, and cruel, Pontiac was considered second only to Tecumseh as the greatest Indian leader of early American history.

Pontiac was born in Ohio in 1712, the son of an Ottawa chief and a Chippewa mother. He led the Ottawa and Chippewa at the English General Braddock's defeat. In 1760 he agreed to the surrender of Detroit to the British when he heard that his allies, the French, had been defeated in Canada. For a time after that Pontiac appeared friendly to the British, but considered King George only as an "uncle," because he felt that he had not received from the British Crown the recognition he deserved as a great sovereign.

But three years later Pontiac entered into a conspiracy with the French to attack the settlements and garrisons of the British on the Great Lakes. He formed a confederacy of the Ottawa, Wyandot, Potawatomi, Shawnee, Winnebago, and other tribes, and planned for each tribe to attack the nearest fort on the same day—this Indian D-Day being in May, 1763.

Pontiac determined to take Detroit himself. The Indians successfully captured ten of the fourteen British posts from Pennsylvania to Lake Superior, but failed to take Niagara, Fort Pitt, Ligonier, and Detroit. An Indian girl is said to have informed a British officer of the plot to capture Detroit, and Pontiac found the British there well prepared. He began a siege which lasted five months.

When informed of a treaty of peace between France and England Pontiac was forced to raise the siege at Detroit. He went west and made an unsuccessful attempt to stir up the tribes along the Mississippi River. Pontiac finally entered into a formal treaty of peace at Detroit on August 17, 1765. Four years later, while engaged in a drinking bout at Cahokia, Illinois, he was murdered by a Kaskaskia Indian. See BRANT, ILLINOIS, KING PHILIP, MIAMI, OTTAWA, POTAWATOMI, SHABONEE, SHAWNEE, TECUMSEH.

**PONY SIGNALS.** See SIGNALS.

**POPCORN.** See MAIZE.

**PORCUPINE.** An animal of the rodent family, whose body is covered with coarse hair and sharp horny spines. The spines or quills of the porcupine were valued by Indians, as Indian women flattened them, colored them, and used them in decorating clothes, saddle pads, quivers, and other articles. See BEADS, COSTUME, QUILLWORK.

**PORTAGE** (port'-ij). The act of carrying a canoe across land from one body of water to another. A portage also means that route taken in transporting a canoe or supplies. Many portages, situated at falls on rivers, became trading posts and later cities. See TRAILS.

**POTAWATOMI** (pot-a-wat'-o-mi). A prominent tribe of the Algonquian family, formerly inhabiting the lower end of Lake Michigan, around where Chicago now stands, and extending southward to the Wabash River and westward into central Illinois. These Indians were at one time associated with the Ottawa and Chippewa and all were grouped under the name "The Three Fires."

The Potawatomi were aligned with the French during early history and were with Pontiac at the siege of Detroit. In the War of 1812 they fought on the English side, and were the chief actors in the Fort Dearborn massacre at Chicago. In the form of Pottawatomie the name is applied to counties in Kansas and Oklahoma, and a town in Kansas; and as Pottawattamie, to a county in Iowa. See CHIPPEWA, OTTAWA, POKAGON, PONTIAC, SHABONEE.

**POTLATCH** (pot'-lach). An Indian feast at which gifts were given and received. The word is Chinook, signifying "gift." The custom was observed in the Northwest, in Canada, and in southern Alaska. In recent years the Canadian government has forbidden potlatch.

At the feasts a chief, to demonstrate his greatness, would give away most of his goods to others—but he would expect the others to return gifts of far greater value. In demonstrating that he was the better man, a chief might break up his canoe, and destroy his blankets and other valuables. Unless his rival did the same or better, his name was considered "broken."

The chief observers of potlatch were the Tlingit, a tribe of totem-pole-makers. See TLINGIT.

**POTOMAC.** The name of an Indian tribe and an Indian town on what is now the Potomac River. Explorers of the river, on being told the name of the town, mistook it for the name of the river. The Potomac tribe of the Powhatan Confederacy formerly occupied the south bank of the river in Stafford and King George counties in Virginia.

**POTTERY.** The making of pottery or vessels of clay was practiced by practically all Indians of the United States east of the Rocky Mountains and in the Southwest. Most Indians of the Great Plains made pottery before the coming of the horse. Pottery was made in the Southeast long before the Christian era.

Indian pottery was not made with a wheel. Instead it was usually built up of spirals of clay.

Pottery had many uses, the chief of which was for cooking purposes. The early pottery of the Indians would stand direct contact with the fire, but modern Indian pottery not only will not stand fire, but will not hold water as it is made primarily for decorative purposes.

The Pueblo tribes were the most expert makers of pottery and probably learned the art from the Indians of Mexico. Among the Zuñi there is a tradition of how the people learned pottery making. They were in the habit of lining baskets with clay when they parched corn. Later they found that these clay linings, when dried out and hardened by fire, could be removed from the baskets and used by themselves. In this way they learned to make pottery.

At the beginning of this century a Hopi Indian woman, Nampeo, became famous for her pottery. The art had almost become lost until she revived it. Another woman, Maria Martinez, of San Ildefonso Village, near Santa Fe, New Mexico, more recently became noted for her black pottery with its highly polished designs in black. See BASKETS, DISHES, PUEBLO INDIANS, ZUÑI.

**POWHATAN** (pow-ha-tan'). One of the most famous Indian chiefs of his time, the founder of the Powhatan Confederacy composed of the Algonquian Virginia tribes. Powhatan's Indian name was *Wahunsonacock,* but, as his favorite residence at the time Captain John Smith arrived was at Powhatan on the James River Falls where the city of Richmond now stands, the whites called him Powhatan. Powhatan was the father of the famed Indian maiden, Pocahontas.

When first known the Powhatan Confederacy of some thirty tribes or subtribes had nearly 200 villages, of which more than 160 were mentioned by Captain John Smith in his writings. These villages, composed of oblong houses with rounded roofs, were enclosed within palisades. The Powhatan raised maize, beans, melons, pumpkins, and some fruit trees. They used the decimal system in counting, and reckoned their years by winters, or by *cohonks,* a name in imitation of the cry of the wild geese that visited them each winter.

Except for some petty warfare with the whites, these Indians were very friendly during Chief Powhatan's time. When Powhatan died in 1618 his younger brother, Opechancanough, became chief and began planning a secret uprising against the colonists. Four years later 347 English were killed and the colonists began a war of extermination against the Indians, finally defeating more than 1,000 and burning their villages.

Peace lasted until 1641 when in another uprising the Indians killed 500 colonists. A year later Opechancanough was captured and shot and the Powhatan Confederacy was broken up.

Several hundred survivors of this once-powerful confederacy still live in Virginia. There are towns named Powhatan in Alabama, Arkansas, Louisiana, and West Virginia; a county and county seat in Virginia; a Powhatan Point in Ohio; and a town called Powhattan in Kansas. See CALENDAR, CHICAHOMINY, CONFEDERATION, COUNTING, POCAHONTAS, SMITH.

**POWWOW.** A term formerly applied to feasts, dances, and public meetings of Indians prior to a grand hunt, a war expedition, or a council. Later it became known as the council itself, where problems and difficulties facing the people were discussed and straightened out.

The term "powwow" was also used to denote a medicine man or "powwow doctor," as well as the conjuring of a medicine man over a patient. The white man took the term, from the Massachuset Indian word *pauwau,* and used it to mean a political conference or talk.

In most tribes almost everyone held a council, or powwow, to decide various matters. The family held a council to settle family problems. The clans held councils, and the chiefs of the clans formed the tribal council. On occasions of great emergencies, a grand council was held, which was composed of chiefs and subchiefs, the women and head warriors of the families, and the leading men of the tribe.

The largest council was that of the Confederacy, where representatives of all the allied tribes met. See CHIEF, CLAN.

**PRAIRIE INDIANS.** Indians inhabiting the vast, fertile, and sometimes treeless plains which extended from western Ohio and southern Michigan across the states of Indiana, Illinois, Missouri, Arkansas, Iowa, Kansas, Nebraska, and North and South Dakota, including the southern portions of Wisconsin and Minnesota. The name "prairie" was given this section by early French explorers.

**PRAYER STICKS.** Sacred sticks, called *pahos*, decorated with feathers, used by the Pueblo, Navajo, and Apache Indians in ceremonies. These sticks usually were painted in various colors and most were about the length of the hand with the fingers extended. To some, small bags of meal or pollen were attached as offerings to the gods.

Prayer sticks were made with great care and all discarded parts in the making, such as chips of wood, ends of cord, and bits of feathers, were destroyed. The sticks were used in trying to gain the good will of the Indian gods. See APACHE, FEATHERWORK, NAVAJO, PUEBLO INDIANS.

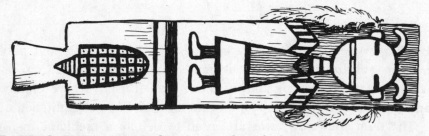

**PRAYING INDIANS.** Indians of colonial days who accepted the teachings of the missionaries. They were organized into villages, known as "praying villages." Chief of these was Natick, Massachusetts, near the present village of the same name, where John Eliot made a great number of converts in 1650–1651. Most of these were remnants of the Massachuset tribe.

After King Philip's War those who would not join the Indians in the praying villages were sold into slavery.

Catholic Iroquois and those who followed the teachings of the Moravian brethren also were known as praying Indians. See ELIOT BIBLE, KING PHILIP, MASSACHUSET, SLAVES.

**PUEBLO** (pweb'-lo) **INDIANS.** A general name for Indians who lived in permanent stone or adobe houses grouped in villages in southern Colorado, central Utah, New Mexico, and Arizona. The term was first used by the early Spaniards, *pueblo* being their term for "town" or "village." It is much the same as calling other Indians "Tepee Indians," or "Wigwam Indians," or the more general terms "Plains Indians" and "Woodland Indians."

Pueblo is not a tribal name or even a language group name. Pueblo Indians actually belong to several distinct language families and to many tribes. But as Pueblo Indians they have become famous because of their peculiar customs and ceremonies, for instance, such a custom as men instead of women working in the fields, as is common to the Acoma Indians, and such ceremonies as the Snake Dance of the Hopis.

Artists and writers have shown great interest in the Pueblo Indians in recent years. Architects, too, have studied their structures and sought to base a style of architecture on them. Scientists have excavated the stone ruins of the Southwest—structures which are believed to have been built by the early Pueblo Indians. Historians are interested because descendants of these people are still living today in one of the two sections of the United States first colonized by Europeans.

The term "Pueblo Indians" is often applied to the Pima and Papago, as well as to the true Pueblo tribes. See ACOMA, ADOBE, CLIFF DWELLERS, HOPI, KERESAN PUEBLO, PIMA, PISÉ, POTTERY, PRAYER STICKS, RANCHERIA, SNAKE DANCE, TANOAN PUEBLOS, ZUÑI. See also illustration, page 232.

**QUAPAW** (kwa'-pa). A group of Siouan Indians whose name meant "Downstream People," as they lived near the mouth of the Arkansas River. They were called *Arkansa* or *Arkansas* by the Illinois and other Algonquian Indians of that section. Early explorers found that they lived in walled villages and also erected large mounds, sometimes placing their chief buildings upon them. White settlers found these Indians so "troublesome" and reluctant to give up their land that after a series of treaties, the Quapaw were allotted land in the Indian Territory. See ARKANSAS, MOUND BUILDERS.

**QUILLWORK.** A type of decoration used by many Indian tribes on various articles of dress, bags and pouches, pipes, and horse gear. Quillwork, which later was replaced almost entirely by beadwork, was done with the quills of porcupines and those of bird feathers.

The Cree, Dakota, Cheyenne, and Arapaho were the principal quill-working tribes, although in earlier days porcupine quills had been employed in decorative embroidery from Maine to Virginia and west to the Rocky Mountains north of the Arkansas River.

The work was done chiefly on dressed skin, but some of the Woodland tribes decorated birch bark with quillwork. The split quills of feathers were used by the Eskimo; other tribes, mainly Algonquian, employed the hair of the porcupine as well as the quills.

The same designs and same color schemes were used in beadwork as had been used in the older craft. See illustration above.

It was the duty of the man to kill the porcupine and pluck the quills as soon as possible after the animal's death. The women sorted them according to length, since they varied from one to four inches. As the quill of the porcupine is a round hollow tube which ends in a barbed point, it was necessary to flatten it before using. A woman would moisten the quill in her mouth, and then draw it between her fingernails or teeth. Sometimes a bone quill-flattener was used.

The quill itself was white and was dyed in various ways before being applied to the buckskin or other material. The red dye was made from the buffalo berry, yellow from the petals of wild sunflowers, and black from the wild grape. Quills were plaited if they were to be wrapped around a pipe stem, and if they were to be sewed on buckskin they were wound around or folded over the sinew after it had been run through the buckskin. See BAGS AND POUCHES, BEADS, CALUMET, COSTUME, KNIFE SHEATH, MOCCASIN, PAPOOSE, PORCUPINE, QUIVER, SINEW, WOMEN.

**QUIRT.** A short riding whip about fifteen inches long, with a wood, bone, or horn handle, a wrist strap at one end and at the other end a double lash of rawhide from twenty to twenty-four inches long. The quirt of the mounted Indian had a hole burned through the handle about two inches from the lash end and a rawhide lash passed through the hole. Both ends of the lash were brought down to the butt of the handle where each end passed through a slit in the other. This secured the lash to the handle. One or two inches from the butt end another hole was burned, through which a wrist strap was passed. See HORSE, RAWHIDE, SADDLE.

**QUIVER.** A container for arrows, made from skins or wood. Many tribes east of the Rockies used deerskin, often beautifully decorated. On the Pacific Coast quivers were made of cedar wood. Otter, mountain lion, and coyote skins were popular among many Indians for quivers. See ARROW, BEADS, BOW, COYOTE, MOUNTAIN LION, OTTER, PARFLECHE, QUILLWORK.

R

**RABBIT-SKIN WEAVING.** A method by which the far western Indian tribes made blankets and robes from rabbit skins. The skins were cut into long strips, twisted with the fur side out, so that they were in rolls about the size of the finger. These rolls formed the warp and were held in place by rows of woven stout cord or babiche. They were extremely warm as blankets. See BABICHE, BLANKET, HAIR-WORK.

**RABBIT STICK.** A type of boomerang used by the Hopi Indians to kill rabbits and other small game. Although the rabbit stick did not return to the thrower as did the trick Australian boomerang, it was constructed on the same airplane principle. See HOPI. See also illustration above.

**RAIN-IN-THE-FACE.** A noted Sioux warrior and chief of the Hunkpapa tribe. He was born in 1835 near the forks of the Cheyenne River in North Dakota.

He received his name after fighting all day in the rain. It had been his habit to paint his face half red and half black to represent the sun when covered by darkness. The rain caused his red and black paint to run and his face became streaked.

Rain-in-the-Face went on the warpath many times, but his first

important experience as a warrior was in the attack on Fort Phil Kearney, Wyoming, in December, 1866, when Captain Fetterman and his command of eighty men were killed.

Rain-in-the-Face was arrested once by Colonel Tom Custer, brother of General Custer, and after escaping he swore he would some day cut out Tom Custer's heart "and eat it." He was with Sitting Bull at the Custer battle and it was claimed that he killed both General Custer and Tom Custer. He denied killing General Custer, but did admit in an interview at Coney Island years later that he had killed Tom Custer and cut out his heart. In more sober moments he is said to have denied this, too.

Rain-in-the-Face fled to Canada with Sitting Bull, but finally surrendered in 1880. See CUSTER'S LAST STAND, DAKOTA, INDIAN NAMES, RED CLOUD, SITTING BULL.

**RALEIGH, SIR WALTER.** See CROATAN, ROANOKE.

**RANCHERIA** (ran-tcha-ree'-ah). A small village of Indians, as compared to the larger pueblos in the Southwest. Rancherias usually were occupied by scattered tribes. Rancheria Grande was a name applied to a large composite band of Indians who settled on the Brazos River in Texas in the first half of the eighteenth century, for defense and protection against the Spanish and Apache. See PUEBLO INDIANS.

**RATTLES.** See MUSICAL
INSTRUMENTS.
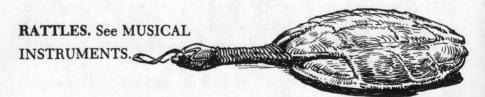

**RAWHIDE.** Untanned hide, one of the most important of all materials to the Indian, was used in innumerable ways.

To make rawhide, the green hide was first stretched on a frame or on the ground and the flesh and fat were removed. After it had been allowed to dry or "set" for several days, the hide was removed from the frame and placed in a stream of running water for four or five days or buried in the ground with a sprinkling of wood ashes on the hair side. This loosened the hair and made it easy to remove.

When properly treated rawhide would not shrink, but green hide, taken directly from the animal, would shrink in drying, becoming very hard. This hardened hide was known as *shaganappi*, or "Indian iron." The Indian took advantage of the shrinking of green hide for securing handles to war clubs, making drumheads, lashing lodge poles, and mending broken objects. See BABICHE, BUCKSKIN, BUFFALO, BULLBOAT, CARIBOU, DEER, DISHES, LARIAT, MOCCASIN, PARFLECHE, QUIRT, SADDLE, SHAGANAPPI, SHIELD. See also illustration, page 258.

**RED BONES.** See CROATAN.

**RED CLOUD.** Most famous chief of the Oglala Teton Sioux (largest band of the Dakota nation). He was born in 1822.

In 1865 Red Cloud claimed the Government's building of a road from Fort Laramie, Wyoming, to the gold regions of Montana would spoil the best buffalo-hunting grounds. Assembling 2,000 warriors, he annihilated a detachment of eighty troops near Fort Phil Kearney in December, 1866. The Government finally agreed to abandon the road and Red Cloud gave no more trouble even during the Sioux war of 1876. He was later forced to cede the Black Hills.

A counter of eighty coups, Red Cloud was a general, a statesman, an orator, and patriotic representative of his tribe. He died in 1909. Red Cloud, Nebraska, and Red Cloud Peak, Colorado, were named in his honor. See DAKOTA, ORATORS, RAIN-IN-THE-FACE, SPOTTED TAIL, YOUNG-MAN-AFRAID-OF-HIS-HORSES.

**RED JACKET.** A noted orator and chief of the Wolf Clan of the Seneca Indians, born about 1756 in Seneca County, New York. His Indian name was *Sagoyewatha,* which meant "He Who Causes Them to Be Awake."

He obtained the name Red Jacket during the Revolutionary War when a British officer, attracted by the chief's ability and brilliance, gave him a red jacket, which in time became characteristic of him.

Cornplanter, the great Iroquois chief, once termed Red Jacket a coward to his face, and urged his wife to leave him.

Although Red Jacket made peace with the Americans after the Revolution, he consistently opposed the white man's way as being neither good nor proper for the Indian. In 1792 when he visited Philadelphia, he was presented by George Washington with a medal bearing the President's own likeness. This medal is now in the Buffalo Historical Society.

Before the War of 1812, the Canadians tried to persuade Red Jacket to join the Algonkins and help the British gain the territory of the Ohio Valley, but he refused. When war actually started Red Jacket fought on the American side.

Red Jacket died January 20, 1830, and his final resting place is Forest Lawn Cemetery in Buffalo where a monument was unveiled to the great chief on June 22, 1891. See BRANT, BURIAL, CORNPLANTER, IROQUOIS, ORATORS, PARKER (ELI), TARHE.

**RED MAN.** A name first applied to the Beothuk Indians of Newfoundland because they colored their bodies, utensils, and weapons with red ocher. Sebastian Cabot, the English navigator, on discovering Newfoundland, mentioned "people painted with red ocher." Other writers later commented on this and soon the name Beothuk was translated by the white man as "Red Indian," or "Red Man." The Beothuk actually were light brown in color. See INDIAN, PAINT.

**RED STICKS.** A term applied by the white man to warriors of the Creek and Seminole Indians. It was the custom of these tribes to erect tall red poles in the village public squares when war was declared. These poles or "red sticks" were in charge of men known as "bearers of the red," and so the men themselves became known as "Red Sticks." See CREEK, PAINT, SEMINOLE.

**REE.** Another name for the Arikara or Arickaree Indians. There also was a band of Northern Cheyenne Indians nicknamed the "Ree Band," because some were related to the Ree or Arikara. See ARIKARA.

**RICE (WILD).** A plant growing on the margins of lakes and in the backwaters of rivers. It was one of the chief foods of the Indians of the North Central states. The colonists termed it "wild oats" or "wild wheat," because at that time the white men of America and Europe were not familiar with rice.

The chief consumers of wild rice were the Algonquian tribes of the Great Lakes region, particularly the Menominee, whose name came from the Chippewa term meaning "wild rice." See FOOD, ME-NOMINEE.

**RIDDLE, TOBY.** A Modoc Indian woman, known to her tribe as *Winema,* or "Woman Chief." At fifteen she gained her Indian name by rallying Modoc warriors after they had been attacked by enemies.

Winema married Frank Riddle, a miner from Kentucky, who later became an interpreter. She was with her tribe when troops sought to round it up during the Modoc War. She saved the life of Commissioner A. B. Meacham, when he and others were attacked while trying to bring about peace. Congress later voted Toby Riddle a pension and she and her husband and child moved east with Meacham. See MODOC, WOMEN.

**ROANOKE** (ro'-a-nok). An early tribe of Indians living on the island by that name off the coast of North Carolina. It was on this island that Sir Walter Raleigh's colony first was established in 1585–1586. The colony was to become known as the "lost colony of the Croatan."

The term "roanoke" was used by Virginia colonists to designate shell beads, or wampum. Captain John Smith in his writings reported the Powhatan name for such beads as *rawrenock*. See BEADS, CROATAN, WAMPUM.

**ROBBIBOE** (rob-bib'-o). A soup of flour and pemmican made by hunters, trappers, and frontiersmen throughout the Northwest. The word is believed to have come from the Chippewa *nabob*, meaning "broth," which in some dialects is *rabob*. See PEMMICAN.

**ROBE.** See BLANKET.

**ROLFE, JOHN.** Husband of Pocahontas. See POCAHONTAS.

**ROLFE, THOMAS.** Son of John Rolfe and Pocahontas. See POCAHONTAS.

**ROMAN NOSE.** A chief of the Pointed Lance Men Society, warrior group of the powerful Southern Cheyenne, whose Indian name was *Sauts*, or "Bat." He led the attack at Aricaree Fork, Colorado, in 1868, when fifty-two scouts, commanded by Colonel G. A. Forsyth, held off several hundred Cheyenne warriors. Roman Nose was killed in the first day's fight. See CHEYENNE.


**ROOTS AND ROOTCRAFT.** Indians used roots for food, medicine, and dyes; for making baskets, cloth, rope, and salt; and for chewing and flavoring.

Roots of species of the lily were used widely as food, as was the camas, which was found from the Wasatch Mountains in Utah, north to the Canadian border and west to the Pacific Coast. The root of the *kouse*, a word derived from the Nez Percé *kowish*, also known as "biscuit root," was used by them to make thin cakes a foot wide and three feet long.

The Plains Indians prized the *pomme blanche*, Indian turnip or Indian potato, pounded and cooked with jerked meat and corn. The Miami, Shawnee, and other tribes were fond of Jerusalem artichokes.

The Hopi and Zuñi, as well as other southern and eastern tribes, used the wild potato; the Navajo were fond of eating it with clay. The Seminole converted *coonti*, a starchy root, into flour for bread. This became popular with the whites and at one time several Florida mills produced coonti flour.

Sweet roots were chewed and scores of roots were used for medicinal purposes. Ginseng, later exported to China by white men, was used by some Indian medicine men, who believed it gave them power.

Dye was made from root bark by the California Indians, from bloodroot by the northern and eastern tribes, and hair dye was extracted from a small root by the Virginia Indians.

The Hopi Indians burned an incense root during ceremonies. Fish were drugged with soaproot in California, and with a variety of poisonous roots by the Iroquois and other tribes of the East.

Rope, cordage, and baskets were made from the trailing roots of spruce, tamarack, hemlock, red cedar, and cottonwood. See BASKETS, CAMAS, FISHING, FOOD, MEDICINE.


**RUNNING THE GANTLET.** See TORTURE.

S

**SACAJAWEA** (sak-a-ja-we'-ah). A Shoshoni Indian woman, famous for guiding the Lewis and Clark expedition. Sacajawea, or the Bird Woman, as the whites called her, was born about 1787 in a camp of the Shoshoni or Snake Indians. At fourteen she was captured by a Hidatsa war party, and sold to Toussaint Charbonneau, a French Canadian voyageur, who lived with the Hidatsa in their village in North Dakota. He later married her.

When Lewis and Clark arrived in Hidatsa territory in 1804, they engaged Charbonneau as an interpreter and guide. Sacajawea had just given birth to a son, but she went along with the party, carrying her papoose on her back, anxious to visit her own people, who ranged from Three Forks, Montana, westward into Idaho.

It was not long before Sacajawea, and not her husband, guided the party. She and her son are mentioned almost daily in the explorers' famous journal and her many services are praised. When the party reached Three Forks, Montana, Sacajawea met her own people and learned that her brother had become chief of the Shoshoni. She was able to obtain aid and ponies from the Indians, without which the party would not have been able to continue.

On the way back from the Pacific Coast, Sacajawea continued as guide. When they reached a Mandan village on the Missouri River, Lewis and Clark paid Charbonneau for his services and dismissed him. Sacajawea remained with her husband.

The little boy, Jean Baptiste Charbonneau, had become a great favorite with both Lewis and Clark. Captain Clark told Charbonneau that if he would bring the child to him he would educate him "and treat him as my own son."

Clark became Agent of Indian Affairs in the Territory of Louisiana in 1807. A little-known *Letter from the Secretary of War Transmitting Information in Relation to the Superintendency of Indian Affairs in the Territory of Michigan During the Year 1820 and Part of 1821* indicates that Clark kept his promise. However, it was the Government, not Captain Clark personally, who paid the innumerable itemized expenses.

It is questionable what happened to Jean Baptiste after the age of about sixteen although he was reported years later in New Orleans. His father was last reported as having been seen in 1838, but what became of Sacajawea remains a mystery.

In 1811 a fur trader reported her death at the age of twenty-five. But in 1875 a missionary found an old woman among the Shoshoni who claimed to be the original Sacajawea. She died near Fort Washakie in Wyoming on April 9, 1884, almost one hundred years old. Her grave is marked by a brass tablet, and a bronze tablet to Sacajawea was erected in City Park, Portland, Oregon, in 1905. See CHARBONNEAU, GROS VENTRE, LEWIS, SHOSHONI, WOMEN.

**SACHEM** (say'-chem). The supreme Indian ruler of a territory inhabited by a number of allied tribes. Each tribe was governed by a sagamore. The office of sachem appears to have been inherited. This form of government was confined to the Indians of Massachusetts, but writers later applied the term sachem to chiefs of tribes in other sections. See CHIEF, NATCHEZ, SAGAMORE.

**SACRED BUNDLES.** Treasured objects which were supposed greatly to influence the destiny of the tribes that owned them. A type of tribal "medicine," they were carefully guarded and sometimes prayer and even sacrifice were made to them. They were shown publicly only on important occasions. Many times these bundles were carried into battle to insure victory,

When the Cherokees' sacred box was captured by the Delaware, they believed bad luck came to them. The sacred metal plates, which the Creek Indians claimed they received from a god, were said to have given out a miraculous ringing sound at times without being touched.

The *taimé* of the Kiowa, a small stone bust of a man, decorated with down feathers and with images of the sun and the moon crescent painted on its breast, is said still to exist. It was kept in a parfleche container and shown only once a year at the Sun Dance.

The Cheyenne treasured a sacred bundle which contained a hat made from the hide and hair of a buffalo cow, and four arrows—two for hunting and two for war. These objects, which were carried into battle, the Cheyenne claimed were given them by their Supreme Being. However, when the Pawnee captured this sacred bundle, the keeper manufactured four more "medicine arrows" to replace those lost. This was believed to have been done with the consent of their god.

Among the Arapaho Indians a "flat pipe" was treasured, as well as an ear of corn and a stone turtle. They believed they had had this sacred bundle since the beginning of the world. It was said never to have touched the ground, and when moving it the priest in charge had to carry it on his back if he were mounted, as it could not even touch his horse. See CHEYENNE, MAN-BEING, MEDICINE.

**SADDLE.** A seat of leather, with or without a horn and cantle, which was secured to the horse's back. Indian saddles were of two general types—the pad saddle and the frame saddle. While all mounted Indians had some form of saddle, in hunting buffalo and for battle the Indian usually rode bareback. The pad saddle was commonly used by Indians of the northern Plains and those living west of the Rockies. Made of two

pieces of soft tanned hide sewed together and stuffed with hair or grass, it was really little more than a stuffed pillow, held on with a rawhide cinch and having short stirrups. On horse-stealing expeditions Indians often carried with them empty pads to be stuffed with grass and used after the horses had been stolen. This type of saddle was popular with the Blackfoot, Nez Percé, Atsina, Mandan, Assiniboin, and Hidatsa.

Some Indians, mainly the Ute, Crow, and Shoshoni, were partial to what is termed the "frame saddle." The frame usually was of cottonwood, shaped and covered with green rawhide which held the parts tightly together after it had dried and shrunk. This saddle had two horns or pommels, one before and one behind, both ten or more inches high. The seat of hide was swung hammock-like between the bow and the cantle.

This type of saddle resembled the Moorish saddle used by the Spanish conquistadores, but though it was used in the Southwest by the Navajo and others, it is believed the Indians developed it independently. Among the Blackfoot and other tribes this was strictly a woman's saddle, although much the same type was used as a packsaddle.

Another type of frame saddle had a low-arched pommel and cantle made of elk or deer horn. It was used by the Comanche, Cheyenne, Arapaho, Dakota, Cree, and also by the Assiniboin, Mandan, and Blackfoot. The elk or deer horn was cut and bent to resemble an inverted "Y" and attached to the side bars before and behind, the prongs of the horn lashed to the bars on either side and the whole covered with green rawhide. Some such saddles had a pommel of deer or elk horn to which the lariat was attached.

All saddles were attached with a single cinch, or girth, made of a strip of hide or woven hair. A special ornamental saddle blanket was used by women among the Dakota, Ute, Crow, and Shoshoni, but most saddle blankets used with frame saddles were composed of two or three folds of soft dressed buffalo hide. See HAIRWORK, HORSE, LARIAT, QUIRT, RAWHIDE.

**SAGAMORE** (sag'-a-mor). Among the Algonquian Indians, a lesser chief or chief of a tribe which was part of a confederation. See SACHEM.

**SAGE.** Any one of several shrubby plants of the aster family. The largest type was used by Indians as a fuel. A smaller white species was used for making tea, treating fevers, and for fumigating. Some Plains tribes hung white sage on the poles of a tepee as protection against lightning.

One kind of sage was used by Indian scouts to keep themselves awake and alert when passing through enemy territory. See MEDICINE.

**SALISH** (sa'-leesh). See FLATHEADS.

**SAMOSET** (sam'-o-set). A Pemaquid Indian sagamore who was the first to greet the Pilgrims when they landed on Cape Cod in 1620. He is reported to have exclaimed in English, "Welcome, Englishmen!" Samoset, who had learned English from some fishermen he had met previously, introduced the Pilgrims to Massasoit.

In 1625 Samoset helped execute the first deed made between the Indians and the English, conveying 12,000 acres of Pemaquid territory to John Brown of New Harbor, Maine. Shortly before his death, he signed another deed in 1653, turning over 1,000 acres to Englishmen. See PILGRIMS.

**SAND PAINTING.** A form of ceremonial art practiced by Indians of the Southwest. This art reached its highest development among the Navajo.

The Navajo, who claimed that sand painting was practiced by the Cliff Dwellers, made their pictures only during religious ceremonies. The five colors most sacred in Navajo mythology were used. Each color had a meaning. White, yellow, and red were made from powdered sand of those colors; black was powdered charcoal; and blue, which was actually gray, was a mixture of white sand and charcoal.

First a blanket of white sand was spread over the lodge floor. Then the artist picked up some of the powder between his first and second fingers and thumb and allowed it to run slowly out as he moved his hand. The pictures represented various gods, lightning, sunbeams, rainbows, mountains, animals, and plants.

While some Pueblo Indians allowed the pictures to remain for several days, the Navajo destroyed all pictures on the day they were made. The Cheyenne, during their Sun Dance ceremony, made sand pictures to represent the Morning Star. The Hopi made theirs in secret, first indicating the north by yellow, the west by green or blue, the south by red, and the east by white. See CHEYENNE, HOPI, NAVAJO, PAINT.

**SARATOGA.** A name said to have come from a band of Mohawk Indians who occupied the west bank of the Hudson River, near the present towns of Saratoga and Stillwater in Saratoga County, New York.

**SATURIBA** (sa-tu-reeb'-ah). A war chief of the Timucua tribe, at one time numbering some thirteen thousand, who fought the Spanish in Florida in the sixteenth century. The tribe has long since disappeared. But Saturiba has lived in history for the dramatic speech he made to a war party just before it set out. Flinging water into the air, he said, "As I have done with this water so I pray that you do with the blood of your enemies."

**SAUK AND FOX.** Two closely allied tribes of Algonquian Indians who spoke almost the same language, observed the same customs, and were found together by the French in 1650. They lived originally in the Great Lakes region and later in Iowa and Kansas. The actual confederation of the two tribes appears to have been formed in 1760 and was strengthened when they fought together in the Black Hawk War in 1832.

The Sauk and Fox were Woodland Indians, lived in bark lodges, and used the canoe. They ate wild rice, and cultivated maize, beans, squash, and tobacco. Their headdress was striking—usually a tuft of deer hair dyed red and tied in the manner of a scalp lock, with the rest of the head shaved bare. They wore moccasins, leggings, and breechcloth, with the upper part of the body bare. Warriors were known by the white clay print of a hand on their backs or shoulders.

The Sauk, sometimes called Sac, were known in the Indian language as "Yellow Earth People," as distinguished from the Fox, who were "Red Earth People."

Father Allouez, a Jesuit priest, reported that the Sauk and Fox were the most savage of all forest tribes. He claimed they would kill a white man because they could not bear the sight of whiskers. Other Indians knew them as brave, but stingy and inclined to thievery.

The Sauk and Fox were continually at war with the French and the Chippewa. The two great Sauk leaders were Black Hawk and Keokuk.

The Sauk gave their name to the Sauk River in Minnesota; to a county in Wisconsin; to Sauk City and Saukville in Wisconsin; to a town in Washington; and Sauk Rapids and Sauk Center in Minnesota. As Sac the name is applied to a county and county seat in Iowa, a river in Missouri, and a small place in Tennessee.

The Fox have given their name to a river in Wisconsin, as well as to a second river, also called the Pishtaka, which rises in Wisconsin and flows through Illinois into the Illinois River. Small places in other sections also have been named for them. See BLACK HAWK, CHIPPEWA, KEOKUK, KICKAPOO, WINNEBAGO.

**SAUVAGE** (so-vaje'). Early French term for an Indian, meaning "savage." See INDIAN, SIWASH.

**SCALP DANCE.** A dance of the Plains Indians, performed only by women, in which the scalps taken by the warriors were carried. Most artists and writers show and tell about warriors dancing the scalp dance, but the dance of the men was actually a victory dance. See DANCE, SCALPING, WOMEN.

**SCALP HOAX.** To embarrass the British during the Revolutionary War, Benjamin Franklin, then living in France, published in a newspaper printed in his shop at Passy, a fictitious story including an imaginary letter, which, it was claimed, had accompanied a large package of colonists' scalps being shipped to the King of England. According to the newspaper account, both package and letter had been intercepted by the Americans.

Although several of Franklin's biographers have explained the affair, many reputable historians have quoted the letter as fact.

**SCALPING.** The removal of the hair from the head of an enemy as a trophy. Not all Indians practiced scalping, and it is believed that the custom was not widespread in America before the coming of the white man. Scalping appears to have been the practice of the early Iroquois and Creek and other allied tribes of the East, and some Plains Indians. Among these tribes the head rather than just the scalp, frequently was cut off by the victor.

Scalping is claimed by some historians to have become popular when the colonists and the Government offered bounties for scalps of certain unfriendly Indians. White men as well as Indians took scalps.

While the practice of scalping has been identified with the American Indian, the Greek historian Herodotus records that the ancient Scythians scalped their enemies in Asia Minor. The American Indian made scalping a ceremonial and religious custom, some sacrificing enemy scalps to their gods. Others held ceremonial scalp dances.

At first Indians did not care about white men's scalps, preferring the scalps of Indian enemies. Plains Indians would not scalp Negroes —or "Buffalo Soldiers," as they called them—because their hair reminded them of a buffalo. The Pima Indian would not scalp the Apache.

Scalping was not always fatal. Many times Indians scalped live enemies and allowed them to return in shame to their tribes. Some white men were scalped and lived to tell about it. The warrior who killed an enemy did not always scalp him.

Among the Plains Indians, touching a live enemy with a coup stick was an even greater honor than killing and scalping him. If a brave did kill his enemy he might leave the scalping to others. Several men might take a portion of a fallen enemy's scalp, or one man might take the entire scalp and divide it with others later. No warrior measured his honors by the number of scalps he had taken.

Some Plains Indians believed that a man would not go to the Hereafter if he had been scalped. For this reason they always scalped enemies and made every effort to save their own dead or wounded from being scalped.

The scalp was not always preserved. Sometimes it was left on the scene of battle. It might be offered as a sacrifice to the sun, in which case it was held toward the sun with a short prayer and then placed on a buffalo chip. Other times it might be sacrificed to water and thrown into a river or stream.

If the scalp was to be preserved it was stretched in a hoop about six inches in diameter. When dry the skin side was painted red, or red and black. The hoops containing the scalps were carried at the end of a stick by women at the time of the scalp dance.

Often scalps were used for decoration on shields, lances, robes, and as pendants on bridles. The Dakota saved a scalp for a year, during which period the spirit of the scalped man was supposed to remain near. Then at a great feast all scalps were destroyed and the spirits freed. The Arikara hung scalps in their Medicine Lodge as a sacrifice to their gods. See COUP, DANCE, HORSE, KNIFE, PIMA, SCALP DANCE, SCALP LOCK, SHIELD. See also illustration, page 268.

**SCALPING KNIFE.** See KNIFE.

**SCALP LOCK.** Portion of hair worn by warriors to defy the enemy, by a sort of come-and-take-it attitude. See HAIR, SCALPING.

**SCHOOLCRAFT, HENRY ROWE** (1793–1864). One of the most famous writers on the American Indian. In 1822 Schoolcraft was made Indian agent at Mackinac and acting superintendent of Indian Affairs in the Michigan area. Ten years later he commanded an expedition to discover the sources of the Mississippi River.

Schoolcraft lived among Indians and married a Chippewa woman. He wrote extensively on his travels and his experiences among Indians from 1820 to 1857. His *Historical and Statistical Information Respecting the History, Conditions and Prospects of the Indian Tribes of the United States,* in five volumes, was authorized and ordered published by Congress.

Schoolcraft also negotiated treaties with various Indian tribes whereby the Government obtained 16,000,000 acres of land. The hero of Longfellow's poem *Hiawatha* is drawn from Schoolcraft's writings. However, Schoolcraft confused the real Hiawatha with a Chippewa deity. As a result nothing in Longfellow's poem relates to the great Iroquois reformer and statesman. See CHIPPEWA, HIAWATHA, LONGFELLOW, SQUAW MAN.

**SEATTLE.** A chief of the allied tribes of Puget Sound, Washington. *Seathl,* as his Indian name was spelled, was the first signer of the treaty by which the Puget Sound Indians agreed to live on reservations. He was friendly to the whites and the city of Seattle, Washington, was named for him. As this occurred before his death, and he believed that the mention of his name after he died would disturb his spirit, he made the people of Seattle pay him a small tribute each year. Seattle died in 1866 at the age of seventy-six, and a monument was erected to him in Seattle twenty-four years later. See INDIAN NAMES.

**SECRET SOCIETIES.** Indians, like most other people throughout the world, had their secret orders and societies. The majority of Indian societies had to do with religion or healing of the sick, while a lesser number were for carrying on tribal myths, preserving records, making rain, and even for keeping their women well in hand.

The head man of a religious or ceremonial society usually was what the white man termed a priest. He was similar to the shaman or medicine man in that he acted as a go-between for the world of spirits and the world of men. But while the shaman acted alone and depended on his individual ability, the priest acted in some fashion for the tribe or the society.

Many of the secret societies of the Plains Indians were military societies, but there were others like the Buffalo Society, which was devoted to curing sick people. The Cheyenne had a society called "Big-Bellied Men," whose members were trained to walk barefoot on fires or red-hot coals.

One of the largest and most important secret societies was the Midewiwin Society—the Grand Medicine Society—of the Chippewa and associated tribes. This society had four degrees, or lodges, and a member could advance to a higher lodge by expending more and more property on feasts. These members learned the secrets of curing diseases and the medicinal virtues of plants. The Delaware Indians had a similar society called the "Great Snake," whose members roamed from band to band to cure diseases by magic and officiate at funerals.

The Zuñi had thirteen secret societies, some for healing the sick and others for such important matters as making rain. Among the Pomo the men had a society which conjured up all sorts of infernal horrors to frighten women and keep them in subjection. See MEDICINE, MILITARY SOCIETIES.

**SEMINOLE** (sem'-e-nol). A tribe of the Muskhogean family allied to the Hitchiti and Creek. The Seminole formerly lived in southern Georgia and northern Florida. They are usually thought of as being inhabitants of the semitropical, swampy country of Florida, but they did not enter the Everglades section until after a long and bitter war with the white man.

Seminole men usually were tall and well proportioned. They wore long, knee-length shirts of striped material, tied around the waist by a cord from which hung bags or pouches for pockets. They also wore a turban wound round their head Turkish fashion, which sometimes was decorated with plumes. These Indians lived on game—deer, turkeys, fish, and even turtles which they roasted in their shells. Their houses were made mostly from the palmetto and were open on all sides, much like a covered platform.

Trouble between the Seminole and the Americans began in the War of 1812, but became serious in 1817–1818 during what has been called the First Seminole War. This war was brought on when the Seminole were accused of protecting runaway slaves. Army troops under General Andrew Jackson invaded Florida, and more than 300 Seminole were killed. The remaining Indians fled to the swamps.

In 1819 Spain ceded Florida to the United States, which was pledged to treat the Indians fairly and deal justly with them—a pledge which it is doubtful was ever fulfilled.

In 1834 an attempt was made to force the Seminole on a reservation and as a result the Second Seminole War started. For almost eight years the Indians fought off the American troops. Finally when Osceola, their chief, sought to talk peace he was imprisoned. The Indians were rounded up and sent to Oklahoma where they became known as the Seminole Nation and one of the Five Civilized Tribes. Some, escaping capture, remained in the Everglades section of Florida where they were later assigned reservations.

The county in Oklahoma where most of the Seminole were sent at the end of the war bears their name, as does a county in Florida. Towns and villages of the name are in Alabama, Oklahoma, Pennsylvania, and Texas. See CREEK, FIVE CIVILIZED TRIBES, OSCEOLA, RED STICKS, SLAVES, TATTOOING.

**SENECA** (sen'-e-ka). The most numerous and warlike of the Iroquois Confederacy. See IROQUOIS.

**SEQUOYA** (se-kwoi'-a). The famous inventor of the Cherokee alphabet. He was born in the Cherokee town of Taskigi, Tennessee, about 1760, the son of a white man and a Cherokee woman. Indians called him *Sikwayi*, but he also was known by the name of George Gist, or as some say, Guess or Guest, the name of his father.

Sequoya grew up with his tribe and at an early age showed his ability as an inventive genius and a natural mechanic. He became an expert silver craftsman. A hunting accident crippled him for life.

Sequoya then found much time to study and think. He began to realize that the arts of writing and printing were the greatest instruments and weapons of the white man's civilization and he wished to make these arts available to his own people. Despite the ridicule of other young men of his tribe, he began to work out a system of writing in the Cherokee language.

In 1821 he submitted his alphabet to the head men of the Cherokee Nation, and after their approval the members of the tribe began to study it. It is said that after a few months thousands of Cherokee Indians could read and write in their own language. Later, parts of the Bible were translated into Cherokee, and in 1828 *The Cherokee Phoenix,* a weekly newspaper in Cherokee and English, was printed.

Sequoya died in 1843 in Mexico where he had gone to try to locate a lost band of Cherokee. The giant redwood in California is named for him. See CHEROKEE, HALF-BREED, INDIAN LANGUAGE, PICTURE WRITING.

**SERPENT MOUND.** Great earthworks, shaped in the form of a serpent, located in northern Adams County, Ohio. The Serpent Mound, it has been determined, was built by the Adena people long before the arrival of Columbus. In 1900 Harvard College donated the mound to the Ohio Archeological and Historical Society. There is a smaller serpent mound near Galena, Illinois. See MOUND BUILDERS.

**SEWAN** (se'-wan). The name for loose shell money much used by Dutch settlers in the New Netherlands. It is from the Narraganset Indian word *siwan*. A string or band of sewan was known as wampum. See WAMPUM.

**SHABONEE** (shab-o-neh'). A noted chief of the Potawatomi Indians and grandnephew of Pontiac. Shabonee's father was an Ottawa Indian who fought under the great chief, Pontiac. Shabonee was one of Tecumseh's lieutenants and was at the side of that celebrated Shawnee leader when he was killed in the War of 1812.

Shabonee became angered at the treatment of the Indian allies by the British after Tecumseh's death, and he joined the Potawatomi and was chosen their peace chief. From that time on he was a friend of the Americans and kept the Potawatomi from joining in the Black Hawk War.

On several occasions Shabonee warned settlers of danger from hostile Indians and one night after a hard ride from Princeton, Illinois, he reached Chicago in time to put the citizens on their guard against an attack. He died in Morris, Illinois, in 1859 at the age of eighty-four. A monument, consisting of a large granite boulder, was erected over his grave in Evergreen Cemetery, Morris, Illinois, in 1903. See BLACK HAWK, PONTIAC, POTAWATOMI, TECUMSEH.

**SHAGANAPPI** (shag'-a-napi). Thongs or strings of rawhide used for making cord or rope. See RAWHIDE.

**SHAMAN** (sha'-man). A priest, conjurer, or medicine man. See MEDICINE MAN, SECRET SOCIETIES.

**SHASTA** (shas'-ta). A tribe of Indians of California, now practically extinct, who at one time lived along the Klamath River. Their name is preserved in Mount Shasta.

**SHAWNEE** (shaw'-nee). A leading tribe of Algonquian Indians, who formerly lived in what is now South Carolina, Tennessee, Pennsylvania, and Ohio. The Shawnee—whose name meant "southerners"— were also called *Shawano, Savannuca,* and *Savannah.* They are best known for strongly opposing the advance of settlements through the Ohio Valley, and because of their celebrated chief, Tecumseh.

The Shawnee early came under the influence of the French and fought on their side. They were with Pontiac at the siege of Detroit, and for a period of forty years from the beginning of the French and Indian War until 1795, were at war with the English or the Americans. From the latter date their great chief Black Hoof kept the majority of his tribe friendly to the Americans.

Later, however, a part of the Shawnee joined with the Creek and Cherokee in the south, while the more hostile went with the Delaware in Indiana. It was this latter group—stirred by the preaching of a medicine man, Tenskwátawa, called "The Prophet," and a brother of Tecumseh—who gathered at the mouth of the Tippecanoe River in Indiana, where they were defeated in 1811 by General William Henry Harrison.

In the War of 1812 Tecumseh led the hostile group of Shawnee and allied tribes on the side of the British. Following his defeat and death in 1813 at the battle of the Thames River in Canada, most of the tribes accepted peace terms.

Today the Shawnee live in Oklahoma. Their name is preserved in various forms in several states, but most prominently in Georgia where the Savannah River and the city of Savannah are named for them. There are towns named Shawnee in Colorado, Kansas, Ohio, and Wyoming; Shawnee-on-Delaware in Pennsylvania; Shawnee in Tennessee; Shawano in Wisconsin; and Shawneetown both in Illinois and Missouri. See BLACK HOOF, CORNSTALK, PONTIAC, TECUMSEH, TIPPECANOE.

**SHEEPEATERS.** See SHOSHONI.

**SHIELD.** A piece of protective armor made of a rawhide-covered frame which was carried into battle by mounted Indians. In the days of the bow and arrow and the lance, the shield was an important part of a warrior's equipment.

As shields were considered sacred objects and were believed to bring good luck, some were preserved by tribes even after the use of firearms became general. These shields were hung on poles to the east of warriors' lodges as charms to ward off danger.

A warrior prized his shield from the time he first received it until his death, when it was laid under his head in his final resting place—unless he had given it to some worthy younger warrior before that.

In a dream or vision, the "shield spirit" told a warrior exactly how his shield should be made, painted, and decorated. The warrior then explained this to a medicine man who made the shield. Enemy scalps might be added as a part of the decoration.

Shields were fashioned from the thick hide of the neck or shoulder of the buffalo. To prepare this hide for a war shield, it was staked down on the bottom of a hole six or eight inches deep and covered with dirt. A fire was kept burning over it for several days. After this processing, the hide would be shrunken and very thick.

The shield was carried into battle on the left arm by a band which passed over the shoulder in such a way as not to interfere with the use of the left hand in holding the bow. When not in use it was swung around and hung down the back. See FEATHERWORK, FIRE MAKING, LANCE, RAWHIDE, SCALPING.

**SHOSHONI** (sho-sho'-ne). A branch of the Uto-Aztecan family, who formerly occupied a vast area including what is now southeastern Oregon, Idaho, western and southern Montana, northern Utah, Nevada, and western Wyoming. They also were called Snakes and the tribe was known as the Snake Nation. The largest group was the Wind River Shoshoni of Wyoming.

The name Snakes had already been given these Indians when Lewis and Clark came across them at the headwaters of the Missouri River in 1805. Some say it came from their former habit of eating snakes. However, the term Snakes later was applied to those living on the Snake River in Idaho and a few bands in Oregon. Another band was known as "Sheep-eaters," a name said to have been given them because they lived on the flesh of mountain sheep at a time when they fled from their enemies.

The northern and eastern Shoshoni early obtained horses from their kinsmen, the Comanche. They soon became horse and buffalo-hunting Indians and lived in tepees. Others, however, in the sagebrush country, lived in roofless grass huts which were little more than windbreaks.

Shoshoni men were smaller than the average Indian. The women, too, were short in stature, with rounded faces. Men wore headdresses imitating those of the Crow, Flathead, and Dakota.

The Shoshoni were at war in the early days with the Blackfoot, Dakota, Cheyenne, and Arapaho. With the Kiowa and Comanche they formed a long line of defense from Montana to Mexico, with the Rockies at their back.

The name Shoshoni has been applied to rivers and mountains in Wyoming and Nevada; to a lake in Yellowstone National Park; to Shoshoni Falls on the Snake River; a county in Idaho; and places in California, Idaho, Nevada, and Wyoming. See BANNOCK, COMANCHE, HORSE, HORSE INDIANS, KIOWA, LEWIS, SACAJAWEA.

**SIGNALS.** Signs made by Indians to communicate information over great distances. Signals were made with the pony, blanket, mirror, smoke, fire-arrow, and many other things.

In signaling with a pony an Indian rode in a circle, or backward and forward. In some tribes the size of the circle, or the distance ridden up and down the crest of a hill, denoted the size of the party seen by the signaler or the quantity of game spotted. Should the Indian, after giving his signal, suddenly hide himself and his pony, this meant danger.

The blanket signal could be seen for long distances. The Indian would grasp the corners of the blanket with his right and left hands and swing it back and forth before him in a vertical curve. As the blanket went to the left, the left hand almost touched the ground, and the same when it went to the right. Indians could give many signals with a blanket. Sweeping it two or three times in front as described above was the sign for question, and usually was the first signal given. If the blanket was brought near the ground and almost spread out, the signal meant an armistice or cessation of hostilities.

Indians had an extensive code in signaling with mirrors. The principal use of the mirror was to attract attention, give warning, or by a number of flashes agreed upon by sender and receiver, to convey a message. Naturally the mirror could be used only when the sun shone. A young man, in courting a girl, sometimes used a mirror to attract her attention, signaling from a small hill near camp.

Smoke signals were much like those of the mirror, in that codes were used. A small fire was built of dry wood and then grass or green brush was thrown on it. A blanket was held over the fire and removed at intervals, sending up puffs of smoke that spelled out a message.

Indians also used fire-arrows at night. Sometimes, too, figures or pictures were made on the ground or on trees or rocks to convey information to other members of the tribe, or to members of another tribe. If a pipe were drawn on a rock, for instance, it meant peace; if a tomahawk, war. See COWBOY, SIGN LANGUAGE.

**SIGN LANGUAGE.** A language of signs and gestures closely related to the Indian's picture writing, by which different tribes of Plains Indians communicated with one another. It was similar in a way to the sign language of deaf-mutes, only Indians had no alphabet and could not spell out words, but made signs for things and ideas.

The sign language is said to have originated in the buffalo country when different tribes came together during a hunt and by signs and gestures indicated whether they were friendly or hostile. It spread throughout the Plains

country and in time reached such a stage of perfection that it was easily understood by Indians of different tribes. Indians living close together, such as the Cheyenne and the Arapaho, did not trouble to learn each other's language, but communicated by the sign language.

In the sign language one or both hands was used. The Indian pointed to the position in the sky where the sun would be to say that a certain event happened at a certain time of day. To indicate a full day he would point to the east and move his finger over his head to the west. If an Indian wanted to hold a private conversation with someone, he would first point to himself, then to the other and finally to the place where they could be alone—or out of sight of others.

The sign for "man" was made by throwing out the hand, back outward, with the index finger extended upward, showing man was an animal that walked erect. "Woman" was indicated by a sweeping downward movement of the hand at the side of the head, with fingers extended toward the hair, to denote the combing of long hair. To designate a Blackfoot Indian the sign-talker would touch his moccasin and then rub his finger on something black.

Just as some languages please the ear, Indian sign language "talked" by experts, pleased the eye. Said one writer: "In fluent grace of movement a conversation in the sign language between a Cheyenne and a Kiowa is the very poetry of motion." See ARAPAHO, CHEYENNE, CHINOOK JARGON, COUNTING, INDIAN LANGUAGE, PICTURE WRITING, SIGNALS, TRADING LANGUAGES.


**SINEW.** Animal fiber used by Indians mainly as thread for sewing or stitching articles together. This fiber consisted of the large tendon lying along each side of the backbone—just back of the neck joint— of the buffalo, cow, horse, deer, and other animals. The tendon usually was about two feet long.

The tendon was stripped out and dried. When needed it was pounded to soften it, and then shredded into any thickness desired. Sometimes several small shreds would be twisted together by rolling them on the thigh with the palm of the hand. Indian women chewed sinew to soften it before use.

Sinew was employed in all kinds of sewing, and for attaching beads and porcupine quills. Moccasins and clothing were stitched with it. Bows were strengthened by backing them with sinew, and arrowheads and feathers were lashed to the arrow shaft with sinew. The Hidatsa made an arrowhead of buffalo sinew. See ARROW, BEADS, BOW, QUILLWORK.

**SIOUAN** (soo'-an) **FAMILY.** The language family of Indians next largest to the Algonquian, the major portion of whom lived from the west bank of the Mississippi River northward from Arkansas nearly to the Rocky Mountains.

**SIOUX** (soo). See DAKOTA, SOUTHERN SIOUX.

**SISSETON** (si-se'-ton). A tribe of the Dakota Sioux now grouped under Santee. Also a reservation in North Dakota. See DAKOTA.

**SITTING BULL.** Famous Sioux warrior, medicine man, tribal chief of the Hunkpapa Sioux, and leader of the allied tribes in the Custer battle. Sitting Bull was born in 1834 on the Grand River in South Dakota. As a boy he was known as Jumping Badger.

He was barely ten when he went on his first buffalo hunt and at fourteen he counted his first coup on a fallen enemy when he accompanied a war party against the Crow Indians. He took the name Four Horns, and not until 1857 when he "made medicine" did he change his name to *Tatanka Yotanka,* or Sitting Buffalo Bull.

Sitting Bull was on the warpath continually from 1869 to 1876. It was in this latter year that he and others of his tribe refused to go on a reservation. In an attempt to round up the Indians, General Custer met disaster at Little Big Horn where Sitting Bull had concentrated between 2,500 and 3,000 Indian warriors. At the time of the actual battle Sitting Bull was said to have been in the hills "making medicine," but this was later refuted.

He took a party of Sioux into Canada where they remained until 1881. Upon surrendering they were placed on reservations.

Sitting Bull encouraged the organizing of the first Ghost Dance at the Standing Rock Agency in North Dakota, becoming the recognized leader of the Ghost Dance religion. He was killed by Indian police on December 15, 1890, when they claimed he resisted arrest.

The story of the early life of this remarkable Indian is preserved in picture writing, drawn by himself shortly before his death.

Sitting Bull was buried in Fort Yates, North Dakota. In 1953 his bones were dug up by Gray Eagle and a band from Bullhead, South Dakota, and transferred to Mobridge, South Dakota. A dispute arose among the authorities as to which state was entitled to Sitting Bull's remains. However, it is now unlikely they will ever be moved again. See AMERICAN HORSE, BURIAL, CRAZY HORSE, CUSTER'S LAST STAND, DAKOTA, GALL, GHOST DANCE, LANCE, MEDICINE MAN, PICTURE WRITING, RAIN-IN-THE-FACE.

**SIWASH** (si'-wosh). A Chinook jargon term for Indian, derived from the French *sauvage.* There were no Siwash Indians, as some believe. See CHINOOK JARGON, SAUVAGE.

**SIX NATIONS. See IROQUOIS.**

**SLAVES.** Persons held as property by others. Slavery was common to some Indian tribes in America. Until the coming of the white man, slaves usually were other Indians captured in war and held within the tribe. Later Indians learned the trading value of slaves.

The Navajo, after the Spanish had taken some of their tribesmen into slavery, began to make slaves of Mexican and Spanish men, women, and children.

Although there is little evidence that slavery was widespread in pre-Columbus days, it is known that the Tlingit of the Northwest were old-time slaveholders. Their slaves were war prisoners and often were killed either in anger or as a sacrifice. The Tlingit had a special implement known as a "slave killer."

The French in the early days obtained many Pawnee slaves, captured by other tribes especially for sale to the French. Such slaves were known as *Panis,* another word for Pawnee, but which later became a word meaning any Indian slave. The last auction of Indian slaves was held in Montreal in 1797.

The Natchez of the South owned many Negro slaves. It has been recorded that in 1825 the Cherokee owned Negro slaves, the tribe as a whole having 1,275 in that year. The Creek, Choctaw, and Chickasaw also learned the value of such slaves and when runaway Negroes fell into their hands they held them. It was not long before all these tribes were buying and selling slaves. The Seminole, on the other hand, treated runaway slaves differently and adopted them into the tribe. It was this practice that brought on the First Seminole War.

Following the Civil War all Indian nations holding slaves were forced to free them. This, of course, included the Cherokee, Creek, Choctaw, and Chickasaw, of the Five Civilized Tribes of Oklahoma. In many cases the freed slaves were adopted into the tribes.

There are many stories of the early white settlers using Indians as slaves. Those of South Carolina at one time carried back to Charleston the entire population of seven Indian villages—1,400 persons—and sold them among other settlers as slaves. In New England the early colonists gave vanquished Indians the choice of entering villages of "Praying Indians" or being sold into slavery. See CAPTIVES, FIVE CIVILIZED TRIBES, NATCHEZ, PAWNEE, PRAYING INDIANS, SEMINOLE, TLINGIT, TORTURE.

**SLEEP.** An Indian term for a day. See CALENDAR.

**SMITH, CAPTAIN JOHN** (1580–1631). An English explorer and adventurer, who in 1605 joined a London Company expedition to colonize Virginia. He was captured by Powhatan and his life allegedly was saved by Pocahontas.

Captain Smith was elected president of the colony in 1608, but returned to England the following year. Two years later he was back in Virginia and remained there for seven years. See POCAHONTAS, POWHATAN.

**SMOKE SIGNAL.** See SIGNALS.

**SNAKE DANCE.** The Snake Ceremony of the Hopi Indians. This dance was a prayer for rain in which the snake priests carried live snakes—bull snakes, whip snakes, and rattlesnakes—in their mouths while they danced around the plaza of their village. At the end of the dance the snakes were carried to the edge of the village and turned loose as messengers to the rain gods, with whom they were supposed to win favor.

The only venomous snake used in this dance was the rattlesnake. As far as is known the fangs of the rattlers were not removed, but the priests, because of their skill in handling these dangerous reptiles, seldom were bitten. But just in case they should be bitten, tribal medicine was made before the dance. Among common cures for snake-bite in the Southwest was the placing of a part of the belly of the snake on the wound. See DANCE, HOPI, PUEBLO INDIANS.


**SNAKES.** See SHOSHONI.


**SONGS.** The Indian had a song for almost every occasion. Songs were a part of tribal life; there were songs for every public ceremony, as well as a song for each important act in the career of an individual.

Some songs had no words but were sung with vocal sounds, much like parts of cowboys' songs which go "com-ma, ti-yi-youpy, ya." But with the Indian, once these vocables were set to melodies they were never changed.

Songs belonged to clans, societies, and to individuals. Clans and societies had special officers to see that the songs were sung properly by the members who had a right to sing them, and if anyone made a mistake in singing he had to pay a penalty. Also, when a mistake was made, the dance or ceremony was stopped and begun over again.

An individual had songs which often came to him during fasting and in his dreams, taught him, he believed, by his protecting spirit. Only the individual could sing his song, unless, as was a practice among some tribes, the privilege was purchased by another. There was a song for setting traps, courtship, playing games, and for facing death. The so-called death song of an Indian was not one sung in defiance, but one sung as an appeal to his protector to save him.

During ceremonies dancers followed the beat of the drum, which usually differed from the rhythm of the song being sung. The beat of the drum was supposed to govern the movements of the legs, body, and arms, while the song, in a different rhythm, had to do with the feelings. At times there were as many as three rhythms, or a rhythm within a rhythm in the singing, and a different rhythm for the drum.

When men and women sang together, the women usually sang in a higher octave than the men singers. Among the Cherokee and other southern tribes "round singing" was common, with sometimes as many as two or three hundred men and women joining in.

Women composed and sang the lullaby and spinning and grinding songs. Among the Pueblo Indians, men joined in, while women ground grain and beat time on the floor or ground. Women also composed and sang songs to encourage warriors or hunters when they left camp for battle or the hunt. See DANCE, DRUM, MUSICAL INSTRUMENTS, WOMEN.


**SOUTHERN SIOUX** (soo). Siouan tribes which included the Iowa, Kansa, Missouri, Omaha, Osage, Oto, and Ponca. These tribes differed from those of the Dakota group in that, besides being buffalo-hunters, they also were farmers and did not live in tepees except when on the march. Their regular houses were oven-shaped, covered with earth, and grouped into villages. It is notable that three of these tribes gave their names to states.

The Iowa Indians at one time lived on the Platte River in Iowa. In 1824 they ceded all their lands to the Government and moved sometime later to reservations. The Oto were closely associated with the Iowa. The Kansa, sometimes called the Kaw, formerly lived on the Kansas River. The Missouri roamed that section of the Missouri River near the mouth of the Grand River. Warfare and disease almost wiped out this tribe.

The Omaha were at the mouth of the Missouri River for a time and later crossed into Iowa with the Ponca, but both were driven back by the powerful Dakota. The Ponca went into the Black Hills and the Omaha settled in Nebraska.

The Osage were once on the lower Missouri River but later ceded their lands, including most of Missouri and a part of Arkansas, to the whites. This tribe became one of the richest in the United States. By 1906 they had $8,562,690 in the United States Treasury after oil had been discovered on their Oklahoma reservation. For a time their individual income was greater than that of any other people on the earth.

The Iowa gave their name to the state, to two rivers, and a county;

to places in Wisconsin, Kansas, California, Louisiana, and Texas.

The Kansa Indians furnished the names for the river and state as well as the cities, and to places in Alabama, Illinois, Ohio, and Oklahoma; as Kaw, to places in Oklahoma, Kansas, and Wisconsin. The Omaha Indians provided the name for Omaha, Nebraska; and for places in Arkansas, Georgia, Illinois, Texas, Kentucky, and Virginia.

The name of the Osage Indians is preserved in that of the Osage River in Kansas and Missouri; a county in Oklahoma; places in Arkansas, Illinois, Oklahoma, Texas, and West Virginia; Osage Beach and Osage City, both in Missouri; and Osage City, Kansas. One of the popular names for *bois d'arc*, the favorite wood for making bows among the tribes of the southern Plains, is Osage orange.

The Oto Indians have places in Iowa and Missouri named for them; and in the form of Otoe, the name is given to a county and a village in Nebraska. The Ponca Indians gave their name to the Ponca River in South Dakota and Ponca City, Oklahoma; as well as places in Arkansas and Nebraska.

The name of the Missouri Indians is associated with the river and state; also Missouri City, Missouri; Missouri City, Texas; Missouri Valley, Iowa; and Missouri Branch, West Virginia. See DAKOTA, MISSOURI, WINNEBAGO.


**SPEAR.** See LANCE.


**SPOKAN.** A tribe of Indians who once lived on the Spokane and Little Spokane rivers in the state of Washington. They gave their name to the city of Spokane, as well as the river in Washington and Idaho.


**SPOTTED TAIL.** A Brûlé Teton Sioux who, like Chief Red Cloud, rose from the ranks. When he was nineteen years old he won his wife by fighting a knife duel with a subchief, in which he was severely

wounded. When Spotted Tail recovered from his wounds he found himself famous.

Later, when his tribe was to be punished for killing some soldiers, Spotted Tail and two others marched into Fort Laramie, Wyoming, in full war dress, chanting their death songs, and gave themselves up as the killers so that their tribe might be spared. He was subsequently released. In 1865, when thirty-two years old, he became chief of the Lower Brûlé.

During the troubles with the Sioux after the discovery of gold in the Black Hills and the Custer disaster, Spotted Tail was appointed chief of all the Dakota Sioux agencies. This was his reward from the Government for not having taken part in the troubles. He arranged for the surrender of his nephew, Crazy Horse, who had led the Oglala Sioux in the Custer battle.

Spotted Tail was killed near the Rosebud agency in South Dakota on August 5, 1881, by a tribesman named Crow Dog. It was charged that Spotted Tail was leading a hostile party against Crow Dog at the time, and Crow Dog shot in self-defense. Spotted Tail was sixty-eight at the time of his death. See BIG MOUTH, CRAZY HORSE, DAKOTA, RED CLOUD.

**SQUANTO** (skwan'-to). A Wampanoag Indian very friendly to the Pilgrims, often mentioned in their chronicles as an interpreter and guide. His Indian name was *Tisquantum*. See PILGRIMS.

**SQUAW.** A Narraganset Indian word for "woman." This term was adopted into the white man's language to mean an Indian wife. See WOMEN.

**SQUAW MAN.** The name given to a white man who was married to an Indian woman. The term "squaw man" was sometimes used as one of contempt, but it was by no means justified in this sense. Many prominent men married Indian women.

Granville Stuart, one of the biggest cattlemen in Montana, and author of *Forty Years on the Frontier*, married an Indian woman. When she died he married another. E. C. Abbot, known as "Teddy Blue," and also a prominent Montana rancher, married one of Stuart's daughters. In his book *We Pointed Them North* he said that all white men he had ever known who were married to Indian women "thought the world of them." Henry Rowe Schoolcraft, the authority on the American Indian, was happily married to an Indian woman.

While it was true that some white men deserted their Indian wives when white women came to the frontier country, the majority of them remained loyal. See HALF-BREED, POCAHONTAS, SCHOOL-CRAFT, WOMEN.

**STANDING BEAR.** A Ponca Indian chief who had the distinction of having brought about the first ruling in the U.S. courts that "an Indian is a person within the meaning of the law of the United States." This ruling was given by Judge Dundy. See BRIGHT EYES, INDIAN.

**STANDISH, MILES** (1584–1656). Military leader of the Pilgrims in their fights with the Indians. Miles Standish, a native of Lancashire, England, had previously served with the British army in the Netherlands. He sailed with the *Mayflower* colony to Massachusetts in 1620, but five years later, the colony being in distress, he was sent back to England. He returned the following year, and later settled at Duxbury, Massachusetts, serving as magistrate for life. See PILGRIMS.

**STARS.** Indians were keen and interested observers of the stars. Just as a rock, a river, a tree, the earth, the night, the storm—everything in nature—was a spirit or man-being to them, so was a star in the Indian's mythology. Some worshiped certain stars, while others believed they foretold important events, such as weather conditions.

The Great Dipper, known as "The Clock of the Yaquis," was used in the Southwest to tell the time of night. The Great Dipper swung around the North Star every twenty-four hours, the clock's "hands" being the stars known to the white man as Alpha and Beta. By the relation of these "hands" to the North Star, the progress of the night could be determined. Cowboys learned this from the Indians and were able to "tell time" during the long hours of night herding.

The Arapaho called the Great Dipper the "Broken Back." Mars they termed "The Big Star"; Jupiter, "The Morning Star," and when it was an evening star they called it "The Lance." Other tribes called Jupiter "The Winter Star." Venus was "The Day Star."

The Pawnee Indians worshiped the Morning Star. They knew enough about stars, they claimed, to foretell weather conditions by them, and the proper time to plant maize.

The Dakota believed that Ursa Major, or the Great Bear, represented a band of foxes. The king of the foxes had been killed in the "Bear's Tepee," which was that cluster of stars to the left of the Dipper. The four stars, Alpha, Beta, Gamma, and Delta, which form the square, were those who were carrying the dead king in a blanket.

The Dakota termed Epsilon, or Alioth, in the Great Bear, the "Medicine Man." Zeta, or Mizar, the middle star in the Dipper handle, was "the woman with the baby on her back," the baby being Alcor, the little star just above Mizar. Alcor, barely visible to the naked eye, was used by the Dakota as well as other Indians to test the keenness of a warrior's eyesight.

Some Indians while smoking, would point the stem of the pipe at these stars, and pray that they would be released so that they would not have to wander continually on their circular trail. See MAN-BEING, PAWNEE, PETALESHARO.


**STEAM HORSE.** Indian term for a railroad locomotive.

**STINKERS.** See NATCHEZ.

**STOCKBRIDGE INDIANS.** See MAHICAN.

**STONE BOILING.** A method of heating water for cooking by placing hot stones in it. This was one of the earliest forms of cooking among Indians, and was practiced when containers were too fragile to stand direct contact with the fire.

Stone boiling was done in baskets made watertight by being lined with clay or pitch, or in bark containers. Among some of the Plains Indians a hole was made in the ground, which was lined with a hide, or a buffalo's or deer's paunch was suspended from four sticks stuck in the ground. Such containers were filled with water, and the stones to be added were placed in a fire and heated red hot. They were lifted one by one with a pair of sticks, or tongs, and dropped into the water. When the water began to boil the food was placed in it. See BARK CRAFT, BASKETS, BUFFALO, DEER, FOOD.

**SUCCOTASH** (suk'-o-tash). The Narraganset Indian name for an ear of corn. The white man later used the term to describe an Indian dish of green corn and green beans.

**SUN DANCE.** The greatest and most important ceremony of the Plains Indians. The Sun Dance was a religious ceremony, in which the Indian fulfilled a vow made to some mysterious force in nature. For instance, when surrounded by foes, he promised the god in the sun—or what the white man termed the Great Spirit—that if he were delivered from the hands of his enemy he would, when the time came, dance the Sun Dance. Also he might promise to perform this dance if some sick relative or friend were restored to health.

Thus the Indian made his vow that in return for help he would submit to physical suffering and torture as well as to fasting. He believed that this god, as well as all other gods, could be moved to pity if one were willing to suffer pain and anguish long enough.

The Sun Dance usually was held during the full moon in June. It lasted several days. First the Sun Dance pole, a straight tall tree, was selected by the medicine man. This tree was cut down and brought with much ceremony to the place of the dance, four halts being made while the Indians smoked and prayed to the Sun God. Finally on the second day a feast was held and the pole was planted in the ground.

An army officer, Captain W. P. Clark, who attended a Sun Dance in the camp of the Sioux chief, Crazy Horse, in 1877, described it thus:

"Those who were to dance only had for clothing a wrapping about their loins; sometimes, I was told, they only wore a breech-cloth. They each had an attendant, who painted him, filled his pipe, rubbed the palms of his hands with sage and other green herbs, and talked encouragingly to him. They seemed to need the encouragement, for they were faint and weak from fasting and the fear of the horrible torture awaiting them.

"Around them were feasting and laughter. The circular shed was filled with people, who had brought huge kettles of food. Later the women kinsfolk, wives, sisters, and sweethearts, came in singing and had their arms slashed by the medicine man's knife, thus endeavoring to support with their suffering the pain and the torture being undergone by the men.

"Finally one of the dancers was laid with his head near the foot of the Sun Dance pole, and two holes were cut in the muscles of his chest, through which two sticks or skewers were thrust. To each of these sticks a string was fastened; then the victim was lifted up, and the strings were fastened to a lariat hanging from the pole. The victim now blew on a whistle made from the bone of an eagle's wing, looked at the sun and its course from its rising to its setting, and until he could free himself by tearing out the flesh and muscles, dancing, whistling, praying for deliverance, and making other requests."

The Sun Dance was performed by the Arapaho, Cheyenne, Siksika, Cree, Dakota, Assiniboin, Mandan, Crow, Ponca, Omaha, Pawnee, Kiowa, Shoshoni, and Ute. Of all these tribes the Cheyenne and Arapaho are said to have performed the dance in its most complete form. Today it is held only as a ceremony and without any of the torture or hardships. See ARAPAHO, CAMP, CHEYENNE, DANCE, EAGLE, WHISTLE.

**SUNS.** See NATCHEZ.

**SURROUND, THE.** An Indian method of hunting buffalo. See BUFFALO.

**SUSQUEHANNA** (sus-kwe-han'-a). An Iroquois tribe, also known as Conestoga, which lived on the Susquehanna River in New York, Pennsylvania, and Maryland. It is believed the last of this tribe was killed by whites in 1763. The name Susquehanna was given the river, a county, and a town; as was Conestoga to three places in Pennsylvania. See CONESTOGA HORSE.

**SWEAT HOUSE.** See WICKIUP.

# T

**TAENSA** (ten'-sa). A tribe of Indians who at one time lived in southern Louisiana. They were noted for their peculiar customs, which were similar to those of the Natchez. The early French reported that they practiced human sacrifice. Their name was given to a parish, a river, and a bayou in Louisiana, and to a river and a village in Alabama. The tribe is believed to be extinct. See NATCHEZ.

**TAMMANY** (tam'-a-nee). A noted Delaware chief who was one of the signers of the deed to William Penn in 1683 for lands near Philadelphia. His name appears on the document as *Tamanen,* although the Indian form of the name was usually spelled *Tamanend.*

Tammany was held in high esteem among the Delaware of those days. Many legends surrounded him and his fame extended to the whites, who began to call him "Saint Tammany." As Patron Saint of America his name appeared on old calendars and Saint Tammany's Festival was celebrated on May 1 of each year. In 1786 a Saint Tammany Society was formed by veterans of the Revolutionary War. The society became so popular that it had thirteen state organizations.

In later years the Tammany Society continued to exist only as an eastern political organization. See DELAWARE, PENN.

**TANOAN** (ta'-no-an) **PUEBLOS.** Twelve pueblos or villages of the Pueblo Indians, the most famous of which are Taos, Isleta, San Ildefonso, and San Juan. Taos, fifty-two miles northeast of Santa Fé, New Mexico, was first visited by the Spaniards in 1540. It was later the home of Kit Carson. Isleta, twelve miles south of Albuquerque, New Mexico, also was discovered in 1540 and is said to stand today on the original site. San Ildefonso, eighteen miles northwest of Santa Fé, was the seat of a Spanish mission in 1617. San Juan, twenty-five miles northwest of Santa Fé, was the headquarters of the Spanish provisional government in 1598.

Other pueblos are Hano, Jemez, Nambe, Pojoaque, Picuris, Sandia, Santa Clara, and Tesuque, all in New Mexico. See CARSON, PUEBLO INDIANS.

**TARHE** (tar'-he). A noted Wyandot chief who was known by the French as Monsieur Grue (Crane) and by the English as Crane—both being translations of his Indian name. Tarhe fought under Chief Cornstalk at Point Pleasant, West Virginia, in 1774 and was one of the thirteen chiefs who participated in the Battle of Fallen Timbers in 1794 when the Indian allies met a disastrous defeat at the hands of General Anthony Wayne.

After this battle Tarhe sided with the Americans, and although seventy years old, led his warriors through the whole of General William Henry Harrison's campaign in the War of 1812. He was present when Tecumseh was slain at the Battle of the Thames.

Until his death at Cranetown, Ohio, in 1816, he was a friend of the Americans, and as chief priest of his tribe was keeper of the calumet which bound the tribes north of the Ohio River in a confederation for mutual benefit and protection. A mourning council at which the celebrated Red Jacket was present, was held after his death. See CORNSTALK, HURON, RED JACKET, TECUMSEH.

**TATTOOING.** The pricking and marking of the skin in patterns with indelible inks or pigments. The custom of tattooing was common to many Indian tribes throughout the United States.

Tattooing was practiced by the Seminole, Creek, Cherokee, and other Indians of the South. A boy was "scratched" when first named, and again "scratched" when he proved himself a warrior. The Wichita Indians were lavish in the use of this decoration. The Kiowa tattooed a circle on the forehead of women as a tribal mark. The Omaha pricked a small round dot on the forehead of a girl, and if her father or a near male relative had committed a brave deed, a four-pointed star was tattooed on her back and breast to honor this achievement.

Among the Osage Indians the keeper of the sacred pipe carried a tattooed design on his body, and if he had been successful in war and had cut off an enemy's head, he was entitled to have a skull tattooed on his back or breast. The Hupa Indians had ten lines tattooed along the inside of the left arm for the purpose of measuring strings of shell money. The Chippewa sometimes used tattooing to relieve pain, especially toothache. Mandan warriors had black parallel stripes tattooed on the left breast and arm. An Eskimo girl at maturity had a line tattooed at the edge of her lower lip. When she married two more lines were added. Eskimo men sometimes kept a record or tally of whales they had killed by tattoo marks on their cheeks, chests, or arms. Tattooing was done with steel needles, sharp flints, or cactus thorns tied in a bundle in the form of a brush. Inks were made from charcoal or charred box-elder wood, while the dyes injected to give color to the design varied in different sections of the country. See CHEROKEE, CHIPPEWA, CREEK, ESKIMO, HUPA, MANDAN, PAINT, PICTURE WRITING, SEMINOLE, WOMEN.

**TECUMSEH** (te-kum'-se). The celebrated Shawnee chief who sought to create a great Indian state in the Ohio Valley and the Great Lakes region by uniting the various tribes under one leader. Tecumseh is considered the most extraordinary Indian in United States history.

Tecumseh, the son of a chief, was born in 1768 near what is now Springfield, Ohio. His birthplace, a village called Piqua, later was destroyed by Kentuckians. His Indian name *Tikamthi* or *Tecumtha* indicated that he belonged to the clan of the Great Medicine Panther, or Meteor, and was interpreted "Crouching Panther," or "Sleeping Star."

This remarkable chief distinguished himself as a leader and for his humane qualities of character. His great influence with his own people is seen in the fact that he persuaded them to discontinue one of their most cherished customs—the practice of torturing prisoners.

Tecumseh opposed the advance of the white man, and denied the right of the Government to purchase land from a single tribe, claiming that the territory belonged to all tribes. To put an end to what he thought was an unjust practice, he sought to form a confederacy of all the western and southern tribes. He visited tribes from Florida to the headwaters of the Missouri River trying to bring them into his union.

But while Tecumseh was organizing the Indians, his brother, Tenskwatawa, "The Prophet," upset his plans by engaging the whites at the Battle of Tippecanoe in Indiana. The Indians were defeated.

Tecumseh then went to Canada and was there when the War of 1812 started. He was made a brigadier-general in command of some 2,000 warriors of allied tribes friendly to the British. He fought in many battles, but met defeat and death at the Battle of the Thames in Canada on October 5, 1813. He is said to have foreseen his fate, and wishing to die as an Indian, had removed his general's uniform and dressed himself in buckskin for the battle. For this reason it was difficult to identify his body. See KICKAPOO, KING PHILIP, LEATHER-LIPS, LITTLE TURTLE, PONTIAC, SHABONEE, SHAWNEE, TARHE, TIPPECANOE, TORTURE.

**TEKAKWITHA** (tek-a-kwith´-a), **CATHERINE.** A Mohawk Indian woman who became famous as "Lily of the Mohawks." She was also called "the Indian Saint" and was the first Indian to become a Catholic nun.

Catherine, or Kateri as she is sometimes called, was born in 1656 at Caugnahwaga, a palisaded town on the Mohawk River above Auriesville, New York. When she was twelve years old some Jesuit priests visited her village and stopped with her uncle, a bitter opponent of Christianity. However, the uncle, with whom Catherine lived, offered them the traditional Indian hospitality and the young girl waited on the priests, gaining her first knowledge of Christian faith and practice.

When on Easter Sunday, 1675, Catherine was baptized by Father Lamberville, she became the object of contempt and derision to many of her tribe. Her refusal to marry angered her aunt. When she observed the Sabbath and refused to work in the cornfields on that day, she was denied food and stoned. A young Mohawk warrior became so angered at her that he raised his tomahawk menacingly over her head, but the young girl awaited the blow with such calmness that the warrior became ashamed and slunk away.

Two years later some Catholic Christian Iroquois visited the village and, finding the young girl persecuted, carried her away in a canoe to Sault Saint Louis. Later she visited Montreal, took the vow of chastity, and became a nun.

Following Catherine's death on April 17, 1680, a priest while at prayer "had a vision in which Catherine arrayed in glory appeared to him." Both Indians and whites came to visit her tomb near the La Chine Rapids on the St. Lawrence River, and it was claimed that many who were sick became well. A memorial cross was erected to her at Auriesville, New York; and at St. Joseph's Seminary, Dunwoodie, New York, a statue stands in memory of her. See WOMEN.

**TENNESSEE.** The name of a state and river derived from that of two or more Cherokee settlements called by the Indians *Ta-nasi* or *Tansi*. The main Cherokee settlement of this name was on the Little Tennessee River, a short distance above the point at which it joins the main stream. Another settlement was on the extreme head branch of the Tuckasegee River above the present town of Webster, North Carolina.

**TENSKWATAWA** (ten-skwa'-ta-wa). Twin brother of Tecumseh, sometimes called "The Prophet." See SHAWNEE, TECUMSEH.

**TEPEE.** The dwelling or lodge of the Plains Indians. The word is from the Dakota *tipi*, meaning "the place where one lives." The Indian's tepee was found to be so ideal for prairie life that General Henry Hastings Sibley took it as a model for the famous Sibley tent of the United States Army.

The erection of a tepee was the work of women. First, three poles about 25 feet in length were lashed together at one end and set up to form a tripod—one pole to the east, one to the north, and one to the south. The east pole was the left-hand doorpost, as lodges always faced the east. From thirteen to twenty-three poles were then leaned against this tripod so that their bases formed a circle about 15 feet in diameter. The final pole to be set up was used to hoist the buffalo-hide covering, which was tied to it.

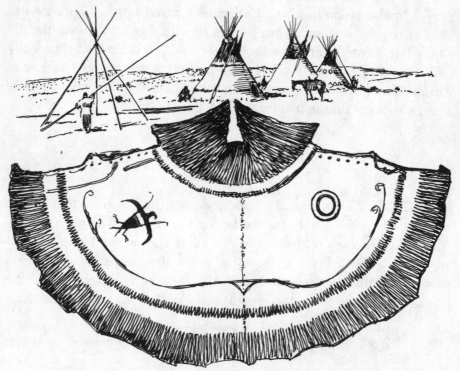

The tepee covering was made of fifteen to eighteen dressed buffalo hides, cut and fitted together and sewed so that they formed a large sheet nearly semicircular in shape. When placed on the framework of poles the edges of the covering were brought together in front and fastened by wooden pins. A space was left for the doorway, the "door" of which was a piece of dressed skin, usually ornamented.

The lower rim of the tepee was kept down by pegs driven into the ground. Flaps were left at the top as a kind of flue for regulating the smoke. These flaps could be adjusted by two poles, and when the wind changed the flaps were set so the flue would draw properly. The fire pit was in the center of the tepee. Beds were arranged on both sides of the door and in the back.

The skin covering of a tepee was decorated with symbols of the owner's own choosing. After a warrior had counted coup on an enemy tepee he could use this tepee's decoration on his own.

When camp was to be moved, women took down the tepees. The poles were lashed to the sides of dogs or horses to form a travois, the covering rolled up and packed on it. See CAMP, COUP, HOGAN, LODGE, PAINT, TRAVOIS, WICKIUP, WIGWAM, WOMEN.

**TETON** (te'-ton). See DAKOTA.


**TEXAS.** In the form of *Tejas* (tay'-has) this term was formerly applied by the Spaniards to the Hasinai Indian tribes of Angelina and the Upper Neches valleys and later to the territory they occupied—the state of Texas. However, before the coming of the Spaniards, the tribes of east Texas used the word as one of greeting, meaning "Welcome," or "Hello, friend!" It also meant "friends" or "allies."

The word "texas" was used later as a name for the "third story," surrounding the pilothouse, of a Mississippi River steamboat. See CADDO, COMANCHE.


**THAYENDANEGEA** (thay-en-dan'-ge). A celebrated Mohawk chief, popularly known as Joseph Brant. See BRANT.


**THORPE, JAMES FRANCIS (JIM).** The famous Indian football player of Carlisle School, considered by many to be the greatest all-around athlete of all time. In 1950 the Associated Press poll named him the outstanding athlete for the first half of the twentieth century, with Babe Ruth and Jack Dempsey as second and third.

Jim Thorpe's grandmother was a granddaughter of the Sauk and Fox chief, Black Hawk. Jim, whose Indian name was *Wathohuck* (Bright Path), was born in a one-room log cabin near Shawnee, Oklahoma, May 28, 1888. His twin brother died at the age of eight.

Jim Thorpe entered Carlisle in 1907, beginning his football career. In the 1912 Olympics, he set point totals in the decathlon and pentathlon which stood for twenty years.

Jim Thorpe died in Los Angeles, March 28, 1953, at the age of sixty-four. A few years later the boroughs of Mauch Chunk and East Mauch Chunk in Pennsylvania, voted to unite under the name of Jim Thorpe,

Pennsylvania. Thorpe's body was moved there in 1957 and a granite tomb dedicated to his memory. See CARLISLE.


**THROWING STICK.** A sling device, or grooved stick, for hurling a lance or spear. It was used before the introduction of the bow and arrow. The throwing stick was a sort of extension of the arm, and by placing the lance in the groove, greater force could be exerted in hurling the weapon. See BANNER STONES, LANCE.


**THUNDERBIRD.** A fabulous bird of great size which Indians believed produced thunder and lightning. While Plains Indians thought of this being as an actual bird, among some tribes of the Northwest it was not a bird but a giant who put on a dress of birdskin with head, wings, and all complete, by means of which it flew through the air in search of its prey.

The Thunderbird's shadow was the storm cloud, the flapping of its wings made the sound of thunder, and the rapid opening and closing of its flashing eyes sent forth the lightning. The heavy rainfall, which usually accompanied thunder and lightning, came from a lake of fresh water the bird carried on its back. Some Plains tribes believed that the thunderstorm resulted from a battle between the Thunderbird and a giant rattlesnake.

The Thunderbird usually had its dwelling on some high mountain or rocky elevation. Within the territory of those tribes who believed in this myth several places were known as Thunder's Nest. Thunder Bay of Lake Huron in lower Michigan obtained its name in this way.

The Thunderbird symbol was often used in Indian design. In Indian picture writing the Thunderbird is shown with zigzag lines running out from its heart to represent the lightning. The Thunderbird of the

Cheyenne and Arapaho carried in its talons a number of arrows with which to strike its enemy. These Indians recognized the eagle on United States coins as this same bird and called it *baa*, the name they gave the Thunderbird. See BULL-ROARER, EAGLE.

**TIPPECANOE** (tip-e-ka-noo'). The Miami Indian name for a river in Indiana, meaning "buffalo-fish place." It was also the name of a noted village site on the west bank of the Wabash River just below the mouth of the Tippecanoe River in the same state. The village was first occupied by the Miami and later by the Shawnee Indians.

It was here on November 7, 1811, that the Shawnee and their allies led by Tenskwatawa, "The Prophet," suffered one of their worst defeats by the United States troops, under General William Henry Harrison.

General Harrison won the name "Old Tippecanoe," and in the 1840 presidential campaign, with John Tyler as his running mate, he was swept into office with the slogan "Tippecanoe and Tyler, too." See SHAWNEE, TECUMSEH.

**TLINGIT** (tling'-git). A tribe of seafaring Indians and totem-pole-makers who lived along the southern coast and islands of Alaska. The Russian capital, when Russia owned Alaska, and the first American territorial capital, Sitka, was on Tlingit land, as is the present state capital, Juneau. The ports of the Tlingit Indians figured prominently in the great Klondike gold rush.

The Tlingit were expert fishermen and sea hunters. They put to sea in dugouts, some of them as long as sixty feet. They built their houses of planks split from the great cedar trees along the coast, and in front of each house was an elaborately carved totem pole. Totem poles were not made, however, until these Indians had received iron tools from the white man at about the beginning of the nineteenth century.

One of the odd customs of the Tlingit was the practicing of "potlatch," which meant the giving of a feast and the distribution of a

large amount of property. At such special feasts after the death of one of their tribe, slaves and property were given away. However, those who gave away property usually expected greater gifts in return. A wealthy man, as a way of boasting of his wealth, might kill a slave or two. Sometimes before a totem pole was placed in the ground a slave was killed and thrown into the hole. Special clubs were used as "slave killers," and these are eagerly sought today by white collectors.

The Tlingit never had a real war with the white people. Today the several thousand in Alaska are gradually adopting the ways of the whites. See ESKIMO, POTLATCH, SLAVES, TOTEM POLES. See also illustration, page 302.

**TOBACCO.** A sacred plant of the early Indians which was used in making offerings to their gods, in curing diseases, bringing good luck, and in sealing agreements and binding treaties. Early Europeans arriving in America found tobacco being used by the natives in many ways—in pipes, as cigarettes, and as cigars.

Indians made good will offerings to Columbus with tobacco leaves, and later he saw them smoking tobacco in the form of cigars. "These *muskets* as we call them, they call *tobacos*," one early Spanish writer recorded.

The astonishing thing about tobacco is that in less than a century after its discovery by the white man, its use had circled the globe. It was first introduced into Portugal and Spain in 1518; into France by Jean Nicot—from whose name came the word *nicotine*—in 1559; into Italy in 1560; Turkey, 1605; Russia, 1634; and into Arabia in 1663. It was carried to the Philippines by the Spanish, cultivated there, and exported to China, thence to Siberia and then to Alaska.

Some Indians along the Atlantic seaboard smoked for pleasure, but the general use of tobacco among Indians was of a ceremonial nature. It was used long before the coming of Columbus, as shown by pipes dug up at many prehistoric sites.

Indians usually did not like straight tobacco and mixed it with barks and herbs. This mixture was termed *kinnikinnick* by the Algonkin. The scarcity of tobacco, too, might have accounted in some cases for such a mixture. Among most Indians tobacco was cultivated by men alone and smoked only by them.

While Europeans later raised, cured, and compressed tobacco into cakes and sold it to the Indians, in their ceremonies the Indians would not use this tobacco. See CALUMET, KINNIKINNICK, PETUN.

**TOBACCO NATION.** Name given by the French to one division of the Huron because of their cultivation of tobacco.

**TOLOWA** (tol'-o-wa). A tribe of Indians who roamed the extreme northwest of California. What few there were abandoned their reservation in 1868 to shift for themselves. Some are believed still to live in California.

**TOMAHAWK.** A term given to a weapon of war or a group of such weapons in use by the early Algonquian tribes of the eastern United States. The word came from *tommahick, tomahack, tamahake,* or *tamahaac* of Virginian Indian dialects.

The tomahawk is usually thought of as a metal hatchet-shaped weapon, often with a pipe bowl on the end opposite the blade. In reality, such tomahawks were of European manufacture and were traded to Indians throughout America. The earlier native Indian tomahawks were in the form of war clubs, or hatchet-shaped stones lashed to handles of wood. See AX, BURY THE HATCHET, WAR CLUB.

**TOMOCHICHI** (to-mo-chi-chi'). A Creek chief noted in the early history of Georgia. For some reason he was outlawed by his people, and with a few followers settled on the spot where Savannah, Georgia, now stands, At the time of the founding of the Georgia Colony in 1733, he became friendly with the whites and helped bring about a treaty of alliance with the colonists and the Lower Creek Indians. At the same time his differences with his own tribe were settled.

The following year Tomochichi accompanied James Edward Oglethorpe, founder of the colony, to England. He was entertained, given many presents, and his portrait was painted. He remained a friend of the colonists until his death in 1739. He was given a public funeral at Savannah, where a monument to his memory was erected in 1899 by the Colonial Dames of America. See CREEK.

**TOM-TOM.** See DRUM.

**TOPEKA.** An Indian name for a potato-like root, which originally grew in the vicinity of the present city of Topeka, Kansas.

**TORTURE.** To inflict or subject to intense physical pain. Torturing their captive enemies seems to have been common practice among the early Indians. Indians only tortured prisoners when they had plenty of leisure time and were in the best of humor. It has been shown by historians that Indians never resorted to torture when they were angry. At such a time they might kill their enemy, but it was only when they were in good spirits and wanted to amuse themselves that they indulged in refined elements of torture and cruelty.

Victims sought in every way to make their tormentors angry, knowing that then they would quickly be killed and put out of pain.

There was another aspect to torturing. It gave the victims a chance to show their fortitude and bravery. They would taunt their captors and appear to relish the most terrible pain to show their scorn. But at the same time the victim would sing his death chant, which was actually an appeal to his protecting gods to save him, or to give him more courage to stand the pain.

Thus while the Indian during his spare time would delight in thinking up novel and more horrible ways to torture any prisoner who fell into his hands—to make him cry out in pain—he would also discipline himself to stand all kinds of pain so that he might never show by a groan or expression that he suffered under torture. When captured and tortured he wanted to prove a brave and honorable warrior.

Torture, then, was a kind of grim game—played by both the captor and the captive. There were cases when Indians who could undergo the most terrible torture without showing their pain by word or expression, were so admired by their captors that they were set free.

Women were notoriously more fiendish than men in torturing enemies. They would work themselves into fits of frenzy and would beat and stone prisoners to death. Old frontiersmen, finding the body of a victim with the head smashed by stones, would know this had been the work of women.

Fire was often used in various ways. Among Plains Indians, a victim might be staked out on an ant hill, where he would live for days. Or he might be buried up to his neck in the ground. Sometimes victims were sewed up in green rawhide and left in the sun. The rawhide would gradually shrink and crush them to death.

Running the gantlet was a favorite method of torture with the

Iroquois and allied tribes. The prisoner would be made to run between two lines of people armed with clubs, tomahawks, and other weapons. He would be spared if he reached the chief's house or some other place pointed out to him beforehand. Among the Creek any prisoner who broke away and hid in a chief's house was safe.

In early history some Indian tribes ate some of the flesh of their victims in order to acquire their virtues. Such an act was not one of true cannibalism. See CAPTIVES, HIAWATHA, SLAVES, TECUMSEH, WOMEN.

**TOTEM.** A natural object, usually an animal, taken by a tribe, a family, or a single individual, as a patron or guarding spirit. The word comes from the Chippewa *ototeman,* meaning "his brother-sister kin." The totem was the Indian's coat-of-arms.

Most Indians believed they had an animal-human ancestor. Such an ancestor usually was a bear, wolf, beaver, fox, or perhaps an owl, eagle, or raven. A trader among the Chippewa in the late 1700's wrote:

"One part of the religious superstition of the Savages, consists in each of them having his *totam,* or favorite spirit, which he believes watches over him. This *totam* they conceive assumes the shape of some beast or other, and therefore they never kill, hunt or eat the animal whose form they think this *totam* bears."

Indians had various ways of finding their totem. Among the Omaha, for instance, a youth acquired his totem through a vision after a fast. He might have seen a bear or something having to do with a bear. In such a case his individual totem was the bear. Thus he might become a member of the Bear Society of the tribe, which consisted of others who had the bear as their totem. See BEAR, CLAN, DREAMS, FASTING, FOOD, MEDICINE, TOTEM POLES, TRIBE.

**TOTEM POLES.** Carved cedar posts erected by some Indian tribes along the Pacific Coast and in Alaska. The animals shown on the totem pole comprised the family coat-of-arms, and indicated the different clans which had married into the family. The poles were brilliantly painted. See CLAN AND GENS, PAINT, TLINGIT, TOTEM. See also illustration, page 302.

**TRADING LANGUAGES.** Common languages used for purposes of trade between Indians of different tribes, and sometimes between Indians and whites. See CHINOOK JARGON, CHOCTAW, COMANCHE, MOBILE, SIGN LANGUAGE.

**TRADING POSTS.** Posts established by the white man for trade or commerce with the Indians. The earliest trade was between Indians of the Northeast and Basque sailors who followed the whale to the fishing banks of Newfoundland. The most famous of the trading posts were those of the Hudson's Bay Company, which obtained an English royal charter in 1670.

President George Washington in 1796 established the first official trading posts of the United States, with the object of seeing that Indians got a fair return for their furs and other articles, and to protect them from the evils of liquor. In 1806 the office of Superintendent of Indian Trade was created, but sixteen years later all official trading houses were abolished by law, because of the opposition of private traders.

From colonial days until the falling off of the fur trade in the last century, wars were frequent between whites and Indians because of the rivalry of traders. Posts were scattered along the rivers from the Great Lakes region to the Pacific Coast. St. Louis was one of the great outfitting centers for traders.

Many important cities grew out of old-time trading posts. Kansas City today marks the spot where traders journeying up the Missouri River by boat parted from those going by land. The Oregon Trail, branching into the Santa Fé Trail 41 miles to the west of Kansas City, was the trade route to the Southwest, with Santa Fé, New Mexico, as the terminus.

Trading posts established along the Oregon Trail—Forts Laramie, Bridger, Hall, Boise, Wallawalla, Vancouver, and Astoria—also are cities today. The same is true of the principal posts along the lakes and rivers. Detroit, Prairie du Chien, Council Bluffs, Pierre, Mandan, Spokane, and many other cities today stand on the sites of old trading posts. See FUR TRADE, TRAILS.


**TRAIL (TO).** To follow a series of "sign." Sign, always used in the singular, meant any evidence that something or someone had been on the ground. A broken blade of grass, a stone that had been moved, a moccasin track, a bead, or a feather that had been dropped—all these were sign and might lead to a trail.

So to the Indian—and the white frontier scout—trailing was the art of making a trail out of sign. A trailer needed good, sharp eyes, perfect knowledge of the appearance and character of the sign made by whatever was being trailed, and familiarity with the country and habits of other Indians and of animals.

Trailing was one of the most important and necessary parts of the education of the Indian. Without this knowledge he could not disguise his own trail, or follow the trail of his enemies, and in many parts of the country he would have starved to death if he could not read sign of food animals. He was taught from childhood to note every mark on the ground, to know what made this mark, how old it was, and everything about it of importance to himself. His daily life as a hunter made him familiar with the habits of all animals and how to read sign.

In traveling the Indian relied on landmarks. He would note certain clumps of trees, certain hills, streams, rock formations, and many other things which would enable him to find his way back on a trail, or pick out a trail to a certain point. Indians, knowing how their enemies depended on the same things, could follow them by being certain they, too, were relying on such landmarks. After a time those who were trailing might be able to determine just where the others were headed and so take a short cut and intercept them.

By moccasin tracks an Indian trailer might determine the tribe to which the one he was trailing belonged. He could tell whether the other was running or walking. If running, only the ball of the foot touched the ground. If the fugitive were trying to throw his pursuer off the trail by walking backwards, his steps were shorter, and the pursuer would notice this. In following pony tracks the trailer could tell whether the pony was carrying a weight by the depth of the tracks. The position of the hoof mark would show whether the pony was walking, trotting, or galloping.

The Indian trailer was alert to everything. If the one he trailed did not leave tracks, the trailer might determine the direction in which the other was going by noting the tracks of animals frightened out of his path. Flocks of birds rising over wooded sections showed that someone was moving along on the ground and frightening them.

If a fugitive tried to cover his tracks by wading up or down a stream, the trailer first looked for the trail on the same side of the water where the other had entered it. Usually a man would come out of the water on this same side. But there was always the question of whether he had done this deliberately or through force of habit, and so the trailer had to reason out whether he had a cunning or a thoughtless man to deal with. Trailing became a game and a matching of wits between the pursuer and the pursued. See COWBOY, INDIAN SIGN, MOCCASIN.

**TRAIL-BLAZING.** A method used by Indians and white men in marking a trail. Sometimes trees were blazed by chipping off or peeling off the bark. Other times young saplings were bent in an elbow-shape. Tufts of tall grass might be tied and bent in the direction of the trail. Piles of stones were sometimes used, especially where the trails led up a steep hill or incline. These stones accumulated because of the custom of the Indian, when approaching a steep grade, of picking up and throwing a stone ahead, which he claimed would keep him from feeling tired. See TRAILS.

**TRAILS.** Paths worn or beaten by people or animals in going from place to place. At one time the United States was marked with a network of trails and paths throughout the length and breadth of the country. Many of these trails were made by deer, buffalo, and other animals in moving to and from feeding grounds, watering places, or salt licks. Others were Indian trails, sometimes marked by bent trees, piles of stones, or other trail-blazing devices. Some Indian trails showed that early tribes were familiar with places hundreds of miles from them and that they always traveled over the same route going or coming.

Trails of the eastern section were very narrow, because these Indians marched in single file. Yet they were much used by hunters, traders, moving bands of Indians, and war parties. The Iroquois of central New York were familiar with country as far west as the Black Hills of South Dakota, from which they brought back prisoners. They also were familiar with trails to South Carolina where they attacked the Catawba and to Florida where they fought the Creek.

The great highway leading through the Cumberland Gap to the mouth of the Scioto River in Ohio was known as Warriors' Path. Daniel Boone traveled this route into Kentucky.

The trails of the Plains were wide roads beaten down by large numbers of passing horses, dragging tepee poles and travois. Some of these trails were well marked, being depressed in some instances as much as two feet below the surface. Some Plains Indians had trails and routes down into Mexico, where they raided from time to time.

The Comanche war parties traveled from the Texas Panhandle down across the border every year. Western Indians, too, had routes to the South where they traveled to obtain blankets from the Pueblo tribes.

In the Southwest there were long trails by which the Hopi and other Pueblo tribes traveled to and from the sources of supply of salt, shells, turquoise, clay for pottery, and other things.

The trails of animals and Indians were followed later by the trapper and the trader, and still later by the missionary, the white hunter, the soldier, and finally the white settler. Some trails today are motor roads and highways and others are routes of the "Iron Horse." See BOONE, CATAWBA, COMANCHE, CREEK, FUR TRADE, HOPI, IROQUOIS, PORTAGE, TRAIL-BLAZING, TRADING POSTS.

**TRAVOIS** (tra-voi'). A type of carrier drawn by a dog or horse, much used by the Plains Indians. The travois consisted of two trailing poles which served as shafts, sometimes bearing a platform of rawhide or wood, or a wickerwork basket for the load.

While special poles were used, often lodge or tepee poles served the purpose. The poles were fastened at their smaller ends by a rope or heavy rawhide thong. They were then passed over the withers of the horse or shoulders of the dog, one pole on each side so the large ends of the poles would drag on the ground. The poles acted as shafts and the load was fastened onto them just behind the animal.

Small children, puppies, and perhaps the more fragile and cherished family effects were usually placed in a wickerwork basket fastened to the poles. For transporting the sick and wounded, a piece of rawhide or rope was fastened to the poles, forming a bed upon which the person reclined. See DOG, HORSE, TEPEE, WOMEN.

**TREE BURIAL. See BURIAL.**

**TRIBE.** A group of Indians comprising a series of families or clans, usually bound together by blood ties and believing all came from a common origin. Members of a tribe spoke the same language, and were under the authority of a chief. The Government in making treaties usually dealt with tribes.

However, a broader meaning has developed for the term "tribe." For example, the Bureau of Indian Affairs today deals with what they term a "tribal entity" in the state of Minnesota. They call this the Minnesota Chippewa Tribe. Yet this tribal organization is composed of six separate bands of Chippewa Indians, and each band can be considered a tribe for many purposes. In addition, there are a number of other bands or groups of Chippewa, each of which can qualify as a tribe.

Also, the Indians of the Fort Berthold Reservation, North Dakota, are dealt with as one tribal entity, even though they are actually made up of three Indian tribes—the Arikara, Gros Ventre, and the Mandan. Altogether the Bureau lists 279 "tribal entities" throughout the United States. See BAND, CHIEF, CLAN AND GENS, CONFEDERATION, TOTEM.

**TUMPLINE.** A pack strap or portage strap used by Indians in carrying heavy loads on their backs. The strap, attached at both ends to the pack, went across the forehead.

**TUNICA** (too-ne'-ka). A leading tribe of the Tunica group of Indians who lived on the lower Yazoo River in Mississippi. They were prominent in early history, especially for their faithful service to the French in fighting the Natchez and their allies. Their name is preserved in Tunica County and Tunica Oldfields in Mississippi, and in a village in Louisiana. There was only one alive in 1930. See NATCHEZ.

**TURK (THE).** The nickname (El Turco) given by members of Coronado's expedition in 1540–1542 to a Pawnee Indian who acted as a guide, because of a type of turban headdress he wore.

The Turk had been a slave in New Mexico and wanted to return to his own people. Therefore he told Coronado a mythical story of much gold which might be found to the north, and offered to lead the Spaniard there. However, he took the expedition on a wild-goose chase and finally Coronado realized what he was doing.

The Turk was placed in irons and later strangled to death. See CORONADO, PAWNEE.

**TUSCARORA** (tus-ka-ro′-ra). See IROQUOIS.

**UMATILLA** (yu-ma-til′-a). A tribe of Indians who lived on the banks of the Columbia River and the Umatilla River in Oregon. An Indian reservation is named for them, as well as the river, a county and a village in Oregon, and a place in Florida. See illustration above.

**UNCAS** (ung′-kas). A famous Mohegan chief who is noted in fiction as the hero of James Fenimore Cooper's novel *The Last of the Mohicans,* but in real life for his services to the white colonists. To have been correct Cooper should have called his novel *The Last of the Mohegans,* as the Mohicans, or Mahicans, while related, were a different tribe from the Mohegans.

The true Uncas married a daughter of the chief of the Pequot, but later was banished from that tribe. He then warred against the Pequot, Narraganset, and allied tribes. After taking Miantonomo, chief of the Narraganset, prisoner, he turned him over to the English, who ordered Uncas to execute him.

Uncas died around 1682. A monument to his memory was erected by the citizens of Norwich, Connecticut, in 1847, the cornerstone of which had been laid by President Andrew Jackson fourteen years earlier. Another memorial consisting of a bronze statue on a large boulder was erected on the site of James Fenimore Cooper's home at

Cooperstown, New York. See COOPER, MAHICAN, MIANTO-NOMO, MOHEGAN, NARRAGANSET.


UTE (yute). An important division of the Shoshoni, closely related to the so-called Paiute and the Bannock Indians. The Ute at one time roamed the entire central and western portions of Colorado, parts of eastern Utah, and portions of New Mexico.

The Ute early obtained horses and were a warlike people. While considered hostile to the whites, they were engaged in few of the early wars, since they occupied territory beyond the advancing frontier. But they were noted for their raids on surrounding tribes and Mexican settlements.

The Utes had a custom of handing over all female prisoners to their own women to be tortured, while warrior prisoners who had distinguished themselves usually were set free.

Between the years 1863 and 1868 the Government assigned to the Ute their own reservations in Utah, Colorado, and New Mexico. In 1879 one hundred of them left the White River Agency in Colorado to roam southern Wyoming, but were rounded up after an Indian agent and several others were killed.

The last trouble with the Ute was in 1906 when four hundred of them decided to leave Utah and settle on the Pine Ridge Reservation in South Dakota. They later surrendered and were sent back to their reservation at their own request.

In 1950 the United States Court of Claims awarded the Ute Indians $31,700,000 in payment for the loss of 15,000,000 acres of their territory when gold was discovered in Utah and Colorado in the 1870's. Not only this, but oil and natural gas have been found on one of their reservations and royalties from leases are constantly being added to the claims fund.

The state of Utah derives its name from the Ute. Utah also is the name of a county and lake in the state. There is a Utahville in Pennsylvania; places named Ute in Colorado and Iowa; and a Ute Park in New Mexico. See BANNOCK, MOUNTAIN LION, OTTER, OURAY, PAIUTE.

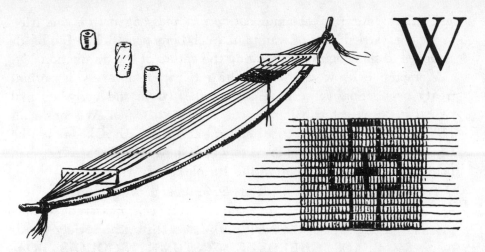

**WAMPUM** (wam'-pum). The shell money of the early Indians. It also was worn as necklaces, bracelets, belts, and used in other ways for decoration. Wampum was important in transactions between tribes, and especially in the binding of treaties.

Wampum consisted of beads made from the interior parts of shells, such as those of the hard-shell clam and the periwinkle. It was usually strung on thread. The beads were of two colors, white and purple. The purple varied in shade from a pink violet to a dark rich purple, and was worth twice as much as the white. The beads themselves were from ⅛" to ³⁄₁₆" in diameter and from ⅛" to ⁷⁄₁₆" in length.

As money, wampum was calculated in fathoms, or six feet to the string. A string of this length consisted of 360 white beads and 180 black or purple beads and in colonial days was worth five shillings, or approximately one dollar. Some Indians had tattooed on the inside of the left forearm a set of lines or a measuring scale by which they could measure the several standard lengths of wampum.

Like all money, wampum was counterfeited, and on May 30, 1650, an ordinance was passed by the Director of Council of New Netherlands in an attempt to remedy this evil. The best wampum was termed "Manhattan wampum." The inferior, consisting of unpolished and unperforated beads, was fixed at a smaller valuation, and the counterfeit was declared worthless.

While wampum was used as money between whites and Indians, the most important use among the Indians themselves was in giving authority to intertribal communications. All messengers from one tribe to another carried belts of wampum. Such belts usually had the beads arranged to show figures, suggesting the nature of the transaction.

Wampum belts were used in the ratification of every important treaty negotiation with the eastern tribes, from the early colonial period to the great tribal treaty of Prairie du Chien, Wisconsin, in 1830. In 1843 at the intertribal council at Tahlequah, Oklahoma, the Cherokee produced wampum belts which showed the peace they had made with the Iroquois before the Revolutionary War.

The Iroquois themselves still preserve several of these ancient record belts. Others of historic importance have been preserved, such as those in the archives of the New York State Historical Society at Albany. See BEADS, CHEROKEE, COSTUME, IROQUOIS, ROANOKE, SEWAN. See also illustration, page 329.

**WAR BONNET.** See HEADDRESS.

**WAR CLUB.** A striking weapon of stone, bone, or wood, in the shape of a club. There were several varieties of war clubs, some of which were called tomahawks in the early days.

Indians of the northern Plains made a war club from a rock, worked into shape to about three inches in diameter and five inches in length, pointed at both ends. A slight depression or groove was made around the center and a piece of green rawhide was then used to fasten a four-foot handle to the rock. A scalp, buffalo tail, or eagle feather usually was used as decoration.

Sometimes the war club simply was a heavy piece of wood, of which one end was trimmed down into a handle and the other into a ball-like shape. Large bones were fashioned in the same manner. Some wooden war clubs had several butcher-knife blades sunk in the striking end. See TOMAHAWK.

**WAR DANCE.** A dance of Indian braves before going to war. In the West it was called "striking the post," or the trunk of a tree from six inches to a foot in diameter, which was planted in the center of the camp.

War parties usually were made up of volunteers. The chief who was to command the expedition sent criers through the camp, beating tom-toms and calling on all warriors to come up to the post. The entire camp would become aroused, and the warriors who volunteered would circle the post and strike it with a weapon or a coup stick.

As the dancers became more excited, others would join the circle. After a warrior had struck the post nothing but death or the worst kind of illness could keep him from fulfilling his vow, as it was a matter of honor with him to acompany the war party. See COUP STICK, DANCE.

**WARD, NANCY.** A noted Cherokee half-breed woman, who held the tribal title of "Beloved Woman," or "Pretty Woman," which entitled her to speak in councils and decide the fate of captives. She was a friend of the colonists and through her influence was able to save the lives of many who had been taken prisoner.

Nancy Ward's father was said to have been a British officer named Ward and her mother a sister of the chief of the Cherokee Nation. The exact dates of her birth and death are not known. She is credited with introducing the first cows into the Cherokee Nation around 1819, and by her own influence and that of her children, improving the ways and conditions of the Cherokee. Her descendants still are to be found today in the Cherokee Nation. See CHEROKEE, WOMEN.

**WARM SPRINGS INDIANS.** A tribe of Oregon Indians whose own name was *Tenino*. A few are living among the Yakima and associated bands on a reservation in Oregon. Tenino, Washington, is named for them.

**WAR PAINT.** See PAINT.

**WARPATH.** A path to war. A term which meant that Indians had been aroused to a state of war.

**WAR PONY.** See HORSE.

**WASCO** (was'-ko). An Upper Chinook tribe, which formerly roamed Oregon in the neighborhood of the city, The Dalles. The name is preserved in Wasco County and a town in Oregon, and villages in California and Illinois.

**WET HEADS.** Pueblo Indian name for missionaries who believed in baptism.

**WHISTLE.** Indians fashioned whistles from wing bones of eagles, hawks, geese, and other birds. But a whistle made from an eagle's wing bone was the most highly prized.

The sound from the whistle was exactly like that of the bird whose wing bone had been used. For example, the turkey wing-bone whistle reproduced the plaintive note of the turkey's cry.

Whistles were worn attached to a thong around the neck and were used for various purposes. In dances, in courting an Indian maiden, or making a signal for a meeting with her; in battle during a charge; and when small parties were scouting, to give the alarm telling whether wild game or the enemy had been sighted—all these sounds were understood, whether the low love note or the shrill war signal. See EAGLE, MUSICAL INSTRUMENTS, SUN DANCE.

**WHITE DOG SACRIFICE.** See DOG, FIRE MAKING.

**WHITE MAN.** Indians had no general name for the white man, except "Pale Face," which the white man himself gave them. Different tribes called the white man by some term which referred to his personal appearance, his arrival in ships, his arms or his clothes, his actions, or perhaps the merchandise he brought with him to trade.

Many tribes used a term to indicate that the white man's skin was a lighter color than their own. The Arapaho called a white man "yellow hide," or "white skinned." The Miami spoke of the white man as "he of the hairy chest." The Delaware called him "person from the salt (sea)."

The Navajo used the word "Belagana," which was their pronunciation of the Spanish word *Americano*. The Iroquois, besides using a term which meant white skin, also called the white man a name meaning "he makes axes." The Wyandot used the terms "morning-light people" and "big knife."

To the Kiowa the white men were "hairy mouths," also "ears sticking out." To the Comanche they were "easterners." Among the Sioux the white man was "iron-maker," "rich people," as well as "long knife" or "big knife." "Long knife" was used by eastern Indians to denote American colonists, and the British were called "coat men." See INDIAN NAMES, LONG KNIVES.

**WICHITA.** A confederacy of nine tribes of the Caddo family, closely related to the Pawnee. They formerly ranged from the middle section of the Arkansas River in Kansas south to the Brazos River in Texas.

The Wichita gained fame at an early period when they were visited by Coronado in 1541, the Spaniards hopefully naming the Wichita country the Province of Quivira, a land of wealth and plenty. However, the explorers found it anything but that.

In the early days the Wichita suffered two epidemics of smallpox, which took many lives. They made their first treaty of peace with the United States in 1836.

Although they lived near the buffalo grounds and at times hunted buffalo, the Wichita were more of an agricultural people. Their permanent homes were dome-shaped, from 30 to 50 feet in diameter, made from a framework of poles overlaid with grass. From a distance they looked like haystacks. Around the inside of the house were beds on elevated platforms. A fire hole was sunk in the center of the floor and a smoke hole cut on one side of the roof. The doorways faced east and west.

The Wichita will be remembered principally from the prominence of Wichita, Kansas, which bears their name. It is also the name of counties in Kansas and Texas; the Wichita Mountains in Oklahoma; a river in Texas; and a town in Oklahoma; besides Wichita Falls, Texas. See CADDO, PAWNEE.

**WICKIUP.** The popular term for the brush shelter or mat-covered house of the Paiute, Apache, and other tribes of Nevada, Arizona, and nearby territory. The name also was applied to the small house or sweat-house built by the Plains Indians for taking sweat baths. Several heated stones were placed in the center of the lodge, the framework of which was covered with skins or blankets. The person or persons within poured water over the hot stones to produce steam.

The Cheyenne, Dakota, and Crow, when on the warpath, built small wickiups as temporary lodges when they made camp for the night. These usually were no more than three feet in height. See CAMP, COWBOY, LODGE, TEPEE.

**WIGWAM.** The house of the Indian tribes of the Algonquian family. The term was borrowed by the white man from the Abnaki Indian word *wigwam* and applied by him to dwellings of most of the eastern Indians.

The wigwam was built either as a circular, dome-shaped house or as a long arbor-like structure. A framework was made of saplings or small poles stuck into the ground and bent inward, their tops being lashed together. This frame was covered with bark or mats.

In moving, the Indians carried only the bark or mat covering and cut new frame poles where they made camp. See ABNAKI, BARK CRAFT, CAMP, HOGAN, LODGE, TEPEE.

**WIND RIVER SHOSHONI.** See SHOSHONI.

**WINNEBAGO** (win-e-bag'-o). A tribe of Woodland Indians of the Siouan family, who formerly occupied the territory in the area of Green Bay, Wisconsin. The dialect of the Winnebago was almost identical to that of three other Siouan tribes—the Oto, Iowa, and Missouri —but they lived more like their Algonquian neighbors. In the Sauk and Fox language their name meant "People of the Filthy Water," which caused the English sometimes to refer to them as "Stinkards."

The Winnebago fought beside the English in the Revolutionary War and the War of 1812, and sided with the Sauk and Fox in the Black Hawk War. After the latter war they remained at peace. In 1825 and 1832 they ceded all their lands south of the Wisconsin and Fox rivers and went to live on a reservation west of the Mississippi River.

The name is perpetuated in Winnebago Lake in Wisconsin; the

names of counties in Iowa, Illinois, and Wisconsin; and places in Illinois, Minnesota, Wisconsin, and Nebraska. See BLACK HAWK, SAUK AND FOX, SOUTHERN SIOUX.

**WINTER.** Indian term for a year. See CALENDAR.

**WINTUN** (win'-toon). A tribe of Indians who formerly roamed the west side of the Sacramento Valley in California. Estimated at 10,000 in 1770, today there are only about 58 living in California.

**WISCONSIN.** The name of a state and a river, said to have been applied to a group of tribes, including the Sauk and Fox, who lived on the banks of the river. The early French spoke of them as *Ouesconsins*. The name is from the Chippewa word meaning "Grassy Place." There are others who contend that the name Wisconsin came from still another Chippewa word, *Wishkonsing*, which was translated as "Place of Beaver," or "Muskrat Hole."

**WISHRAM** (wish'-ram). A tribe of Chinook Indians who lived on the north side of the Columbia River in Washington. Today a few live with the Upper Chinook tribes in the same state. Their name is preserved in that of Wishram, Washington.

**WIYOT** (wi'-yot). A tribe of California Indians who lived on the lower Mad River, Humboldt Bay, and the lower Eel River. A few survive in that vicinity today.

**WOMEN.** Indian women were long thought of by the white man as hardly more than slaves or drudges of the men and the tribe in general. The term "squaw," which was a Narraganset Indian word for "woman," was early used by the white man and became the accepted term for an Indian woman, especially an Indian wife. Even Indians of other tribes on reservations throughout the United States adopted it. And usually the word brought to mind a poor, hard-working, burden-bearing woman, who was at the mercy of her husband, and without any rights of her own.

It is true that most Indian women had hard lives, but so did the men. Among the more highly organized tribes, such as the Iroquois, women had many rights. The child of the Iroquois woman always belonged to the mother's clan—in other words, descent was reckoned through the mother. Women selected the sachem, or chief of the clan. They could have this sachem removed from office if they were not satisfied with him. They could forbid their sons to go to war. They owned the tribal fields, the wigwams, and everything in these wigwams. They had the right of life and death over such prisoners as might become their share of the spoils of war. Thus women ruled the tribe, as the men who actually were the chiefs were representatives of the women—not of the men.

Among the Pueblo Indians much the same high position was given women. The husband came to live with the wife and she could get rid of him whenever she wanted to. The children belonged to the woman, or rather to her clan. Men helped the women with the heavier work, such as house-building and fuel-gathering; and even wove blankets and made moccasins for their wives, and worked in the fields.

Women on the Plains possibly had the hardest time. Before they had the dog or horse to drag the travois, they carried all the camp equipment. All hard work was done by them. Men killed the buffalo and left them where they fell. The women followed and skinned the buffalo, cured the hide, cut up the meat, and carried it to camp. They put up and took down tepees, did all the cooking and making of the clothing. Yet they were not without influence and power.

Women did not always remain in camp when their men went on horse-stealing expeditions or to war. The Piegan had a famous woman warrior named Running Eagle who went to war and led many horse raids. She was killed attempting to take horses from the Flatheads.

Women had their own dances and their own games. Some had their own "talk." There were women's societies in some tribes, too, such as the Goose Women, who guarded the corn, and the White Buffalo Cows, whose ceremonies were thought to lure the herds for the buffalo-hunters. In the South some women became rulers of their tribe, such as the Lady of Cofitachiqui, encountered by the Spanish explorer, De Soto. See BEADS, BLANKET, BRIGHT EYES, CLAN, COFITACHIQUI, COSTUME, DANCE, FEASTS, GAMES, HAIR, INDIAN LANGUAGE, INDIAN NAMES, MILLY, MINNEHAHA, MOCCASINS, MOTHER-IN-LAW TABOO, PAINT, POCAHONTAS, QUILLWORK, RIDDLE (TOBY), SACAJAWEA, SCALP DANCE, SONGS, SQUAW, SQUAW MAN, TATTOOING, TEKAKWITHA, TEPEE, TORTURE, TRAVOIS, WARD (NANCY). See illustration, page 328.

**WOODEN INDIAN.** A carved wooden statue of an Indian, used as a cigar- and tobacco-store advertisement, because the Indian was the originator of the use of tobacco. Small wooden Indians were used in England as early as 1600. A century later large life-sized wooden Indians appeared in front of the tobacco shops in the colonies. See ABNAKI.

**WYANDOT** (wi'-an-dot). See ERIE, HURON.

**WYOMING.** The name of a state which was taken from that of a Lenape village in Pennsylvania called *M'cheuwomink,* meaning "Upon the Great Plain." The native name became Chiwaumuc, Wiawamic, Wayomic, Waiomink, and finally Wyoming. By this time it was supposed to mean "Field of Blood." It is not known who suggested the name for the state, but it was probably some emigrant of Pennsylvania.

# Y

**YAKIMA** (yak'-i-ma). A tribe of Indians who lived on the lower course of the Yakima River in Washington. Even as in the early days other tribes were included in the name Yakima, so today it is difficult to tell how many true Yakima live on the reservation of that name in Oregon and Washington. They are farmers and stock-raisers. The name has been preserved in that of the river, a county, and a town in Washington.

**YANA** (ya'-na). A California tribe of the upper Sacramento Valley. The Yana were almost exterminated in a massacre by miners in 1864. It is doubtful if any survive today.

**YANKTON.** See DAKOTA.

**YOKUTS** (yo'-kuts). A California tribe that roamed the entire floor of the San Joaquin Valley. It was customary in this tribe for a husband to go to live at the house of his wife, or his father-in-law. Estimated at 18,000 in 1770, a few survive in California today.

**YOPON** (yo'-pon). Trader's term for a species of holly growing in the southern United States along the coast. The tree is from ten to fifteen feet in height. Indians, especially the Creek during their Busk Dance, prepared a beverage from the leaves. Englishmen termed this the "black drink." The word is also spelled "yaupon." See BUSK, CREEK.

**YOUNG-MAN-AFRAID-OF-HIS-HORSES.** A chief of the Oglala Sioux, and one of Red Cloud's lieutenants in the war of 1866 when the Dakota sought to stop the building of the Montana road through their territory. The proper translation of his name is said by some authorities to be "His-Horses-Are-Afraid," and by others, "They-Fear-Even-His-Horse." After the peace of 1868 he lived at the Pine Ridge Agency in South Dakota, where he died some years later. See DAKOTA, RED CLOUD.

**YUKI** (yoo'-ki). A tribe of Indians who lived along the Eel River in California. Some survive in California today.

**YUMA** (yoo'-ma). A tribe of Arizona Indians who lived on both sides of the Colorado River at and below its junction with the Gila River. Counties in Arizona and Colorado and localities in Arizona, Colorado, Kansas, Kentucky, Michigan, and Tennessee preserve their name.

**YUROK** (yoo'-rok). A California tribe of Indians who lived on the lower Klamath River and along the coast to the north and south of the river.

# Z

ZUÑI (zoo'-nye). An important tribe of Pueblo Indians, and the only members of the Zuñian language family. Zuñi is also the name of the village in which they lived—and still live.

A small village of Zuñi, located on the Zuñi River in New Mexico, probably was the first pueblo seen by the white man. It was visited in 1539 by Fray Marcos of Niza, who carried back to Mexico so glowing an account that the Spanish explorer, Coronado, thinking it the fabulous "Kingdom of Cibola," rich in gold and precious stones, fitted out an expedition the following year. However, Coronado found the "seven cities," as they were termed, to be nothing but ordinary Indian pueblos.

The Zuñi, an agricultural people, joined with the other Pueblo tribes in a revolt against the Spaniards in 1680. The Americans later found them to be a quiet, good-natured, and industrious people. They depended on corn and game for food, were good potters, and raised cotton, which they wove into cloth. They had domesticated the turkey.

The men today wear their hair in bangs, with a headband of cloth, and their belts are adorned with large silver disks. They live on their own reservation in New Mexico. Besides the river, the name Zuñi is borne by a range of mountains in New Mexico, and places in New Mexico and Virginia. See CORONADO, POTTERY, PUEBLO INDIANS.

# THE INDIAN FAMILY TREE OF THOSE TRIBES
## LISTED IN THIS BOOK

It is believed that the forefathers of the American Indians came across eastern Siberia in Asia, and then through Alaska to the territory now known as the United States. These people, who were Mongolians, in time divided into many groups, some remaining in Alaska, some settling in the northwestern section of the United States, some pushing to the South and others to the East. The different groups became known later as "language families," as each gradually developed its own language. In historic times there are believed to have been as many as fifty such language groups. The groups split into tribes and even into bands and when the white man came there were thousands of different languages and dialects spoken in this country. Below are listed the main language family groups and the tribes associated with each as they are known today.

## THE ALGONQUIAN FAMILY

*In the East*

Abnaki
Adirondack
Algonkin
Chickahominy
Delaware
Hatteras
Mahican
Massachuset
Micmac
Mohegan
Munsee
Narraganset
Passamaquoddy
Pennacook
  (Merrimac)
Penobscot
Pequot
Podunk
Potomac
Powhatan

*In the Midwest*

Chippewa (Ojibwa)
Cree
Illinois
Kickapoo
Menominee
Miami
Ottawa
Potawatomi
Sauk and Fox
Shawnee

*In the Plains Area*

Arapaho
Blackfoot
Blood
Cheyenne
Cree
Gros Ventre (Atsina)
Piegan

*In California*

Wiyot
Yurok

# THE ATHAPASCAN FAMILY

| In the South | In the North | On the Pacific Coast |
|---|---|---|
| *Apache Tribes:* | Hupa | Tlingit |
| Chiricahua Apache | Kato | |
| Jicarilla Apache | Tolowa | |
| Kiowa Apache | | |
| Lipan Apache | | |
| Mescalero Apache | | |
| White Mountain Apache | | |
| | | |
| Navajo | | |

# THE CADDOAN FAMILY

| In the South | In the Central Area | In the North |
|---|---|---|
| Caddo Confederacy: | Pawnee Confederacy: | Arikara |
| Caddo | Chaui | (Arikaree, Ree) |
| Kichai | Kitkehahki | |
| Tawakoni | Pitahauerat | |
| Waco | Skidi | |
| Wichita | | |

# THE ESKIMAUAN FAMILY

## In Alaska

Aleut
Eskimo

# THE HOKAN FAMILY

## In the Southwest

| Karok | Pomo | Yuki |
|---|---|---|
| Maricopa | Shasta | Yuma |
| Mojave | Yana | |

343

# THE IROQUOIAN FAMILY

| *In the North* | *Independents* | *In the South* |
|---|---|---|
| The Six Nations: | Erie | Cherokee |
| Cayuga | Huron (Wyandot) | |
| Mohawk | Neutrals | |
| Oneida | Susquehanna | |
| Onondaga | (Conestoga) | |
| Seneca | | |
| Tuscarora | | |

# THE KERESAN FAMILY

*In the Southwest*

Pueblos:
Acoma
Cochiti
Laguna
San Felipe
Santa Ana
Santo Domingo
Sia

# THE MUSKHOGEAN FAMILY

*In the South*

Alibamu
Apalachee
Chickasaw
Choctaw
Creek
Koasati
Mobile
Muskogee
Natchez
Seminole
Taensa
Tunica

# THE PENUTIAN FAMILIES

*In the Northwest*

| *California Tribes:* | Cayuse | Klamath |
|---|---|---|
| Costanoan | Molala | Modoc |
| Maidu | | |
| Miwok | *Chinookan:* | *Shahaptin Group:* |
| Wintun | Chinook | Klickitat |
| Yokuts | Clatsop | Nez Percé |
| | Wasco | Palouse |
| | Wishram | Umatilla |
| | | Warm Springs |
| | | Yakima |

# THE SALISHAN FAMILY

## In the Northwest

Colville
Flatheads (Salish)

Kutenai
Pend d'Oreille (Kalispel)
Spokan

# THE SIOUAN FAMILY

## On the Northern Plains

Assiniboin (Stoney)
Dakota Tribes:
  Eastern Dakota
  Santee
  *Teton
  Yankton

*Teton Divisions:
Blackfeet
Brûlé
Hunkpapa
Miniconjou

Oglala
Sans Arc
Two-Kettle

## On the Lower Mississippi

Southern Sioux Tribes:
Iowa
Kansa

Missouri
Omaha
Osage

Oto
Ponca

## On the Upper Missouri

Crow

Hidatsa

Mandan

## Stragglers

Atakapa
Biloxi
Catawba

Quapaw (Arkansas)
Sisseton

Winnebago

# THE UTO-AZTECAN FAMILY

Shoshonean Branch:

Bannock (Idaho)
Chemehuevi (Arizona and
  Nevada)
Comanche (Oklahoma)
Hopi (Arizona)
Kern River Tribes (California)

Mission Indians (California)
Mono Tribes (California)
Paiute [Diggers] (Nevada)
Shoshoni [Snakes] (Idaho)
Ute (Utah)
Wind River Shoshoni (Wyoming)

### In the Southwest

**Tanoan Group:**

*Pueblos:*

| | | |
|---|---|---|
| Hano | Picuris | San Juan |
| Isleta | Pojoaque | Santa Clara |
| Jemez | Sandia | Taos |
| Nambe | San Ildefonso | Tesuque |
| Pecos | | |

### On the Plains

*Kiowan Group:*

Kiowa

*Aztec Group:*

Papago
Pima

## THE ZUÑIAN FAMILY

*In the Southwest*

Zuñi

## DISTRIBUTION OF INDIAN TRIBES BY STATES

Population figures are based on the census of 1950 *

**Alabama—928**
  Creeks

**Alaska—34,586**

| | | |
|---|---|---|
| Aleuts | Eskimos | Tlingit |
| Athapaskan | Haida | Tsimshian |

---

* As reported in House Report No. 2503, 82nd Congress, *Report with Respect to the House Resolution Authorizing the Committee on Interior and Insular Affairs to Conduct an Investigation of the Bureau of Indian Affairs,* United States Government Printing Office, Washington, D.C., 1953, and the *World Almanac and Book of Facts for 1959,* edited by Harry Hansen, published by the *New York World-Telegram and the Sun,* New York, 1959.

† Figures taken from the *World Almanac and Book of Facts for 1959.*

Where used, the term "urban Indians" signifies those Indians of various tribes living in metropolitan areas. Because the urban Indian population today is so fluid, it is impossible to estimate accurately the totals in various areas. For example, while present census figures show only 1,443 Indians in Illinois, newspapers and agencies estimate that in Chicago alone the Indian population currently totals from 8,000 to 10,000.

Arizona—65,761
  Apache
  Chemehuevi
  Cocopa

  Havasupai
  Hopi

  Hualapai
  Maricopa

California—19,947
  Cahuilla
  Chemehuevi
  Chumash
  Costanoan
  Cupeño
  Diegueño
  Gabrieleño
  Hupa
  Juaneño
  Karok
  Klamath
  Klamath River

  Maidu
  Miwok
  Modoc
  Mono
  Paiute
  Paviotso
  Pomo
  Salinan
  Serrano
  Shasta
  Shoshoni
  Tolowa

  Tubatulabal
  urban Indians
  Wappo
  Washo
  Wintun
  Wiyot
  Yana
  Yokuts
  Yuki
  Yuki-Wappo
  Yuma
  Yurok

Colorado—1,567
  Ute

†Connecticut—333

†Delaware—none

†District of Columbia—330

Florida—1,011
  Seminole

†Georgia—333

Idaho—3,800
  Bannock
  Coeur d'Alene

  Kutenai
  Nez Percé

  Paiute
  Shoshoni

†Illinois—1,443

†Indiana—438
  Miami

Iowa—1,084
  Sauk (Sac) and Fox

Kansas—2,381
  Cherokee (?)
  Chippewa-Munsee
  Iowa

  Kickapoo
  Potawatomi

  Sauk (Sac) and Fox
  urban Indians

†Kentucky—234

†Louisiana—409
  Chitimacha
  Choctaw

  Houma
  Koasati

  Tunica

347

†Maine—1,522
   Abnaki                    Passamaquoddy              Penobscot
   Micmac and Malecite

†Maryland—314

†Massachusetts—1,201

†Michigan—7,000
   Chippewa                  Potawatomi                 urban Indians
   Ottawa

Minnesota—12,533
   Chippewa                  Sioux or Dakota            urban Indians

Mississippi—2,502
   Choctaw

†Missouri—547

Montana—16,606
   Assiniboin                Chippewa                   Sioux or Dakota
   Atsina                    Crow                       urban Indians
   Blackfeet                 Flathead
   Cheyenne                  Sioux

Nebraska—3,954
   Iowa                      Sante Sioux                urban Indians
   Omaha                     Sauk (Sac) and Fox         Winnebago
   Ponca                     Sioux or Dakota

Nevada—5,025
   Paiute                    Shoshoni                   Washo

†New Hampshire—74

†New Jersey—621

New Mexico—40,768
   Apache                    Mescalero Apache           urban Indians
   Jicarilla                 Navajo                     Zuñian Pueblo
   Keresan Pueblo            Tanoan Pueblo

New York—10,640
   Cayuga                    Poosepatuck                Tuscarora
   Mohawk                    Seneca                     urban Indians
   Onondaga                  Seneca and Cayuga
   Oneida                    Shinnecock

North Carolina—5,720
   Cherokee

North Dakota—10,766
Arikara     Hidatsa    Sioux or Dakota
Chippewa    Mandan    urban Indians

†Ohio—1,146

Oklahoma—53,769
Apache     Iowa     Ponca
Arapaho    Kansa or Kaw  Potawatomi
Caddo     Kickapoo   Quapaw
Cherokee   Kiowa    Sauk (Sac) and Fox
Cheyenne   Kiowa Apache Seminole
Chickasaw   Miami and Illinois Shawnee
Choctaw    Osage    Tonkawa
Comanche   Oto and Missouri Wichita and Kichai
Creek     Ottawa    Wyandot
Delaware   Pawnee    Yuchi

Oregon—5,820
Cayuse     Klamath   Umatilla
Chetco     Modoc    urban Indians
Coos      Paiute     Walla Walla
Grand Ronde tribes Shasta     Warm Springs
Kalapooia    Siletz tribes  Warm Springs tribes

Pennsylvania—1,141
Seneca     urban Indians

†Rhode Island—385

†South Carolina—554
Catawba

South Dakota—23,344
Sioux or Dakota

†Tennessee—339

Texas—2,733
Alabama-Coushatta

Utah—4,201
Mattapony   Pamunkey   Ute
Paiute     Shoshoni

†Vermont—30

†Virginia—1,056

Washington—13,816
Chimakum   Makah    Yakima
Chinook    Salish

†West Virginia—160

Wisconsin—12,196

| Chippewa | Potawatomi | urban Indians |
| Menominee | Stockbridge-Munsee | Winnebago |
| Oneida | | |

Wyoming—3,237

| Arapaho | Shoshoni |

## SELECTED LIST OF MUSEUMS

American Museum of Natural History, New York City.
Brooklyn Museum, Brooklyn, New York.
Buffalo Historical Society, Buffalo, New York.
Chicago Natural History Museum, Chicago, Illinois.
City of Milwaukee Museum, Milwaukee, Wisconsin.
Cleveland Museum of Natural History, Cleveland, Ohio.
Denver Art Museum, Denver, Colorado.
Historical Society of Montana, Helena, Montana.
Minnesota Historical Society, St. Paul, Minnesota.
Museum of Anthropology, University of California, Berkeley, California.
Museum of Natural History, University of Kansas, Lawrence, Kansas.
Museum of the American Indian, Heye Foundation, New York City.
Nebraska State Historical Society, Lincoln, Nebraska.
New York State Museum, Albany, New York.
Northern Arizona Society of Science and Art Museum, Flagstaff, Arizona.
Oklahoma Historical Society Museum, Oklahoma City, Oklahoma.
Oshkosh Public Museum, Oshkosh, Wisconsin.
Peabody Museum of Harvard University, Cambridge, Massachusetts.
Pettigrew Museum, Sioux Falls, South Dakota.
Rapid City Indian Museum, Rapid City, South Dakota.
Rochester Museum of Arts and Sciences, Rochester, New York.
Southwest Museum, Los Angeles, California.
State Historical Society Museum, Bismarck, North Dakota.
State Historical Society Museum, University of Wisconsin, Madison, Wisconsin.
The Newark Museum, Newark, New Jersey.
United States National Museum, Smithsonian Institution, Washington, D.C.
University Museum, University of Pennsylvania, Philadelphia, Pennsylvania.

Books to read if you want to know more about:

## INDIANS IN GENERAL

Dorian, Edith, and Wilson, W. N. *Hokahey! American Indians Then and Now.* Whittlesey House, 1957.

Elting, Mary (Folsom). *The First Book of Indians*, Watts, 1950.

Fletcher, Sydney. *The American Indian*, Grosset & Dunlap, 1954.

Hodge, Frederick Webb. *Handbook of American Indians North of Mexico*, Bureau of American Ethnology, Bulletin 30, 2 vols., 1907-1910.

Holling, Holling Clancy. *The Book of Indians*, Platt, 1935.

Raphael, Ralph B. *The Book of American Indians*, Fawcett, 1953.

Stirling, Matthew W. *Indians of the Americas*, National Geographic Society, 1955.

Swanton, John R. *Indian Tribes of North America*, Bureau of American Ethnology, Bulletin 145, 1953.

Wissler, Clark. *Indians of the United States*, American Museum of Natural History, Science Series, 1940.

*World Book Encyclopedia*. "Indian, American," Vol. 9, pp. 3703-3725, Field Enterprises, 1955.

### INDIANS OF THE EAST

Bleeker, Sonia. *Indians of the Longhouse; the Story of the Iroquois*, Morrow, 1950.

Cooper, James Fenimore. *Last of the Mohicans* and *Deerslayer; or the First War-Path*, Scribner, 1929.

Lenski, Lois. *Indian Captive; the Story of Mary Jemison*, Lippincott, 1941.

Shippen, Katherine Binney. *Lightfoot; the Story of an Indian Boy*, Viking, 1950.

### INDIANS OF THE SOUTH

Ball, Zachary. *Swamp Chief*, Holiday House, 1952.

Bleeker, Sonia. *The Cherokee*, Morrow, 1952.

Coblentz, Catharine. *Sequoya*, Longmans, 1946.

### INDIANS OF THE WEST

Balch, Glenn. *Indian Fur*, Crowell, 1951.

Farnsworth, Frances Joyce. *Winged Moccasins; the Story of Sacajawea*, Messner, 1954.

Howard, Helen Addison. *War Chief Joseph*, Caxton Printers, 1952.

Rush, William Marshall. *Red Fox of the Kinapoo; a Tale of the Nez Percé Indians*, Longmans, 1949.

### INDIANS OF THE PLAINS

Bleeker, Sonia. *Crow Indians*, Morrow, 1953.

Garst, Doris. *Sitting Bull; Champion of His People*, Messner, 1946.

Grant, Bruce. *Warpath: A Story of the Plains Indians*, World, 1954.

Penny, Grace Johnson. *Tales of the Cheyennes*, Houghton Mifflin, 1953.

## INDIANS OF THE NORTHWEST

Desmond, Alice. *The Talking Tree*, Macmillan, 1940.
Martin, Frances Gardiner. *Nine Tales of the Raven*, Harper, 1951.
Pinkerton, K. S. *Hidden Harbor* (Tlingit Stories), Harcourt, Brace, 1951.


## INDIANS OF THE SOUTHWEST

Armer, Laura. *Waterless Mountain*, Longmans, 1950.
Bronson, Wilfrid Swancourt. *Pinto's Journey*, Messner, 1948.
Moore, Grace. *Chi-Wee; the Adventures of a Little Indian Girl*, Doubleday, 1925.
Wyatt, Edgar. *Geronimo; the Last Apache War Chief*, McGraw-Hill, 1952.


## INDIAN ARTS, CRAFTS, AND WOODLORE

Griswold, Lester. *Handicraft*, Lester Griswold, 1951.
Jaeger, Ellsworth. *Wildwood Wisdom*, Macmillan, 1945.
Mason, Bernard Sterling. *Book of Indian Crafts and Costumes*, Barnes, 1946.
Salomon, Julian Harris. *Book of Indian Crafts and Indian Lore*, Harper, 1928.